OXFORD LATIN COURSE

PART II
SECOND EDITION

MAURICE BALME & JAMES MORWOOD

OXFORD
UNIVERSITY PRESS

OXFORD
UNIVERSITY PRESS

198 Madison Avenue, New York 10016

Oxford University Press is a department of the University of Oxford.
It furthers the University's objective of excellence in research,
scholarship and education, by publishing worldwide in

Oxford New York
Auckland Bangkok Buenos Aires Cape Town Chennai
Dar es Salaam Delhi Hong Kong Istanbul Karachi Kolkata
Kuala Lumpur Madrid Melbourne Mexico City Mumbai Nairobi
São Paulo Shanghai Singapore Taipei Tokyo Toronto

with an associated company in Berlin

Oxford is a registered trade mark of Oxford University Press
in the UK and in certain other countries

© Oxford University Press 1996
Reprinted 1996, 1997, 1999, 2000, 2001, 2002

Paperback edition: ISBN 0-19-521205-3
Hardback edition: ISBN 0-19-521551-6

Typeset and designed by Positif Press, Oxford
Printed in Italy by G. Canale & C. S.p.A.

Contents

Acknowledgements

The publisher and authors would like to thank the many consultants
in the United Kingdom and the United States for comments and
suggestions that have contributed towards this second edition.
In particular: (UK) Julian Morgan, Deborah Bennett, David Cartwright,
Alison Doubleday, John Powell, Philip Powell, Jeremy Rider, Tim
Reader, F. R. Thorn, Andrew Wilson; (US) John Gruber-Miller, Carlos
Fandal, Dennis Herer, Gilbert Lawall, James Lowe, Diana Stone and
Jeffrey Wills.

*The publishers would like to thank the following for permission to
reproduce photographs*:

© AKG pp. 54, 82 (top); © AKG/John Hios p. 81; © AKG/Eric Lessing pp. 22,
23, 109; Alinari-Giraudon p. 85; Ancient Art & Architecture Collection pp. 42,
49 (right), 69, 70, 100; Archivi Alinari pp. 16, 75; Bildarchiv Preussischer
Kulturbesitz pp. 8, 41(right), 44, 46, 82 (bottom); John Brennan, Oxford p. 30;
© British Museum p. 51 (bottom); Peter Clayton pp. 9, 68, 87 (top), 106 (top);
Peter Connolly p. 20; Donald Cooper © Photostage p. 67; Roger Dalladay p. 8
(right); C. M. Dixon pp. 73, 110; Fitzwilliam Museum, Cambridge p. 87
(bottom); Giraudon pp. 27, 36 (left); The Ronald Grant Archive p. 41 (left);
© Michael Holford pp. 1, 88, 90; © 1989, Loyola University Chicago, R. V.
Schoder SJ, photographer p. 80; James Morwood pp. 60, 61, 63, 76, 77, 106
(bottom); Musée archéologique, Pella/G. Dagli Orti p. 101; Musée
archéologique, Timgad/G. Dagli Orti p. 48; Musée du Louvre/© photo R.M.N.
p. 55; Museo d'Arte Moderno di Ca Pesaro, Venice/The Bridgeman Art
Library, London pp. 28, 29; Alfredo Dagli Orti/Bildarchiv Preussischer
Kulturbesitz pp. 35, 36 (right); The Royal Collection © Her Majesty Queen
Elizabeth II p. 57; Scala, Florence pp. 10, 14, 19, 33, 49 (left), 51 (top), 52, 62,
66, 92, 94, 98 (right), 104.

Cover photo: Bildarchiv Preussischer Kulturbesitz

The cartoons are by Cathy Balme.
The maps were drawn by John Brennan.

Introduction

The first part of this course centered around the life of a freedman's family in a country town in Apulia, far from Rome and largely unaffected by the political upheavals which were taking place there; the events described in it are fictitious, since we know very little about the early life of our hero, the poet Quintus Horatius Flaccus. In Part II we leave Apulia behind; because Quintus is clever and the local school inadequate, his father decides to take him to Rome, where he attends one of the best schools there. From Rome he goes on to university in Athens. The framework of the story is now historical. We learn a good deal about this stage of Quintus' life from his own poetry, and the momentous political events of the time impinge on his own life more and more closely, until at the end of this part he is about to be drawn into the civil war which took place after the murder of Julius Caesar.

The following chronological table puts the events of Part II into historical perspective:

BC	
65	Quintus Horatius Flaccus born at Venusia
51?	Flaccus takes Quintus to Rome
50	Quintus meets young Marcus Cicero (fiction)
49–46	Civil war – Julius Caesar versus Pompey and the senate
46	Julius Caesar's fourfold triumph
45	Marcus Cicero sent to study in Athens
44	Assassination of Julius Caesar
	Quintus goes to the Academy in Athens
	Brutus visits Athens and recruits undergraduates
43	Cicero murdered by Antony's soldiers
	Civil war – Antony and Octavian versus Brutus and Cassius
	Quintus joins the army of Brutus
42	Quintus commands a legion at the battle of Philippi

Quīntus ad lūdum ambulābat; subitō Gāium vīdit.

Gāius arborem ascendēbat. Quīntus ad arborem festīnāvit.

ānxius erat; clāmāvit: 'quid facis, Gāiī? dēscende.'

Gāius eum audīvit; ad terram rediit Quīntumque salūtāvit.

These captions introduce two different past tenses; you should look at the grammar on p. 112 before you study the vocabulary.

Vocabulary 17

From now on in the vocabularies, verbs will be given with the perfect (1st person sing.) as well as the present infinitive, e.g.

1st conjugation: **parō, parāre, parāvī**
2nd conjugation: **moneō, monēre, monuī**
3rd conjugation: **regō, regere, rēxī**
4th conjugation: **audiō, audīre, audīvī**

The different ways in which 3rd conjugation verbs form their perfect are explained bit by bit in the grammar sections of succeeding chapters.

A number of verbs have 'irregular' principal parts, i.e. they do not follow the regular pattern given above.

verbs		*adverbs*	
sum, esse, *imperfect*: **eram**; *perfect*: **fuī**	I am	**deinde**	then, next
superō, superāre, superāvī	I overcome	**enim**	for
discēdō, discēdere, discessī	I go away, depart	**igitur**	and so, therefore
legō, legere, lēgī,	I read	**tamen**	however, but
crēdō, crēdere, crēdidī + dat.	I believe, trust		
prōmittō, prōmittere, prōmīsī	I promise		
efficiō, efficere, effēcī	I effect, carry out		

nouns		*adjectives*		*conjunction*	
hōra, -ae, f.	hour	**candidus, -a, -um**	white	**cum**	when
pecūnia, -ae, f.	money	**optimus, -a, -um**	best		
dīvitiae, -ārum, f. pl.	riches	**pessimus, -a, -um**	worst		
candidātus, -ī, m.	candidate	**vērus, -a, -um**	true		
numerus, -ī, m.	number	**vēra dīcere**	to speak the truth		
ōrātiō, ōrātiōnis, f.	speech	**gravis, grave**	heavy, serious		
ōrātiōnem habēre	to make a speech				
vulnus, vulneris, n.	wound				

enim, igitur and **tamen** always come second word in their clause,

e.g.　**sērō venīmus; festīnāmus igitur ad lūdum.**
　　　We are coming late, and so we are hurrying to school.
　　　magister īrātus est; sērō enim ad lūdum venīmus.
　　　The master is angry, for we are coming to school late.
　　　lentē ambulāvimus; nōn tamen sērō advēnimus.
　　　We walked slowly, but we did not arrive late.

What do the following English phrases mean and from what Latin words are the words in italics derived: an *impecunious* husband, a *pessimistic* forecast, an *insuperable* problem, *numerical* order, an *optimum* score?

Comitia

comitia iam aderant. cīvēs novōs duovirōs creāre dēbēbant. per omnēs viās in mūrīs casārum nūntiī candidātōrum pictī erant, sīcut:

comitia the elections
creāre to elect; **pictī** painted
sīcut like

5   ORO VOS M. EPIDIUM SABINUM DUOVIRUM
    FACIATIS. CANDIDATUS DIGNUS EST,
    COLONIAE VESTRAE DEFENSOR.

ōrō vōs…faciātis I beg you to make

cīvēs in viās festīnābant et candidātōs spectābant. illī per viās ambulābant; togās candidās gerēbant; turba fautōrum eōs comitābat. ōrātiōnēs habēbant; multa prōmittēbant quae efficere
10 nōn poterant; cīvēs eōs audiēbant, paucī tamen eīs crēdēbant.

turba fautōrum a crowd of supporters
comitābat accompanied

    Flaccus in tabernā sedēbat et colloquium cum amīcīs faciēbat. Ganymēdēs, senex querulus et miser, 'candidātīs crēdere nōn possumus' inquit; 'cum enim magistrātum petunt, omnia prōmittunt. cum duovirī sunt, nihil faciunt. nihil cūrant nisi
15 pecūniam suam.'

tabernā a pub
colloquium conversation
querulus complaining, querulous
magistrātum magistracy, office
nisi except

    Philērus 'vēra dīcis, Ganymēdēs,' inquit; 'omnēs candidātī putidī sunt, sīcut Chrȳsanthus, homō pessimus. ōlim pauper erat, quī parātus fuit quadrantem dē stercore dentibus tollere. nunc dīvitiās innumerābilēs habet. quōmodo illās dīvitiās sibi
20 comparāvit? furcifer est.'

putidī rotten; **ōlim** once
quadrantem a farthing
dē stercore from the dung
dentibus with his teeth
comparāvit did he get?
furcifer a thief; **nūgās** nonsense

    Flaccus tamen amīcōs invītus audīvit: 'nōlī nūgās nārrāre, amīce,' inquit; 'iam dēbēmus ad comitium īre et suffrāgia ferre. surgite, amīcī, et mēcum venīte.' omnēs igitur ad forum prōcessērunt et festīnāvērunt ad comitium. in triviīs duōbus
25 candidātīs occurrērunt quī ad comitium prōcēdēbant. pistōrēs alterī favēbant; alba ferēbant cum hāc īnscrīptiōne:

comitium the polling station
suffrāgia ferre to cast our votes
in triviīs at a crossroads
pistōrēs the bakers; **alterī** (dat.) one
favēbant favored, supported
alba (n. pl.) notice boards

    C. IULIUM POLYBIUM DUOVIRUM ORO VOS
    FACIATIS; PANEM BONUM FACIT.

pānem bread; **alterī** the other

alterī favēbant mūliōnēs.
30   aliī aliōs vituperābant. mox saxa per aurās volābant. multī vulnera accēpērunt, multī timuērunt domumque rediērunt. tandem candidātus quīdam, vir gravis et spectātus, ōrātiōnem ad cīvēs habuit tumultumque sēdāvit. omnēs ad comitium prōcessērunt, suffrāgia tulērunt, novōs duovirōs creāvērunt.
35 fautōrēs eōrum laetī clāmāvērunt victōrēsque triumphantēs domum dūxērunt. Flaccus domum festīnāvit Scintillaeque omnia nārrāvit.

mūliōnēs the muleteers
vituperābant began to abuse
volābant were flying
spectātus respected
tumultum riot
sēdāvit calmed
tulērunt cast
triumphantēs in triumph

Part of an election poster from Pompeii

A Roman bar

Respondē Latīnē

1 cūr cīvēs candidātīs nōn crēdēbant?
2 quid dīxit Ganymēdēs dē candidātīs?
3 quid dīxit Philērus de Chrȳsanthō?
4 quid respondit Flaccus?
5 quid accidit (*happened*) in triviīs?

Word-building

Learn the following compounds of **mittō, mittere, mīsī***:*

admittō, admittere, admīsī	I admit, I commit (a crime)
āmittō, āmittere, āmīsī	I send away, I lose
committō, committere, commīsī	I join together, I entrust
dēmittō, dēmittere, dēmīsī	I send down
dīmittō, dīmittere, dīmīsī	I dismiss (send in different directions)
ēmittō, ēmittere, ēmīsī	I send out
immittō, immittere, immīsī	I send into, I send against
permittō, permittere, permīsī	I permit
prōmittō, prōmittere, prōmīsī	I promise
remittō, remittere, remīsī	I send back

Roman coin
showing a citizen voting

Decimus Quīntum lacessit

lacessit bullies

Translate the first paragraph of the passage below and answer the questions on the second and third

dum Flaccus ad comitia prōcēdit, Quīntus in lūdō sedēbat.
Flāvius arithmēticam docēbat; 'dīc mihi, Gāī,' inquit; 'sī dē
quīnque remōtus est ūnus, quid superest?' Gāius respondit:
'quattuor.' Flāvius 'euge!' inquit, 'tū potes rem tuam servāre.'
5 multī puerōrum etiam nunc numerōs nec addere nec dēdūcere
poterant. Quīntus iamdūdum numerōs didicerat litterāsque facile
legēbat. nunc igitur pictūrās scrībēbat, saepe hiābat, interdum
dormiēbat. tandem Flāvius puerōs domum dīmīsit.

   illī laetī in viam festīnāvērunt. Quīntus cum amīcīs ambulābat,
10 cum accessit Decimus; ille Quīntō invidēbat quod ingeniōsus
erat. ad pugnam eum vocāvit. ille resistere temptāvit, Decimus
tamen eum facile superāvit. ad terram cecidit; tunica scissa erat,
sanguis ē nāribus effluēbat. surrēxit et domum cucurrit.

   ubi domum rediit, Scintilla eum rogāvit: 'Quīnte, cūr tam
15 sordidus es? cur tunica scissa est?' Quīntus mātrī omnia nārrāvit.
illa nihil respondit sed casam trīstis intrāvit.

remōtus removed, subtracted
superest is left; **euge!** good!
rem tuam your fortune
dēdūcere subtract
iamdūdum long ago
didicerat had learnt; **facile** easily
hiābat was yawning
interdum from time to time
ingeniōsus clever
cecidit fell; **scissa** torn
sanguis blood
ē nāribus from his nostrils, nose
effluēbat was pouring
cucurrit ran; **sordidus** dirty

1 Why was Decimus envious of Quintus? [1]
2 How did Quintus come off in the fight? [5]
3 What did Scintilla ask him when he got home? [2]
4 How did she react to his reply? [2]

Cursus Honorum
Course of Honor

ELECTIONS

As in modern democracies, so in both Rome and the provincial towns elections were of key importance. At Rome there were annual elections at which the citizen body elected the magistrates, who were the executives of the whole system of government. There were four 'colleges' of magistrates, and those aspiring to high office had to hold each post in succession. The junior post was that of quaestor (treasury official); next were the aediles, who had general administrative duties; then came the praetors, who were in charge of judicial administration; and finally the two consuls, the chief executives of the state.

Roman magistrates

The magistrates held office for one year only and there was a minimum age at which candidates were allowed to stand. On becoming a quaestor, you automatically joined the senate for life, and so at the elections the people not only chose those who were to hold office for a year but also the members of the senate, who advised and in fact controlled the magistrates.

However, the system was not as democratic as it sounds since in the elective assemblies there were elaborate arrangements by which the votes of the richer citizens counted for more than those of the poor. Elections were rigged, bribery was normal, and the common people were only allowed to vote for members of the upper classes. The many conquests which were expanding the empire brought more and more slaves to Rome and they did more and more of the work. There was, therefore, an increasing number of unemployed citizens who had to be supported by subsidized or free grain. There was no good reason for voting for one candidate rather than another except for their short-term promises, and so the common people's vote tended to go to those who gave them the most grain or put on the best shows in the theatre. A Roman poet called Juvenal was to remark, with considerable truth, that the only things that interested them were 'bread and circuses' (*pānem et circēnsēs*).

In provincial towns the local government was modelled on that of Rome. The citizens of a *colōnia* met annually in assembly to elect the two magistrates (*duovirī*) who were to run their town for a year. Corresponding to the senate there was an assembly of 80–100 councillors (*decuriōnēs*) who were recruited from ex-magistrates and held office for life. Like the senate, their function was to advise the *duovirī* and in practice they ran public affairs.

Elections were lively events, hotly contested, as numerous surviving graffiti on the walls of Pompeii make clear. Two of these are included in the Latin story. Here are two more: the first shows the guild system at work in a rather comic way!

Client/Patron

- The guild of Late Drinkers unanimously supports Marcus Cerrinius Vatia as aedile.

- Statia and Petronia ask for your support for Marcus Casellius and Lucius Albucius as aediles. I hope we have citizens like this in our colony for ever.

A letter survives in which Quintus Cicero advises his brother Marcus – who is soon to feature in our story – on how to conduct his election campaign. Here is some of what he says:

- System
- not paid
- larger group = 1 vote
- $ very important
- background
- connected

> A campaign for election to a magistracy can be divided into two kinds of activity: firstly to gain the support of one's friends, secondly to win the good will of the people. The support of one's friends should be secured by kindness done and repaid, by long-standing acquaintance and by a charming and friendly nature. But the word 'friend' has a wider application in an election campaign than in the rest of life. Anyone who shows any sympathy towards you, who pays attention to you, who frequents your house, should be reckoned among your 'friends'… It is necessary to have friends of every kind: for the sake of appearance, make friends with men who are distinguished in rank and title. These, though they may not actively support the campaign, none the less confer some prestige upon the candidate… You should have knowledge of people's names, winning manners, persistence, generosity, reputation and confidence in your public program… You badly need to use flattery, which, though disgraceful in the rest of one's life, is essential while electioneering… All men naturally prefer you to lie to them than to refuse your aid… To make a promise is not definite; it allows postponement, and affects only a few people.

Would Quintus Cicero's advice be helpful to a modern politician?

The word candidate is derived from the Latin word for 'white' (candidus), as candidates would make their togas especially white while running for office. Why do you think they did this?

Here is the full version of the poster painted on the walls of Pompeii which was quoted on page 8:

> *I beg you to elect Marcus Epidius Sabinus duovir; he is a worthy candidate; a defender of your colony, supported by the eminent judge Suedus Clemens and the unanimous voice of the town council, as worthy of our republic because of his services and his honesty. Vote for him.*

Explain what office Sabinus hopes to win, whose support he claims to have, and what grounds he has for hoping that the electors will vote for him. Compare this poster with those put out by candidates in a modern local or national election.

tōtam hiemem Flaccus Quīntusque dīligenter labōrābant.

prīmō diē vēris parātī erant iter inīre; Scintillam Horātiamque valēre iussērunt.

quīnque diēs in Viā Appiā contendēbant sed Rōma adhūc multa mīlia passuum (*miles*) aberat.

nōnō diē Flaccus moenia urbis cōnspexit. decem diēbus Rōmam advēnērunt.

Vocabulary 18

verbs		*nouns*		
absum, abesse, āfuī + abl.	I am away from	**lacrima, -ae,** f.		tear
discō, discere, didicī	I learn	**silva, -ae,** f.		forest
fleō, flēre, flēvī	I weep	**annus, -ī,** m.		year
ineō, inīre, iniī	I enter, begin	**ignis, ignis,** m.		fire
trānseō, trānsīre, trānsiī	I cross	**iter, itineris,** n.		journey
studeō, studēre, studuī + dat.	I study	**tempus, temporis,** n.	time
valēre iubeō	I bid goodbye to	**vēr, vēris,** n.		spring
vendō, vendere, vendidī	I sell	**diēs, diēī,** m.		day
cōnspiciō, cōnspicere, cōnspexī	I catch sight of			

adjective		*adverbs*		*preposition*	
longus, -a, -um	long	**adhūc**	still	**sine** + abl.	without
longē	far	**tam**	so		

What do the following phrases mean, and from what Latin
words are the words in italics derived: an *absent* friend,
an *annual* celebration, a long *itinerary*, a *silvan* glade,
igneous rock, a *studious* pupil?

Quīntus domō discēdit

posterō diē Scintilla Flaccō dīxit: 'Quīntus nihil discit in illō lūdō.   **posterō** the next
ingeniōsus est. dēbet Rōmam īre ad optimum lūdum.' Flaccus   **ingeniōsus** clever
'uxor cāra,' inquit, 'nōn potest Quīntus sōlus iter Rōmam facere.'
Scintilla eī respondit: 'vēra dīcis, mī vir; tū dēbēs eum Rōmam   **mī vir** my husband

5 dūcere.' Flaccus 'nōn satis argentī habēmus,' inquit, 'nec possum   **satis argentī** enough (of) money
tē Horātiamque sōlās relinquere.'

    trēs hōrās rem disserēbant. tandem Scintilla 'agrum' inquit   **rem disserēbant** they discussed the
'dēbēmus vendere. tū Quīntum Rōmam dūcere dēbēs; ego et   matter
Horātia possumus hīc manēre et frūgāliter vīvere.' cōnstituērunt   **frūgāliter** cheaply, frugally

10 dīmidium agrī vendere; dīmidium Scintilla Horātiaque colere   **dīmidium** half
poterant. tōtam hiemem Quīntus domī manēbat parentēsque   **domī** at home
iuvābat. omnēs dīligenter labōrābant. Quīntus agrum colēbat;
Flaccus partēs coāctōris agēbat et sīc multum argentum   **partēs coāctōris agēbat** worked as
comparāvit.   an auctioneer

15   vēr accēdēbat cum Flaccus uxōrī dīxit: 'iam satis argentī   **comparāvit** got, made
habēmus. tempus est Quīntum Rōmam dūcere.' duōbus diēbus
omnia parāta erant. posterō diē Flaccus Quīntusque Scintillam
valēre iussērunt.

    māter flēbat deōsque ōrābat: 'ō deī, servāte fīlium meum.

20 reddite eum mihi incolumem. ō Flacce, fīlium nostrum cūrā! ō
Quīnte, bonus puer estō! dīligenter studē et mox domum redī!'
fīlium virumque amplexū tenēbat; deinde rediit in casam valdē   **amplexū tenēbat** held in her
commōta.   embrace

Horātia Argusque cum eīs ad prīmum mīliārium contendērunt.
25 deinde Horātia eōs valēre iussit Argumque domum redūxit, nōn
sine multīs lacrimīs. tertiā hōrā diēī illī, et trīstēs et laetī, viam
iniērunt quae Rōmam dūcēbat.

quīntō diē Flaccus fīliusque collem ascendērunt. Venusia
longē aberat. Quīntus valdē fessus erat. mīliārium prope viam
30 vīdit. accessit et īnscrīptiōnem lēgit: 'ROMA CENTUM ET
QUINQUAGINTA MILIA PASSUUM'. 'ō pater,' inquit, 'quīnque
diēs contendimus. montēs et flūmina trānsiimus; sed Rōma adhūc
abest centum et quīnquāgintā mīlia passuum. ego valdē fessus
sum. ecce! nox adest. quid facere dēbēmus? nōn possum longius
35 contendere.'

Flaccus respondit: 'nōlī dēspērāre, fīlī. possumus in illā silvā
pernoctāre.' Flaccus Quīntum in silvam dūxit. Quīntus ligna
collēgit et ignem accendit. cēnam celeriter parāvērunt. tum
Quīntus sub arbore cubuit et mox dormiēbat.

mīliārium milestone

vīdit he saw

longius further

pernoctāre to spend the night
ligna (n. pl.) **collēgit** he collected
firewood **cubuit** lay down

Word-building

Learn the following compounds of **eō**, **īre**, **iī**:

abeō, abīre, abiī	I go away
adeō, adīre, adiī	I go to, approach
exeō, exīre, exiī	I go out
ineō, inīre, iniī	I go into, begin
pereō, perīre, periī	I perish
prōdeō, prōdīre, prōdiī	I go forward
redeō, redīre, rediī	I go back, return
trānseō, trānsīre, trānsiī	I cross

A Roman milestone

Quīntus paterque in perīculum cadunt

Translate the first two paragraphs and answer the questions on the third

Quīntus trēs hōrās iam dormīverat cum subitō sonus eum excitāvit; lupōs audīvit procul ululantēs. Flaccus 'nōlī timēre, fīlī,' inquit. 'lupī longē absunt; praetereā ignem timent. nōn audent accēdere.'

5   Quīntus igitur iterum dormīvit. nōn dormīvit Flaccus sed ignem cūrābat; ānxius enim erat perīculumque timēbat. mediā nocte sonum audīvit; hominēs per umbrās ad ignem accēdēbant. Flaccus fīlium celeriter excitāvit; 'tacē' inquit; 'hominēs hūc accēdunt. venī mēcum.' Quīntī manum cēpit et celeriter eum
10 dūxit per umbrās in virgulta; ibi sē cēlāvērunt ānxiīque spectābant.

    trēs hominēs ad ignem accessērunt. statim impedīmenta Flaccī rapuērunt. deinde ipsōs quaerēbant sed invenīre nōn poterant. tandem in silvās abiērunt. Flaccus fīliō 'nōlī timēre, fīlī,' inquit;
15 'iam abiērunt hominēs. sine dubiō illī sunt servī fugitīvī, hominēs scelestī. ē magnō perīculō ēvāsimus. iam dēbēmus hīc manēre in virgultīs cēlātī.'

dormīverat had slept
lupōs wolves **ululantēs** howling
praetereā moreover
audent they dare

umbrās the shadows

manum cēpit took the hand
virgulta (n. pl.) undergrowth, bushes
sē cēlāvērunt they hid (themselves)
impedīmenta (n. pl.) baggage
rapuērunt seized

sine dubiō without doubt
fugitīvī runaway **scelestī** wicked
cēlātī hidden

1 What did Flaccus and Quintus see from their hiding place? [2]
2 Why did Flaccus tell Quintus not to be afraid? [2]
3 What were the men, according to Flaccus? [2]
4 What did Flaccus say they must do now? [2]

[handwritten: Where you were born]

SPQR (Senatus Populusque Romanus)

After the kings had been driven out in 510 BC, the new republic of Rome was governed by the senate, the magistrates and the people. But, as we saw in the last chapter, the magistrates were drawn exclusively from the upper classes, and the senate, which consisted of magistrates and ex-magistrates, thus consisted of the great Roman families, the *nōbilēs* (the patricians). They were only 300 to 600 in number and kept power firmly in their grasp.

[handwritten: → if had a consul in the family]

The chief magistrates, as we have seen, were the two consuls who were elected to hold office for a year. Because there were two of them it made it unlikely that one consul would seize all the power and become another king. They were able to veto each other's proposals (i.e. to stop them being carried out), but the Romans were a practical people and the consuls usually worked out a way of managing affairs in harmony.

The consuls also commanded Roman armies operating in Italy. They were accompanied when on official business by twelve attendants carrying *fascēs*, bundles of rods which were the emblems of their authority. From the end of the first century BC men who had served as consuls could be sent out to govern

*[handwritten: $$ (agriculture)
Patricians
equites → $$$$
plebs → $ -tribune
• freedmen
slaves
Foreigners]*

15

Rome's increasing number of provinces abroad. Here the bundles of rods carried by their attendants contained an axe, which signified their power to carry out the death sentence.

We have seen that the common people, who were called the *plēbs*, had limited power and were often oppressed by the *nōbilēs*. In order to safeguard the rights of the *plēbs*, ten tribunes of the people were appointed. They could veto the senate's measures and it was illegal to lay a finger on them. The senate was a conservative body – that is to say, it preferred to keep things as they always had been – and so in the early days the tribunes of the people proved a valuable force in winning justice for the lower classes of Rome. After 287 BC decrees taken in the Council of the Common People (*concilium plēbis*) bound the whole community. These decrees were called *plēbiscīta* (what English word is derived from this?).

In the later republic a middle class, between the senators and *plēbs*, but far closer to the former, developed increasing power. This class consisted of the equestrians or knights, the *equitēs*. These had to have a large sum of money to qualify for membership. Many were the financiers of Rome, the bankers, money-lenders and collectors of taxes.

Attendants carrying fasces

In this period there was continual conflict between the representatives of the *plēbs*, who called themselves *populārēs*, and of the nobility, who called themselves the *optimātēs*, while the *equitēs* sometimes backed one side, sometimes the other. It was very rare for a new man, i.e. a man whose family did not belong to the old Roman nobility, to get to the top and become consul. Cicero, who is soon to enter our story, was one of the few who did so, making his way by pure ability.

It was in fact Cicero who tried to bring about a harmony between knights and senators. But it was an unreal though noble wish. At the time of our story, each class seemed only interested in what appeared to be best for itself, and the most powerful class, the senate, was hopelessly divided. In the last decades of the republic a succession of individuals set out to establish their own authority and gain supreme power. They would use any means to do so, and violence, intimidation, rioting and anarchy became basic facts of life in Cicero's day. The kings had been driven out in the sixth century BC. Five hundred years later, it looked as if they were on the way back.

Who were the chief magistrates? What was the emblem of their authority?
When the Italian dictator Mussolini called his party the fascists, what point was he aiming to make?
Who were the officials especially elected to protect the plēbs?
Who were the equitēs?

iter tandem cōnfectum erat. Quīntus paterque Rōmam intrāverant.

postrīdiē ad forum contendērunt; Quīntus aedificia tam splendida numquam vīderat.

tandem Flaccus fīliō 'iam omnia spectāvistī,' inquit; 'venī ad lūdum Orbiliī.'

Quīntus nōn omnia spectāverat, sed pater eum ē forō dūxit.

A new tense is introduced in the cartoons. Which verbs are in the new tense? How is it formed and what does it mean?

Vocabulary 19

verbs		nouns	
agō, agere, ēgī	I do; I drive	**aedificium, -ī**, n.	building
claudō, claudere, clausī	I shut	**vestīmenta, -ōrum**, n. pl	clothes
aperiō, aperīre, aperuī	I open	**Iuppiter, Iovis**, m.	Jupiter
apertus, -a, -um	open		

adjectives		adverbs	
altus, -a, -um	high	**continuō**	immediately
cōnfectus, -a, -um	finished	**hūc... illūc**	this way and that
invītus, -a, -um	unwilling	**paene**	nearly
medius, -a, -um	middle	**ubīque**	everywhere
sacer, sacra, sacrum	sacred		
vacuus, -a, -um	empty	preposition		conjunction	
difficilis, difficile	difficult	**extrā** + acc.	outside	**ubi**	where

What do the following English words mean and from what Latin words is each derived:
error, altitude, edifice, vestment, vacuum?

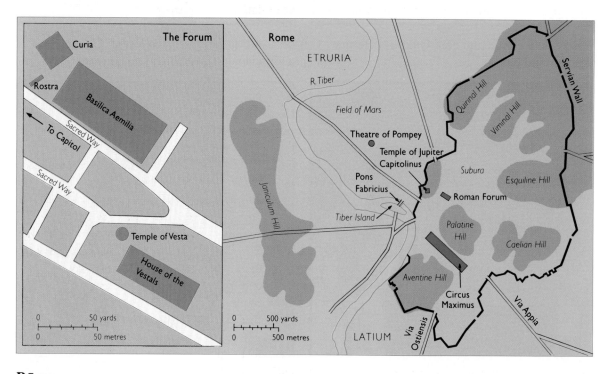

Rōma

dum Scintilla et Horātia Venusiae ānxiae manent, Quīntus
paterque iam novem diēs Rōmam contenderant; montēs et flūmina
trānsierant; iter difficile fuerat et labōriōsum. tandem Rōma nōn
longē aberant. Quīntus valdē fessus erat, sed pater 'nōlī dēspērāre,
5 fīlī,' inquit; 'iter paene cōnfectum est. Rōma nōn longē absumus.'

Venusiae at Venusia

The Porta Appia

postrīdiē moenia urbis conspexērunt et festīnāvērunt ad portās.

nox iam vēnerat cum urbem intrāvērunt. parvam caupōnam **caupōnam** inn
invēnērunt; cēnāvērunt et post cēnam continuō dormīvērunt.
prīmā lūce Flaccus Quīntum excitāvit et 'venī, Quīnte,' inquit;
10 'dēbēmus lūdum Orbiliī quaerere.' lentē prōcēdēbant per viās
urbis.

tandem in Viā Sacrā ambulābant et mox ad forum vēnerant.
nec Quīntus nec pater umquam vīderant aedificia tam magnifica.
diū stābant attonitī; deinde omnia spectābant. hīc erat templum | **attonitī** astonished
15 Vestae, ubi Virginēs Vestālēs ignem perpetuum cūrābant; illīc erat | **illīc** there
Basilica Aemilia, ubi magistrātūs iūs dīcēbant; hīc erant rōstra, | **magistrātūs** (nom. pl.) the magistrates
ubi magistrātūs ōrātiōnēs ad populum habēbant. illīc steterat | **iūs dīcēbant** dispensed justice
cūria; iam ruīnīs iacēbat, in tumultū ambusta. ā fronte erat mōns | **rōstra** (n. pl.) the speaker's platform
Capitōlīnus, ubi stābat ingēns templum Iovis. | **cūria** the senate house

20 omnia diū spectāverant, cum Flaccus 'venī, fīlī,' inquit, | **ruīnīs** in ruins; **in tumultū** in a riot
'Rōmae diū manēbimus. omnia haec saepe vidēbis.' ā forō | **ambusta** burnt; **ā fronte** in front
discessērunt collemque ascendērunt; mox ad lūdum Orbiliī | **manēbimus** we shall stay
advēnerant. extrā iānuam lūdī stetērunt. puerōs audīre poterant | **vidēbis** you will see
recitantēs et Orbilium eōs corrigentem; nōn tamen intrāvērunt. | **recitantēs** reciting
25 Flaccus 'venī, Quīnte,' inquit; 'domicilium dēbēmus invenīre et | **corrigentem** correcting
nova vestīmenta emere.' | **domicilium** a lodging

Quīntus paterque ē mediā urbe discessērunt et prōcēdēbant ad
Subūram, ubi pauperēs habitābant. ibi nūllae erant aedēs magnae | **aedēs** houses
sed altae īnsulae, in quibus habitābant multae familiae. viae | **īnsulae** tenements
30 sordidae erant et artae. multī hominēs hūc illūc currēbant; ubīque | **artae** narrow
clāmor et tumultus. mox ad vestiārium vēnērunt; Flaccus Quīntō | **tumultus** uproar
togam praetextam et tunicam candidam ēmit; Quīntus, quī | **vestiārium** a clothes shop
vestīmenta tam splendida numquam habuerat, patrī grātiās ēgit. | **praetextam** purple-bordered
deinde in Subūram prōcessērunt et domicilium quaerēbant. | **grātiās ēgit** thanked (gave thanks to)

Respondē Latīnē

1 ubi Flaccus Quīntusque ad forum advēnērunt, cūr attonitī erant?
2 quid faciēbant Virginēs Vestālēs?
3 ubi (*where*?) magistratūs iūs dīcēbant?
4 ubi Flaccus Quīntusque ad lūdum Orbiliī advēnērunt, quid audīvērunt?
5 quid ēmit Flaccus in vestiāriō?

Word-building

Learn the following compounds of **sum**, **esse**, **fuī**:

absum, abesse, āfuī	I am away from, I am absent
adsum, adesse, adfuī	I am present
dēsum, dēesse, dēfuī + dat.	I fail
īnsum, inesse, īnfuī + dat.	I am in
intersum, interesse, interfuī	I am among, I take part in
prōsum, prōdesse, prōfuī + dat.	I benefit
supersum, superesse, superfuī	I am left over, I survive

A Roman tenement

Quīntus domum novam invenit

Translate the first paragraph and answer the questions below on the other two paragraphs, without translating

tandem Flaccus īnsulam intrāvit cuius iānua aperta erat
iānitōremque quaerēbat. invēnit eum in aulā dormientem. ēbrius
erat. Flaccus eum excitāvit et dīxit: 'ego fīliusque domum
quaerimus; habēsne domicilium vacuum?' ille non surrēxit sed
5 Flaccō respondit: 'nūllum domicilium habeō vacuum. abī.' sīc
dīxit; oculōs clausit iterumque dormīvit.

cuius of which
iānitōrem the doorkeeper
aulā courtyard
dormientem sleeping; **ēbrius** drunk
domicilium lodging

pater fīliusque in viam trīstēs exierant, cum aliquis eōs
revocāvit; fēmina quaedam ē iānuā festīnāvit, anus rūgōsa, quae
'manēte' inquit; 'marītus meus caudex est et semper ēbrius.
10 errāvit. ūnum cēnāculum habēmus vacuum. venīte.'
    dūxit eōs anhēlāns ad summum tabulātum. ibi erat cēnāculum,
parvum et sordidum. iānitōris uxor 'ecce,' inquit; 'vīsne hoc
cēnāculum condūcere? quīnque dēnāriōs tantum rogō.' Flaccus
īrātus erat; 'nimium rogās,' inquit; 'cēnāculum parvum est et
15 sordidum. trēs dēnāriōs tibi dare volō.' illa 'trēs dēnāriōs dīcis,
furcifer? dā mihi quattuor dēnāriōs, sī cēnāculum condūcere vīs.'
Flaccus invītus concessit et quattuor dēnāriōs eī trādidit. abiit
fēmina ad iānitōrem. Quīntus novam domum trīstis spectāvit.

anus rūgōsa a wrinkled old woman	
caudex blockhead	
cēnāculum garret, attic room	
anhēlāns panting	
summum tabulātum the top storey	
condūcere to rent; **dēnāriōs** denarii	
tantum only; **nimium** too much	
furcifer thief	
concessit gave in	

1 What made Flaccus and Quintus go back into the *īnsula*? [2]
2 What did the doorkeeper's wife tell them? [4]
3 Where did the she lead them? [2]
4 Describe the bargaining between her and Flaccus. [5]
5 Briefly describe the characters of the doorkeeper and his wife. [4]
6 How did Quintus feel about the garret? [1]

Fābella

Persōnae: **Quīntus, Flaccus, iānitor, iānitōris uxor**

*Quīntus Flaccusque per Subūram prōcēdunt, domicilium
quaerentēs.*

quaerentēs looking for

Quīntus: pater, mē manē. nōn possum tē vidēre in tantā turbā.

mē manē wait for me

5 **Flaccus**: festīnā, Quīnte. tē trūde per turbam. ecce, fīlī, illīus
īnsulae iānua aperta est. venī mēcum.

turbā crowd
tē trūde push (yourself)!

Flaccus Quīntum in aulam īnsulae dūcit.

aulam courtyard

Flaccus: euge, adsumus. nunc dēbēmus iānitōrem quaerere.
(*clāmat*) iānitor! iānitor, ubi es?

10 **Quīntus**: nēmō respondet, pater. iānitor abest.

Flaccus: sine dubiō adest alicubi. dēbēmus eum quaerere, tū
illāc quaere, ego hāc.

sine dubiō without doubt
alicubi somewhere or other

Quīntus: pater, venī hūc. iānitōrem invēnī. in illō angulō
dormit.

illāc that way; **hāc** this way
angulō corner

15 **Flaccus**: veniō statim. iānitor, ēvigilā!

iānitor stertit; Flaccus eum vellicat.

stertit is snoring; **vellicat** pinches

iānitor: (*ēvigilat*) quid facis? cūr mē sīc vellicās? abī! sine mē
dormīre. (*iterum dormit*)

sine allow! let!

Quīntus: quid facere dēbēmus, pater? homō plānē ēbrius est.

plānē plainly; **ēbrius** drunk

20 **Flaccus**: dēbēmus eum excitāre. tū, Quīnte, ad fontem festīnā
et urnam aquae mihi fer.

*Quīntus ad fontem currit reditque urnam aquae manibus
ferēns. Flaccus aquam in caput iānitōris īnfundit. iānitor
exsilit, valdē īrātus.*

manibus in his hands
ferēns carrying; **caput** (n.) head
īnfundit pours over; **exsilit** jumps up

25	**iānitor:**	quid facis, furcifer? vīsne mē occīdere? quid cupitis?
	Flaccus:	domicilium condūcere cupimus, iānitor.
	iānitor:	nūllum domicilium habeō vacuum. abīte! cūr mē vexātis? sine mē dormīre.

condūcere to rent

vexātis do you bother?

iānitor recumbit et dormit. Flaccus Quīntusque ex aulā trīstēs
30 *ambulant. subitō fēmina ē iānuā currit et clāmat.*

recumbit lies down again

iānitōris uxor: manēte, redīte. errat marītus meus. caudex est et
semper ēbrius. ūnum cēnāculum habēmus vacuum. in
summō tabulātō est, nōn magnum sed mundum.

marītus husband; **caudex** blockhead
cēnāculum garret
summō tabulātō the top floor

iānitōris uxor anhēlāns eōs ad gradūs dūcit. gradūs ascendunt
35 *ad summum tabulātum. illa iānuam aperit cēnāculumque eīs*
ostendit et minūtum et sordidum, sub tegulīs situm.

mundum clean, neat
anhēlāns panting
gradūs (acc. pl.) steps

iānitōris uxor: ecce, amīcī, domicilium pulchrum, unde
prōspectum habētis ēgregium.

minūtum tiny
sub tegulīs under the roof tiles
situm sited, positioned

Flaccus: domicilium minūtum est et sordidum. quantum rogās?
40 **iānitōris uxor:** volō cēnāculum tibi vīlī locāre. quīnque dēnāriōs
tantum rogō per mēnsem.

unde from where
prōspectum ēgregium an
outstanding view

Flaccus: nimium rogās. trēs dēnāriōs volō tibi dare.
iānitōris uxor: quid dīcis, furcifer? trēs dēnāriōs! nōlī nūgās
nārrāre. dā mihi quattuor dēnāriōs, sī vīs cēnāculum
45 condūcere.

quantum? how much?
vīlī cheaply; **locāre** to let
tantum only; **per mēnsem** per
month; **alterum** another

Quīntus: pecūniam eī trāde, pater. nōn possumus alterum
domicilium invenīre.

Flaccus invītus quattuor dēnāriōs iānitōris uxōrī trādit; illa
discēdit triumphāns. Quīntus cēnāculum trīstis spectat.

triumphāns in triumph

The temple of Vesta, Rome

ROME

Rome was built on the left bank of the river Tiber about 40
miles from where it flows into the sea. A small island in
the river breaks up the strong current here and the water is
shallow and easy to ford. A bridge to this island, the Pons
Fabricius, had been built by Horace's time (in 62 BC). This
is still standing and is in fact used by traffic. Rome's
control of this part of the Tiber was of great importance
since anyone travelling along the western side of Italy
would almost certainly cross the river at this point. Thus
Rome became a key center for inland trade. Dangerous
shoals in the river for a long time stopped Ostia, the port at
the mouth of the Tiber, from becoming as important a
harbor as the more distant Puteoli near Naples. But Rome
was still able to engage in a flourishing trade abroad.

The famous seven hills of the city, especially the rocky Capitoline hill, made it comparatively safe from attack. The Roman orator and politician Cicero, who is soon to enter our story, praised the city's natural strength:

Romulus and the other Roman kings showed great wisdom in laying out the course of the wall along a line of hills which are high and sheer at every point. The one approach, which is between the Esquiline and Quirinal hills, is protected by a huge rampart and ditch. The Capitoline hill is so well fortified by its steep walls of rock that, even in the terrible time when the Gauls invaded, it remained safe and undamaged. The place chosen by Romulus is in addition plentifully supplied with springs, and even if the surrounding marshes are a breeding-ground for malaria, Rome is in fact a healthy site. For the hills channel the breezes and give shade to the valleys.

As Quintus walks with his father along the Sacred Way, the only road of any size in Rome, to the forum, he sees the temple of Vesta where a flame was always kept alight by the Vestal Virgins in honor of the goddess of the hearth, and the great temple of Jupiter on the Capitoline hill, built by Tarquin the Proud. He also passes by the law courts and the platform (*rōstra*) where magistrates stood to address the people. The senate house (*cūria*), the seat of government, had stood close to them on the north side of the forum. It had recently been burnt down by rioters. Horace has arrived in Rome at a very troubled time, as you will see.

The forum, Rome

The forum was certainly no longer the humble market-place which it had once been. Bankers and money-lenders had replaced the shop-keepers and it was now the busy heart of city life. Rome had almost a million inhabitants in Horace's day and it became a city of the greatest splendor. The first emperor, Augustus, boasted that he had found it brick and left it marble. But many squalid areas remained and Horace and his father find a room in once of these, the Subura.

This poor, over-crowded district lay between the Viminal and Esquiline hills. It was such a slum that Augustus, the first emperor, had a wall more than a hundred feet high built in his forum to stop it being seen! Here there were many high-rise blocks of flats of up to four or five storeys. In Horace's time a height limit of 60 feet was enforced, but even so, as the poet Juvenal wrote, these overcrowded, poorly built structures were liable to collapse:

> We live in a city largely held up by thin props, for that is how the real estate agent supports the tottering house. And when he plasters over the gaping cracks on the long-neglected wall, he tells the occupants not to worry and to sleep soundly, though the place is about to crash down.

or to burn:

> If there is a fire panic at the bottom of the stairs, the furthest tenant will go up in smoke, the one who is only protected from the rain by tiles where the soft doves lay their eggs.

A bend in the Tiber enclosed the Campus Martius (Field of Mars), on the other side of the Capitoline hill, to the north-west. This was a huge open space used for military and athletic exercises. The theatre of Pompey was near by, the first stone theatre in Rome. This was completed in 55 BC and could seat an audience of 9,000 to 10,000. Plays both comic and tragic were performed here. The huge Circus Maximus stood between the Palatine and Aventine hills. Here chariot races took place for the amusement of a vast and uncritical audience. The taste of the average Roman was for the violent, sensational and crude.

Rome was the capital city of a great area. Suggest modern equivalents, e.g. in London or Washington, for the buildings described above.

An inscription on a gravestone from Rome reads:

> *All a person needs. Bones reposing sweetly, I am not anxious about suddenly being short of food. I do not suffer from arthritis, and I am not indebted because of being behind in my rent. In fact my lodgings are permanent – and free!*

What does this inscription tell us about the life the dead person has escaped?

Orbilius barbam longam habēbat vultumque
sevērum; in manū ferulam gerēbat.

Orbilius librum Quīntō trādidit iussitque eum
multōs versūs legere.

Orbilius Quīntum in medium dūxit. 'ecce,
puerī,' inquit, 'novum discipulum vōbīs
commendō: nōmen eī est Quīntus Horātius
Flaccus.'

Quīntus miser in angulō scholae sedēbat;
interdum puer quīdam sē vertit et nārēs
fastīdiōsē corrūgāvit.

Vocabulary 20

verbs

appellō, appellāre, appellāvī	I call (by name)
recitō, recitāre, recitāvī	I recite, read aloud
rīdeō, rīdere, rīsī	I laugh
induō, induere, induī	I put on
intellegō, intellegere, intellēxī	I understand

nouns

		adjectives and adverbs	
poēta, -ae, m.	poet	**rēctus, -a, -um**	straight
grātiae, -ārum, f. pl.	thanks	**rēctē**	rightly, correctly
grātiās agō + dat.	I thank	**sevērus, -a, -um**	severe
schola, -ae, f.	school, schoolroom	**facilis, facile**	easy
discipulus, -ī, m.	pupil	**facile**	easily
liber, librī, m.	book		
gradus, gradūs, m.	step		
manus, manūs, f.	hand		
versus, versūs, m.	verse		
vultus, vultūs, m.	face, expression		

What do the following English words mean:
recitation, risible, intellect, library, manufacture, gradually?
From what Latin words is each derived?

Lūdus Orbiliī

prīmā lūce Flaccus Quīntum excitāvit. ille sē lāvit et novam
togam induit. pater fīliusque in viam dēscendērunt et festīnābant
ad Orbiliī lūdum. Flaccus capsulam Quīntī manibus ferēbat   **capsulam** satchel
partēsque paedagōgī agēbat. celeriter contendērunt et ad lūdum   **manibus** in his hands
5   mox advēnerant.   **partēs paedagōgī** the role of tutor

    iānua aperta erat; intrāvērunt et Orbilium quaerēbant.
invēnērunt eum in aulā sedentem. vir gravis erat; longam barbam   **in aulā** in the courtyard
habēbat vultumque sevērum; in manū ferulam gerēbat. Flaccus   **sedentem** sitting; **barbam** beard
accessit et 'ecce!' inquit, 'magister; fīlium meum Quīntum ad tē   **ferulam** cane
10   dūcō.' ille Quīntum īnspēxit et 'venī hūc, Quīnte,' inquit, 'et pauca
mihi respondē.'

    Orbilius multa Quīntum rogāvit, prīmum dē rēbus Rōmānīs;   **rēbus Rōmānīs** Roman history
'quis' inquit 'Rōmam condidit? quis Tarquinium Superbum Rōmā
expulit? quandō Hannibal in Italiam invāsit?' et multa alia.   **invāsit** invaded
15   Quīntus facile respondēre poterat. deinde Orbilius librum eī
trādidit iussitque eum legere; Quīntus librum manibus accēpit et
facile eum legēbat. Orbilius 'euge,' inquit, 'puer bene legere   **euge!** good!
potest.' deinde librum Graecē scrīptum Quīntō trādidit. Flaccus   **Graecē scrīptum** written in Greek
ānxius erat; ad Orbilium prōcessit; 'fīlius meus' inquit 'Graecē
20   nec dīcere nec legere potest.' Orbilius attonitus erat; 'quid?'

inquit, 'quid? puer Graecē nec dīcere nec legere potest? dēbet
statim litterās Graecās discere.' librum Quīntō trādidit Graecē
scrīptum et iussit eum omnēs litterās celeriter discere.

    cēterī puerī iam advēnerant. Orbilius 'venī, puer,' inquit;
25 'tempus est studēre.' Quīntum in scholam dūxit. ubi intrāvērunt,
omnēs puerī surrēxērunt magistrumque salūtāvērunt. ille
Quīntum in medium dūxit et 'ecce, puerī,' inquit, 'novum
discipulum vōbīs commendō. nōmen eī est Quīntus Horātius
Flaccus. barbarus est: Graecē nec dīcere nec legere potest.'
30 omnēs puerī rīdēbant. ille 'tacēte, puerī,' inquit. 'Quīnte, ad
angulum ī et litterās Graecās disce.' itaque Quīntus in angulō
scholae sedēbat litterīsque Graecīs studēbat. Orbilius cēterōs
Iliadem Homērī docēbat; omnēs Homērum facile intellegēbant;
omnēs versūs Graecōs rēctē recitābant. interdum puerōrum
35 quīdam sē vertit et nārēs fastīdiōsē corrūgāvit. Quīntus valdē
miser erat; domum redīre cupiēbat.

commendō I introduce
barbarus a barbarian

angulum corner

interdum from time to time
nārēs corrūgāvit turned up his nose
fastīdiōsē disdainfully

A Roman boy
with his teacher

Word-building

Learn the following compounds of **dō**, **dare**, **dedī**:

addō, addere, addidī	I add
condō, condere, condidī	I found
crēdō, crēdere, crēdidī + dat.	I believe, trust
dēdō, dēdere, dēdidī	I give up, surrender
perdō, perdere, perdidī	I lose, waste
prōdō, prōdere, prōdidī	I betray
reddō, reddere, reddidī	I give back, return
trādō, trādere, trādidī	I hand over

Note that although **dō** is 1st conjugation, all its compounds are 3rd.

Quīntus miser est

Translate the first paragraph and answer the questions on the second without translating

dum Orbilius Iliadem Homērī cēterīs expōnēbat, Quīntus in angulō scholae litterīs Graecīs studēbat. merīdiē magister puerōs dīmīsit et iussit eōs in aulā paulīsper lūdere. omnēs laetī in aulam cucurrērunt. dum cēterī lūdēbant, Quīntus sōlus stābat; nēmō
5 cum eō lūdēbat, nēmō eī quicquam dīxit. tandem puer quīdam ad eum accessit et 'nōlī dēspērāre, Quīnte,' inquit; 'Orbilius sevērus est, sed doctus. puerōs ignāvōs sevērē pūnit; eum appellāmus plāgōsum Orbilium. sed sī dīligenter studēs, cōmis est.' Quīntus eī respondēre volēbat, sed eō ipsō tempore Orbilius puerōs in
10 scholam revocāvit.

post merīdiem poētae Latīnō studēbant; Quīntus aliquid intellegere poterat. tandem Orbilius puerōs dīmīsit. Quīntus cum patre trīstis ad Subūram redībat; 'ō pater,' inquit, 'cēterī puerī magnī et ingeniōsī sunt; omnēs Graecē dīcere possunt. ego
15 parvus sum et vix quicquam intellegere possum. et magister valdē sevērus est.' ille 'nōlī dēspērāre, cāre fīlī,' inquit; 'tū dīligenter studēre cupis. celeriter discēs.'

expōnēbat was explaining
angulō corner
merīdiē at midday
paulīsper for a little while
quicquam anything

doctus learned, clever
ignāvōs idle; **pūnit** he punishes
plāgōsum flogger; **cōmis** friendly

aliquid something

ingeniōsī clever

discēs you will learn

1 Why were things slightly better for Quintus in the afternoon? [3]
2 Why did Quintus despair? [5]
3 How did his father comfort him? [4]
4 List all the things about Orbilius' school (a) which seem familiar to you; (b) which seem unfamiliar. [3/3]

GREECE AND ROME

Why is it so important that Quintus masters the Greek language? You will remember that when the Greeks captured and sacked the city of Troy, Aeneas and his men fled from its smouldering ruins. They established themselves in Italy after many struggles and hardships, intermarried with Italians and founded the Roman race. The Romans established their rule over the whole of Greece in 197 BC. It was a kind of revenge for the defeat which their legendary ancestors had suffered a thousand years before. But the victors were in fact not at all vindictive. The Roman general declared at the Games at Corinth the following year that all Greek states were now free and independent. The enthusiastic shouting of the liberated peoples was so loud that the birds flying overhead are said to have fallen to the ground stunned.

The Romans' attitude to the Greeks was strangely mixed in Horace's day. On the one hand, they despised the present weakness of a nation which had driven huge forces of invading

Persians from their native soil five centuries before, and more recently had conquered the known world under Alexander the Great. On the other hand, they enormously admired their great art and literature. Educated Romans were bilingual, speaking both Greek and Latin, and Quintus was expected to be the same. When he sails to Athens to complete his education in Greek philosophy, he makes a journey that many Romans had travelled before him.

The extraordinary intellectual and creative inventiveness of the Greeks dazzled the Romans. Their discoveries in mathematics (Pythagoras), geometry (Euclid), astronomy (Ptolemy), science (Archimedes) and natural history (Aristotle), their mastery of the art of speaking (Demosthenes), their unrivalled architecture and sculpture (Pheidias, Praxiteles), their great philosophical tradition (Plato) – all seemed wonderful to the Roman nation.

It was perhaps in literature especially that the superiority of the Greeks lay. The poems of Homer, the tragic plays of Aeschylus, Sophocles and Euripides from the fifth century BC, the historical writings of 'the father of history' Herodotus and of his successor Thucydides, and a whole treasury of lyric poetry – here was a great literary inheritance that gave the Romans everything to study and little to invent. So while Rome had captured Greece, Greece captivated Rome. As Horace himself put it: *Graecia capta ferum victōrem cēpit* (Captured Greece captured her wild conqueror).

The Acropolis, Athens

The Pont du Gard, southern France. The people walking on the top show the scale of the structure

However, the Romans still felt superior, even while they admired. They had their feet firmly planted on the ground compared with the talented but unreliable Greeks. They rightly saw themselves as a practical and realistic race in contrast with their neighbors across the Adriatic. Their greatest works of art were impressive but heavy feats of engineering. Their major achievement was not to create but to conquer and rule. In the *Aeneid*, Virgil puts in the mouth of Aeneas' father Anchises a fine statement of the world of difference that lay between the two nations:

> Others [i.e. the Greeks] will hammer out the bronze so that it breathes in softer lines, others will transform marble into living faces, will plead cases in the law courts with superior skill, will trace the movements of the planets with the rod and tell of the rising constellations. You, Roman, must bear in mind how to rule the peoples of the earth under your command (that will be your art), how to create peace and then civilization, how to spare those who submit and to beat down proud resisters.

There have always been some people who admired the Greeks more than the Romans. From what you have read so far, what is your view?

Look up in an encyclopaedia two of the famous Greeks mentioned in the third and fourth paragraphs above and write a paragraph on each of them.

Chapter 21

Marcus Quintum domum suam invitat

posterō diē Quīntus cum patre domum ambulābat cum accurrit Marcus.

ille 'manē, Quīnte,' inquit; 'vīsne domum mēcum venīre patremque meum vīsere?'

Marcus Quīntum domum dūxit; patrem in tablīnō invēnit.

Marcī pater epistolam scrībae dictābat dē rēpūblicā.

Vocabulary 21

verbs		*nouns*	
salvē, salvēte!	greetings!	**epistola, -ae**, f.	letter
sinō, sinere, sīvī	I allow	**dominus, -ī**, m.	master
vīsō, vīsere, vīsī	I visit	**ātrium, -ī**, n.	hall
cōnficiō, cōnficere,		**ingenium, -ī**, n.	character, talents
cōnfēcī	I finish	**studium, -ī**, n.	study
intersum, interesse,		**tablīnum, -ī**, n.	study (the room)
interfuī + dat.	I am among,	**aedēs, aedium**, f. pl.	house
	I take part in	**ōrātor, ōrātōris**, m.	orator, speaker
adjectives		**soror, sorōris**, f.	sister
clārus, -a, -um	clear, bright, famous	**diēs, diēī**, m.	day
ingeniōsus, -a, -um	talented, clever	**merīdiēs, merīdiēī**, m.	midday
lātus, -a, -um	wide, broad	**cotīdiē**	every day
		rēs, reī, f.	thing, matter, property
adverb		**rēspūblica, reīpūblicae**, f.	the republic
praetereā	moreover	**rē vērā**	in truth, in fact, really
		spēs, speī, f.	hope
pronoun			
aliquis, aliquid	someone, something		

Marcus Quīntum domum suam invītat

cotīdiē Flaccus fīlium ad lūdum Orbiliī dūcēbat. Quīntus celeriter
discēbat, et mox Graecē et dīcere et scrībere poterat. Orbilius
eum laudābat, quod bonus discipulus erat. prīmum Quīntus valdē
miser erat. cēterī enim puerī eum vītābant nec cum eō lūdere
     vītābant avoided
5 volēbant; tandem tamen is quī prīmō diē eum salūtāverat accessit
     is quī the one who . . .
et 'Quīnte,' inquit, 'mihi nōmen est Marcus. nōn dēbēs sōlus hīc
stāre. venī mēcum comitēsque salūtā.' Quīntum ad comitēs dūxit
et 'amīcī,' inquit, 'volō vōbīs commendāre Quīntum Horātium
     commendāre to introduce
Flaccum. salūtāte eum et sinite eum lūdīs nostrīs interesse.' cēterī
10 puerī Marcum suspiciēbant, quod puer erat magnus et lautus;
     suspiciēbant looked up to
praetereā pater eius erat vir īnsignis, quī cōnsul fuerat et clārus
     lautus elegant
ōrātor. itaque omnēs Quīntum salūtāvērunt et eum sīvērunt lūdīs
     īnsignis distinguished
suīs interesse.

    paucīs post diēbus ubi Orbilius puerōs dīmīsit, Quīntus
15 domum ambulābat, cum accurrit Marcus. 'Quīnte,' inquit, 'vīsne
domum mēcum venīre patremque meum vīsere?' Quīntus
verēcundus erat; 'rē vērā' inquit 'mē domum tuam vocās? nōnne
     verēcundus shy
pater tuus rēbus occupātus est?' ille respondit: 'pater meus
     rēbus occupātus occupied by things,
semper occupātus est. semper tamen cupit amīcōs meōs vidēre.
     busy
20 trīstis est; hōc annō soror mea, Tullia, dēliciae patris, periit.
     dēliciae (f. pl.) the darling
adhūc eam lūget sed ubi amīcīs meīs occurrit, hilarior fit. venī.'
     lūget is mourning
    forum trānsiērunt et montem Palātīnum ascendērunt. mox ad
     hilarior fit he becomes more
Marcī aedēs advēnērunt. Marcus iānuam pulsāvit; iānitor iānuam
     cheerful; **pulsāvit** knocked

aperuit et Marcum salūtāvit; 'salvē, domine,' inquit; 'intrā.' Marcus
25 eum rogāvit: 'ubi est pater?' ille 'pater tuus' inquit 'est in tablīnō.
occupātus est. epistolās enim scrībae dictat.'

    Marcus Quīntum in ātrium dūxit. ille numquam aedēs tam
magnificās vīderat. ātrium erat et lātum et altum; in omnibus
lateribus erant magnae iānuae. Marcus Quīntum dūxit ad iānuam
30 quae ā fronte stābat et pulsāvit. aliquis vōce blandā 'intrā' inquit.
Marcus iānuam aperuit et Quīntum in tablīnum dūxit.

scrībae to his secretary
dictat is dictating

lateribus sides
ā fronte in front (of them)
blandā pleasant

A grand Roman atrium

Respondē Latīnē

1 cūr Orbilius Quīntum laudāvit?
2 cūr miser erat Quīntus?
3 cūr Marcum suspiciēbant (*looked up to*) cēterī puerī?
4 ubi erant aedēs Marcī?
5 ubi ad aedēs advēnērunt, quid faciēbat Marcī pater?

Word-building

Learn the following compounds of **pōnō, pōnere, posuī** I put, place:

compōnō, compōnere, composuī	I put together, compose
dēpōnō, dēpōnere, dēposuī	I put down
dispōnō, dispōnere, disposuī	I put in different places, arrange
expōnō, expōnere, exposuī	I put out, explain
impōnō, impōnere, imposuī	I put into, put on
repōnō, repōnere, reposuī	I put back

33

Marcus Quīntum patrī commendat

*Translate the first paragraph of the passage below and answer
the questions on the second*

pater Marcī prope mēnsam stābat; vultum trīstem habēbat et
ānxium sed benevolum; togam praetextam gerēbat tabulamque in
manū tenēbat. ubi Marcus intrāvit, eī arrīsit et 'manē paulīsper,'
inquit; 'ego epistolam dictō ad Atticum dē rēbus pūblicīs.' Marcus
5 Quīntō susurrāvit: 'Atticus est amīcus intimus meī patris; pater
semper eī scrībit dē rēbus pūblicīs.' iam Marcī pater epistolam
cōnfēcerat et scrībae dīxit: 'epistolam statim signā et cursōrī
trāde.'
  Cicerō ad puerōs sē vertit. 'venī hūc, Marce,' inquit, 'et
10 amīcum tuum mihi commendā.' Marcus Quīntum ad Cicerōnem
dūxit et 'ecce, pater,' inquit, 'volō amīcum meum Quīntum
Horātium Flaccum tibi commendāre. puer valdē ingeniōsus est.
Orbilius magnam spem pōnit in ingeniō eius.' Cicerō ad Quīntum
sē vertit et eī arrīsit; 'salvē, Quīnte,' inquit; 'gaudeō quod fīlius
15 meus amīcum tam ingeniōsum habet.' deinde pauca Quīntum
rogāvit dē studiīs; ille studia bene exposuit. Cicerō 'euge,' inquit;
'Marcus vērum dīcit; puer rē vērā ingeniōsus es. sī vīs, tibi licet
librōs meōs īnspicere. Marce, dūc Quīntum ad bibliothēcam.'

mēnsam a table
benevolum benevolent, kindly
praetextam purple-bordered
arrīsit smiled at
paulīsper for a little
susurrāvit whispered
intimus closest
scrībae to his secretary
signā seal! **cursōrī** to my courier

tibi licet you may
bibliothēcam library

1 When Cicero turns to the boys, what does he tell
 Marcus to do?   [2]
2 When Marcus introduces Quintus to him, why is
 Cicero pleased?   [2]
3 How does he know that Marcus told the truth
 about Quintus?   [3]
4 What does he tell Marcus to do?   [2]

CICERO

The young Cicero

Marcus Tullius Cicero, the father of Quintus' friend Marcus, was
born in 106 BC near Arpinum, a little hill town about 100 km
from Rome. His father was a wealthy member of the local
nobility, but his family had never played any part in politics in
Rome. Cicero proved a very bright child and his father sent him
to the best teachers in Rome and then to university in Greece,
where he studied law, oratory (rhetoric) and philosophy.

  A series of terrible wars was tearing the Roman world apart
for much of Cicero's life. When he was seventeen, he himself
fought in one of these wars, Rome's conflict with her Italian
allies (see the background section of Part I, chapter 15). Rome
emerged victorious from this, but now a bloody succession of

civil wars was to begin. These were fought between her great generals in a struggle for power. Some of these generals claimed to be supporting the rule of the senate against the attacks of popular politicians. Others thought that the present system of government no longer worked and wished to reform it in the interests of the people. Cicero tried throughout his life to prop up the old system, but it was doomed to collapse.

Cicero the attorney

The young Cicero was ambitious and decided to make his way by practising in the law courts as a attorney. He did well from the start and in 70 BC leapt to fame when the people of Sicily asked him to prosecute their ruthless Roman governor, Verres, who had plundered the island for personal gain. Verres had said when he was elected that he needed to govern Sicily for three years. One year was to cover his election expenses (he had bribed the electors), one year was to get enough money to secure acquittal when he was prosecuted for misgovernment (he intended to bribe the jury) and one year was to make some profit!

Cicero was taking a big risk since Verres was a noble, and had many powerful friends. But he conducted the case so brilliantly that Verres fled into exile before it was even over. So Cicero was acknowledged to be the leading attorney in Rome at the age of thirty-six.

Cicero

Cicero the consul

Cicero had already been elected quaestor in 76 BC and so was a member of the senate. But he was always looked on with suspicion by the old Roman nobility because he was born a member of the equestrian class (a knight). No one could become a consul until he was forty-three, since much experience was necessary for the post. Cicero became consul at the earliest possible age in 63 BC, but the nobility still despised him as a *novus homō*, a self-made man who was not one of them.

While Cicero was consul, a young noble called Catiline, who had failed in his attempts to become consul himself, tried to overthrow the government by force. Cicero acted decisively. He arrested and executed Catiline's chief supporters in Rome and defeated his army in Etruria. He was hailed by the people as *pater patriae*, and never tired of reminding others of this achievement.

The senators and knights had drawn closer together while they united against the conspiracy, and Cicero hoped to keep this alliance working. His political aim was to maintain the *concordia ōrdinum* (the harmony of the senatorial and equestrian classes), but this was a dream never to be fulfilled.

Three powerful men

The three most powerful men in the Roman world were now Gaius Julius Caesar, Marcus Licinius Crassus (whom we saw in chapter 14 leading an army through Venusia) and Gnaeus Pompey, whom Cicero admired as a man and supported as the champion of the knights. In 60 BC these three formed a political alliance called the First Triumvirate (a ruling group of three men) and brushed the authority of the senate aside. You will be reading more about this in chapter 25. Cicero would have nothing to do with them, but this did not worry them much; all the power was in their hands.

Gaius Julius Caesar

Gnaeus Pompey

Caesar was consul in 59 BC and then went out to govern Gaul, where he achieved famous conquests. Meanwhile Rome was becoming a dangerous and frightening place to live. Political gangs were carrying on a reign of terror and the leader of one of them, Clodius, prepared to prosecute Cicero for executing Catiline's supporters illegally. Cicero panicked and fled to Greece. He was allowed back the next year and given a warm welcome by the people of Italy, but he soon realized that it was the Triumvirs who had let him return and that he had to do what they told him. He was no longer independent and was deeply ashamed of the fact.

Then the Triumvirate began to fall to pieces. Caesar and Pompey drifted apart and Crassus was defeated and killed at Carrhae in 53 BC by the Parthians, against whom he was marching in chapter 14 with high hopes of conquest. Cicero himself was sent in 51 BC, very much against his will, to govern a remote province called Cilicia. Here he governed fairly but not very firmly and won a minor military victory of which he was extremely proud, although no one at Rome took it very seriously.

Civil war

He returned home in 50 BC to find that civil war between Caesar and Pompey could not be long delayed. For a time he sat on the fence. Caesar took the trouble to visit him to try to win him over, but in the end he decided to join Pompey's army in Greece. Here he was given nothing to do. When Caesar defeated Pompey at the battle of Pharsalus (48 BC), Cicero was stunned and his political hopes were destroyed. He returned to Italy and was soon reconciled to Caesar, but he now lived largely in retirement. He entered upon the political scene again four years later, however, after the murder of Julius Caesar. As we shall see, this resulted in his death.

Cicero the man

Cicero was one of the most remarkable men who ever lived. He was a brilliant orator, attorney and writer, a philosopher and a capable, if uninspired, poet. He stuck to his principles as a statesman and gave up his life for them.

He was also a great letter writer. After his death, his letters were collected and published in thirty-five books. Sixteen of these are to his family and friends (some with replies from men such as Caesar and Pompey); sixteen are to his closest friend Atticus, to whom he was writing when Quintus met him; and three are to his brother Quintus. Cicero's letters throw an extraordinarily vivid light on the Rome of his day.

Here is part of a letter written to his brother Quintus in February 56 BC, the year after he had returned from exile to find the political gangs at work. Clodius' gang had destroyed Cicero's house on the Palatine hill during his exile, but he received compensation by decree of the senate and quickly rebuilt it. The letter describes a meeting of the people, before whom Clodius was prosecuting the rival gang-leader Milo for using violence in politics. Pompey came forward to speak for Milo:

> On 6 February Milo appeared in court. Pompey spoke, or rather tried to. For as soon as he got up, the gangs of Clodius raised a shout, and this went on throughout his whole speech –

he was interrupted not only by uproar but by insults and abuse. When he had finished his speech (for he was extremely brave: he said the lot and at times even amid silence), but when he had finished, up got Clodius. There was such a shout from our side (for we had decided to return the compliment) that he lost all control of his thoughts, his tongue and his expression. This went on for two hours while every insult and even obscene verses were shouted against Clodius and his sister.

Clodius, furious and pale, in the middle of all this shouting asked his supporters, 'Who wants to starve the people to death?' 'Pompey!' answered the gang. Then, at the ninth hour, as if a signal had been given, Clodius' supporters all began to spit at ours. Tempers flared. Clodius' gang shoved, to push us from our place. Our side made a charge; his gang fled; Clodius was thrown from the platform, and then we fled too, in case we should have trouble from the crowd. The senate was summoned to the senate house. Pompey went home.

The following year Clodius was killed in a brawl outside Rome by Milo and his supporters. In the rioting which followed, Clodius' gangs burned his body in the senate house, which was burnt to the ground and had not been rebuilt when Quintus arrived in Rome.

Here is another letter, which Cicero wrote to a friend when his beloved daughter Tullia died in February 45 BC:

In this lonely place, I don't talk to anyone at all. In the morning I hide myself in a thick, thorny wood and I don't come out of it until the evening. After yourself, my best friend in the world is my solitude. When I am alone, all I talk to is my books, but I keep on bursting into tears. I fight against them as much as I can, but so far it has been an unequal struggle.

After reading this section, compose a date chart outlining Cicero's life.

What does the first of the two letters quoted above suggest about the state of politics in Rome at this time? On what occasions might similar scenes occur today?

paucīs post diēbus Marcus Quīntum ā forō ad Circum Maximum dūxit.

puerī intrāvērunt sed loca spectātōribus vacua vix invēnērunt.

praetor soliō (*chair*) surrēxit signumque dedit.

continuō ē carceribus (*starting cage*) ēvolāvērunt equī.

Vocabulary 22

verbs		nouns	
spērō, spērāre, spērāvī	I hope	**turba, -ae**, f.	crowd
volō, volāre, volāvī	I fly	**lūdī, -ōrum**, m. pl.	the games
faveō, favēre, fāvī + dat.	I favor, support	**signum, -ī**, n.	sign, signal
pāreō, pārēre, pāruī + dat.	I obey	**vesper, vesperis**, m.	evening
frangō, frangere, frēgī	I break	**cāsus, cāsūs**, m.	mishap, misfortune
perdō, perdere, perdidī	I lose, destroy	**currus, currūs**, m.	chariot
rapiō, rapere, rapuī	I snatch, steal	**cursus, cursūs**, m.	running; a course

adverb		adjectives	
quō?	where to?	**contentus, -a, -um**	content
		frāctus, -a, -um	broken
		maximus, -a, -um	greatest, very great
		plūrimus, -a, -um	very many
		nōbilis, nōbile	noble, famous'
		tālis, tāle	such
		vetus, veteris	old

What do the following English words mean and from what Latin words are they derived:
fracture, maximize, perdition, vespers, veteran?

Lūdī circēnsēs

paucīs post diēbus Quīntus cum patre ad lūdum Orbiliī
ambulābat; iam ad forum advēnerat cum aliquem sē vocantem
audīvit. respēxit et Marcum vīdit ad sē currentem. ille, ubi
accessit, 'quō īs, Quīnte?' inquit. Quīntus 'ad lūdum nīmīrum
5   festīnō.' Marcus 'nōlī nūgās nārrāre,' inquit; 'fēriae sunt. hodiē
nēmō ad lūdum īre dēbet. venī mēcum ad Circum Maximum.
praetor lūdōs magnificōs populō dat.' Quīntus, quī lūdōs circēnsēs
numquam vīderat, Marcō pārēre volēbat, sed pater cautus erat;
'multī scelestī' inquit 'tālibus lūdīs adsunt. perīculōsum est.' sed
10 Marcus Quīntum trāns forum iam dūcēbat. Flaccus sē vertit et
domum rediit.
      ubi ad Circum advēnērunt, ingēns turba aderat; multa mīlia
cīvium, virī, fēminae, puerī ad portās concurrēbant. Quīntus
Marcusque intrāre vix poterant; tandem loca vacua invēnērunt et
15 sēdērunt. maxima pompa iam per circum contendēbat; tībīcinēs
pompam dūcēbant, deinde mīlitēs imāginēs deōrum ferēbant,
postrēmō plūrimī agitātōrēs currūs quadriiugōs lentē agēbant.
      tandem pompa cōnfecta erat. duodecim currūs in carceribus

lūdī circēnsēs the circus games

vocantem calling

nīmīrum of course
nūgās nonsense
fēriae sunt it's a holiday
praetor the praetor

cautus cautious; **scelestī** criminals
perīculōsum dangerous

pompa procession
tībīcinēs flute players
imāginēs images; **postrēmō** lastly
agitātōrēs (chariot) drivers
quadriiugōs four-horsed (adj.)
duodecim twelve
carceribus the starting cage

stābant ad prīmum cursum parātī. praetor soliō surrēxit signumque
20 dedit. continuō ē carceribus ēvolāvērunt equī. omnēs spectātōrēs
clāmābant et agitātōrēs incitābant. illī equōs verberābant
mētamque petēbant. prīmus mētam incolumis circumiit; alter
mētae interiōrem rotam īnflīxit; currus frāctus est; ipse ad terram
cecidit, habēnīs involūtus; habēnīs sē expedīvit fūgitque ē cursū.
25 cēterī cursum septiēns circumvolāvērunt sine cāsū; vīcit Venetus.
gaudēbat Marcus, quī illī factiōnī favēbat.

totum diem Quīntus Marcusque cursūs spectābat. vesper iam
aderat cum Marcus 'venī, Quīnte,' inquit, 'tempus est domum
redīre; sine dubiō parentēs nostrī ānxiī sunt.' dum surgit,
30 crumēnam ē sinū togae tollere temptābat; sed nihil sinū inerat;
crumēnam perdiderat. 'dī immortālēs!' inquit, 'aliquis crumēnam
meam rapuit.' Quīntus valdē commōtus erat, sed Marcus 'nūllīus
mōmentī est,' inquit; 'aliam crumēnam domī habeō.'

solio from his chair

incitābant urged on
verberābant lashed
mētam the turning post
circumiit rounded
interiōrem rotam the inner wheel
īnflīxit crashed (x acc. on y dat.)
habēnīs involūtus wrapped up,
  caught in the reins
expedīvit freed from
septiēns seven times
Venetus the Blue; **factiōnī** team
sine dubiō without doubt
crumēnam purse; **sinū** pocket
nūllīus mōmentī of no importance

Word-building

Learn the following compounds of **faciō**, **facere**, **fēcī** I do, I make:

afficiō, afficere, affēcī	I affect
cōnficiō, cōnficere, cōnfēcī	I finish
efficiō, efficere, effēcī	I carry out, effect
interficiō, interficere, interfēcī	I kill
perficiō, perficere, perfēcī	I carry through, complete
reficiō, reficere, refēcī	I remake, repair

The praetor starts
the chariot race

The chariot race
from the film Ben Hur

Fābella: Marcus Quīntusque cursibus adsunt

Persōnae: Marcus, Quīntus, spectātor, puella

Marcus Quīntum in Circum Maximum dūcit.

Marcus: festīnā, Quīnte. dēbēmus locum vacuum quaerere.

Quīntus: tantam turbam hominum numquam vīdī. nūlla loca
5 vacua sunt.

Marcus: ecce, duo loca vacua. pervēnimus. vidē, Quīnte,
puella pulchra proxima sedet. euge! pompa paene
cōnfecta est. tū, quī post nōs spectās, crūra contrahe!
mē trūdis.

10 **spectātor:** ignōsce mihi, iuvenis. crūra mihi longa sunt, līnea
arta.

Quīntus: vidē, Marce, duodecim currūs in carcere stant. praetor
signum dat. iam ēvolant equī.

Marcus: (*clāmat*) festīnā, Venete. equōs verberā. ad mētam
15 festīnā. mē miserum! spatiōsō orbe mētam circumit.
(*clāmat*) quid facis, ignāve? proximus currus tē subit.

Quīntus: quid facis, īnfelīx? tende lōra sinistrā! ecce! fāvimus
ignāvō. Russātus eum superat.

Marcus: (*ad puellam sē vertit*) cūr lacrimās, cārissima? tū
20 quoque Venetō fāvistī?

puella: heu, heu! omnem spem in Venetō posuī, omnem
pecūniam.

Marcus: nōlī tē vexāre. ego cōnsōlātiōnem tibi offerō. (*eam
bāsiāre temptat*)

25 **puella:** nōlī procāx esse, iuvenis. vidē! currūs iterum ad
mētam accēdunt.

Quīntus: Russātus mētam propius circumit. ecce! currum in
mētam illīsit.

puella: ecce! Venetus eum superāvit. iam ad fīnem prīmus
30 advenit. (*Marcō arrīdet*) ille palmam tenet, tū palmam
tuam petere dēbēs.

Marcus puellam bāsiat.

proxima next (to us)
pompa the procession
crūra contrahe pull back your legs
trūdis you are pushing
ignōsce (+ dat.) forgive!
līnea arta the seats (are) narrow

verberā lash!
mē miserum! unhappy me!
spatiōsō orbe in a wide circle
ignāve coward!
subit is catching up
tende lōra pull on the reins
Russātus the Red (team)

bāsiāre to kiss
procāx impertinent

propius too close
illīsit he has crashed
fīnem the finish
arrīdet (+ dat.) smiles at
palmam prize, palm

Chariot racing

Scintilla ad Flaccum scrībit

*Translate the first paragraph of the following passage and
answer the questions on the letter*

paucīs post diēbus Flaccus epistolam accēpit; celeriter signum
frēgit; Scintilla omnia scrīpserat quae Venusiae facta erant, ex
quō Rōmam abierant. Flaccus Quīntum statim vocāvit
epistolamque recitāvit:

5   Scintilla virō fīliōque cārissimīs salūtem plūrimam dat.
          prīmum, ego Horātiaque valēmus et rēs bene agimus.
      iuvenis quī Horātiam amat nōs iuvat; fīlius est veteris tuī
      amīcī Terentiī. ovēs cūrat; omnēs iam tetondit; plūrimam
      lānam habēmus. segetēs mātūrae sunt, sed magna siccitās fuit;
10   ex quō Rōmam abiistis rārō pluit. itaque segetēs nōn bonae
      sunt. vīnētum tamen flōret; plūrimās ūvās habēbimus.
      contentae sumus, sed vōs valdē dēsīderāmus. Argus trīstis est;
      Quīntum semper quaerit.
          et vōs, cārissimī, iter longum cōnfēcistis et Rōmam
15   incolumēs advēnistis? Quīntusne iam in lūdō Orbiliī studet?
      domicilium invēnistis? nōndum epistolam accēpimus. sine
      morā scrībe longam epistolam et nārrā nōbīs omnia quae
      accidērunt. cūrā, mī cārissime vir, ut valeās, et Quīntum
      fīlium nostrum cārissimum dīligenter cūrā.
20   Venusiae data Kalendīs Quīntīlibus.

signum the seal
facta erant had happened
ex quō (tempore) since

cārissimīs dearest; **salūtem
    plūrimam** warmest greetings
valēmus we are well
ovēs sheep; **tetondit** has sheared
lānam wool; **segetēs** crops
mātūrae ripe; **siccitās** drought
rārō pluit it has seldom rained
vīnētum vineyard; **flōret** is
    flourishing; **ūvās** grapes
habēbimus we shall have
dēsīderāmus we miss
domicilium a lodging
nōndum not yet; **morā** delay
accidērunt has happened
ut valeās that you keep well
data (epistola) given (to the postman)
Kalendīs Quīntīlibus on 1 July

1 Scintilla's letter follows the form (beginning and end)
   usual in Roman letters; how does this form differ from
   that of our letters?   [4]
2 How are Scintilla and Horatia managing to run the farm? [3]
3 Why aren't the crops good?   [3]
4 What is the matter with Argus?   [2]
5 What items of news does Scintilla want from Flaccus?   [4]

THE GAMES

In a place such as Rome where so many citizens were poor or
unemployed, the public shows put on for them were of great
importance as something to look forward to in their grim lives.
And mounting these shows gave the magistrates an opportunity to
display their wealth and social status as well as to win popularity –
and votes – among the common people who would noisily express
their appreciation for the free entertainment. At the time of our
story there were sixty-four days of shows in the Roman calendar.
Soon, as politicians such as Julius Caesar went all out for self-
advertisement, the number was to increase dramatically. And of
course shows were held not only at Rome but at towns all over the
Roman world, including Verulamium and Caerleon in Britain.

However, these entertainments did not necessarily defuse social tensions. In 59 AD during the gladiatorial games at Pompeii a riot broke out between the locals and visitors from nearby Nuceria. The amphitheatre was closed for ten years. Sadly, the modern world can offer parallels to such pointless brutality: in 1986 thirty-eight were killed and over four hundred wounded when conflict broke out between soccer fans in the Heysel soccer stadium in Belgium.

Theatre

In Rome during the first century BC the shows would generally begin with performances in the theatre, continue with gladiatorial displays and end with the races. The drama consisted largely of comedies, slapstick, knockabout farce, acrobatics, ballet and mime, an increasingly popular Roman mix of satire and playful antics. Biting references to leading politicians were speedily picked up by the audience. Serious drama was not unknown but it tended to be swamped in spectacle in a bid for popular appeal by the sponsor. Accius' *Clytemnestra* was staged with 600 mules. And Horace tells us that when spectators became bored there were cries of 'We want bears' and 'We want boxers'.

Gladiators

Until Rome's first permanent amphitheatre was built in 29 BC, exhibitions of gladiators and of wild beast fights took place in temporary enclosures in the forum and the Circus Maximus. Pompey exhibited elephants in the latter at his games in 55 BC and when they stampeded and made for the railings enclosing the arena, there was general panic. Julius Caesar's response in 46 BC was to surround the arena with a ditch ten feet wide and ten feet deep.

Gladiators

The gladiatorial show started with a grand parade with the gladiators riding in chariots to the arena dressed in gold and purple robes. Brass and wind instruments and a hydraulic organ supplied the music.

Who were the gladiators? Those who were put in no-hope situations in the arena were criminals who had been condemned to death. The proper gladiators, on the other hand, had at least a little hope. If they survived long enough, they would win their freedom, or they might be given it after a particularly impressive performance. And they could gain an enormous following, especially among the female members of the crowd. Some of them were criminals condemned to the gladiatorial schools; others were slaves, often prisoners of war, who had been sold to them; and some were free citizens who had enrolled voluntarily or been forced to do so by economic necessity. When they signed on, they swore: 'I undertake to be burnt by fire, to be bound in chains, to be beaten, to die by the sword.' These bleak words are appropriate to an activity which goes back to ancient funeral rituals where fights to the finish were staged as a blood offering to the dead.

In the arena they were variously armed and matched against differently equipped opponents. Here we describe three of them. The heavy-armed Samnite carried a large oblong shield, a sword or spear. His head was protected by a visored helmet, his right leg by a greave and his right arm by a protective sleeve. The Thraex also wore a helmet, carried a light shield and was armed with a reversed sickle. The light-footed *rētiārius* fought bare-headed, wore a tunic and was armed with a three-pronged trident and a dagger, and a net to trap his adversary.

If a gladiator was at his opponent's mercy, the crowd would express passionate judgement as to whether he should be finished off. Thumbs down probably meant that his opponent should drop his weapon and spare him, thumbs pointed to one's own chest probably meant kill him. The president of the games would almost always fall in with popular sentiment. The winner received a crown and prize money, and an attendant with the mask of Mercury, the god who escorted souls to the underworld, came on with a hot iron to make sure that the victim was really dead. Boys covered the pools of blood with clean sand.

Brutality did not stop here. Two criminals might be driven into the arena, only one of them armed. And wild beasts were matched against each other or against humans. Vast hunts were staged in which huge numbers of exotic animals were exterminated. (In 80 AD when the emperor Titus inaugurated Rome's famous amphitheatre, the Colosseum, 5,000 wild beasts were killed in a single day.) Incense-burners were set out to overcome the smell of the animals, and slaves would spray clouds of perfume at the audience as they sat under the shade of an awning that covered the entire circle of the amphitheatre.

It is interesting that the gladiatorial combats did not stop when the Roman empire became Christian. And before we condemn this viciously cruel pastime too scornfully, it is as well to remember that public executions were held in Britain until 1868 and that bull-fighting even now has a huge and fanatical following in Spanish-speaking countries and the South of France.

Fighting a leopard

The races

Quintus goes with Marcus to see the races at the Circus Maximus, a huge rectangle with semicircular ends surrounded by seats which held 250,000 spectators. It is located between the Palatine and Aventine hills. Men and women could sit together here (they were kept apart at the theatre and amphitheatre).

When the praetor dropped a white cloth to start the race, the chariots rushed from the twelve staggered starting boxes, beginning counterclockwise on the first of what were usually seven laps of the 1,200 yard track. They dashed along the central division (*spīna* = backbone) of the stadium, keeping it on the right. Each time a lap was finished, an egg and later also a dolphin were lowered. Most thrilling were the turns around the *mētae*, the turning posts which each consisted of three cones of gilded bronze, at either end of the *spīna*. If a team went too wide of these turning posts, it might be overtaken on the inside but if it more than grazed it it would crash. This was a sport involving considerable skill. The distance covered was about 5 miles and the race lasted about fifteen minutes.

Charioteers were mainly slaves, but, like gladiators, they could win immense popularity and might make enough money to be able to buy their freedom. They came from one of four companies of trainers who hired out teams to the promoters who paid the expenses. The charioteers wore the colors of their stables – red, pale green, sea blue and white – and were cheered on by fanatical supporters whose enthusiasm was sharpened by the money they had bet on their team. Gambling was against the law, but it went on on a massive scale both in the circus and in the arena.

Pliny wrote of the racing:

> *The races are on, a spectacle which has not the slightest attraction for me. It lacks novelty and variety. If you have seen it once, you have seen it a thousand times. So it amazes me that thousands and thousands of grown men should be like children, wanting to look at horses running and men standing on chariots over and over again.*

Do you sympathize with Pliny here? Give your reasons.

What are the similarities and the differences between modern and Roman sports and between their fans?

Quīntus, puer summā industriā, librum legēbat cum Marcus eum magnā vōce vocāvit.

Marcus Quīntō 'venī mēcum' inquit 'ad balnea; forō nōn longē absunt.'

in balneīs aliī in piscīnam ingentī clāmōre īnsiliēbant, aliī pilīs lūdēbant.

Quīntus omnia summā admīrātiōne spectābat.

Vocabulary 23

verbs		*nouns*	
retineō, retinēre, retinuī	I hold back	**mora, -ae**, f.	delay
referō, referre, rettulī	I carry back; I report	**nimium, -ī**, n. + gen.	too much, e.g.
īnsum, inesse, īnfuī	I am in, I am among	**nimium vīnī** too much (of) wine	
mālō, mālle, māluī	I prefer	**balnea, -ōrum**, n. pl.	baths
		ānxietās, ānxietātis, f.	anxiety
adverbs		**celeritās, celeritātis**, f.	speed
paulīsper	for a little (time)		
unde?	whence? from where?	*adjective*	
undique	from all sides	**aeger, aegra, aegrum**	sick, ill

In the following sentences explain the meaning of the words in italics by reference to their Latin roots:

1 He has a *retentive* memory.
2 She *related* all that had happened.
3 We had an *ingenious* idea.
4 They returned with the utmost *celerity*.
5 They presented a *petition* to the chairman.

A mosaic at the entrance to a Roman bath house

Marcus Quīntum ad balnea dūcit

Quīntus iam diū in lūdō Orbiliī studuerat. puer erat summā industriā studiīsque gaudēbat. quondam ubi Orbilius puerōs dīmīsit, Marcus Quīntō 'ego' inquit 'ad balnea eō. nōnne vīs mēcum venīre? forō nōn longē absunt.' Quīntus ōtiōsus erat

5 Marcōque pārēre volēbat. continuō ad balnea prōcēdēbant; Flaccus cum Marcī paedagōgō post eōs ambulābat.

    mox advēnērunt. intrāvērunt et circumspectābant. plūrimī hominēs in ātriō erant; clāmōrēs undique circumsonābant. aliī in piscīnam sonō ingentī īnsiliēbant, aliī pilīs lūdēbant. botulāriī

10 crustulāriīque mercēs suās magnā vōce laudābant. Quīntus omnia summā admīrātiōne spectābat cum Marcus amīcum quendam vīdit; Quīntum relīquit et ad eum accessit. Quīntus sōlus ad apodytērium discessit. vestīmenta exuit et in armāriō posuit. prīmum in tepidārium iniit et paulīsper in aquā tepidā iacēbat;

15 deinde in calidārium iit; dēnique in piscīnam īnsiluit et aliquamdiū sē exercēbat.

    tandem ad apodytērium rediit vestīmentaque quaesīvit. sed ubi armārium aperuit, nihil inerat; aliquis vestīmenta rapuerat. Quīntus in ātrium recurrit et circumspectābat. subitō hominem

summā industriā of the greatest industry, extremely hardworking
quondam once
ōtiōsus at leisure

paedagōgō tutor

circumsonābant echoed around
piscīnam the pool
īnsiliēbant were jumping into
pilīs with balls
botulāriī sausage-sellers
crustulāriī cake-sellers
mercēs suās their wares
apodytērium the changing-room
exuit took off; **armāriō** cupboard
tepidārium the warm room
calidārium the hot room
dēnique finally
aliquamdiū for some time

20 cōnspexit ad iānuam festīnantem quī vestīmenta manibus ferēbat.
Quīntus statim magnā vōce clāmāvit: 'dēprehende illum fūrem;
vestīmenta mea aufert.' Flaccus, quī in ātriō manēbat, eum
audīvit, fūrem vīdit, sine morā petīvit. ille iam ad portam
fugiēbat sed Flaccus summā celeritāte cucurrit ipsōque in līmine
25 eum dēprehendit. vestīmenta rapuit rettulitque ad fīlium. Quīntus
patrī grātiās ēgit vestīmentaque celeriter induit.

festīnantem hurrying
dēprehende seize!
fūrem thief

līmine threshold

Respondē Latīnē

1 ubi balnea Quīntus intrāvit, quid vīdit?
2 cūr sōlus ad apodȳtērium Quīntus iit?
3 ubi Quīntus ad apodȳtērium rediit, cūr nōn sē induit?
4 quōmodo Quīntus vestīmenta recēpit?

A hypocaust, a heating system
under the floor

An apodyterium (changing room)

Word-building

Learn the following compounds of **ferō**, **ferre**, **tulī** I carry, bear:

afferō (= **adferō**), **afferre**, **attulī**	I carry to, I report
auferō (= **abferō**), **auferre**, **abstulī**	I carry away
cōnferō, **cōnferre**, **contulī**	I carry together
efferō, **efferre**, **extulī**	I carry out
īnfero, **īnferre**, **intulī**	I carry into, carry against
prōferō, **prōferre**, **prōtulī**	I carry forwards, bring out
referō, **referre**, **rettulī**	I carry back, I report

Marcus ēbrius est

Without translating, answer the questions below the following passage

Quīntus, ubi vestīmenta induit, in ātrium cucurrit Marcumque quaesīvit. diū quaerēbat; tandem eum invēnit in terrā iacentem post columnam. Quīntus eum tollere temptāvit; ille aegrē surrēxit; vacillāvit iterumque ad terram dēcidit. Quīntus eum
5 summā ānxietāte spectābat; sed Marcus nōn aeger erat; nimium vīnī cum amīcīs biberat et plānē ēbrius erat. iam accurrerat eius paedagōgus, quī eum sustulit et domum dūxit. Flaccus, hīs rēbus commōtus, Quīntum domum rapuit.

postrīdiē Marcus ad lūdum nōn vēnit. nam pater, quī valdē
10 īrātus erat, eum domī retinēbat; Cicerō ipse, vir summā doctrīnā, fīliī studia cūrābat. posterō annō Cicerō eum Athēnās mīsit ad Lycēum, ubi philosophiae studēbat. sed Marcus in studiīs nōn multum prōfēcit; nam lūdere mālēbat quam studēre. Quīntus trīstis erat quod amīcum tam bonum perdiderat; neque eum
15 posteā Rōmae vīdit, sed paucīs post annīs eī Athēnīs occurrit; ipse enim eō tempore in Acadēmiā studēbat.

post columnam behind a column
aegrē with difficulty
vacillāvit tottered
plānē completely
paedagōgus tutor
sustulit raised him
rapuit rushed
summā doctrīnā of the greatest learning
posterō annō the next year
Lycēum the Lyceum (one of the two universities in Athens)
prōfēcit made progress
Acadēmiā the Academy (the other university in Athens)

1 Where did Quintus find Marcus? What was the matter with him? [2/2]
2 How did Flaccus feel about the incident? [2]
3 Why didn't Marcus come to school the next day? [3]
4 How did Marcus get on at the Lyceum? [3]
5 Why was Quintus sad? [2]
6 Where and under what circumstances did they meet again? [3]

A DAY AT ROME

Let us now follow the daily round of an ordinary Roman who wishes to climb to a higher social level.

He gets up very early in his simply furnished bedroom and splashes some water on his face and hands. He has slept in his tunic and, before he leaves the house, he puts on his toga. He drapes over himself this large woollen garment, roughly semi-circular in shape, winding it round his shoulders and waist. To wear the toga marked a man out as a Roman citizen.

If he bothers with breakfast, it is a light one, consisting of bread with cheese or with honey, washed down with some milk. Then he sets off to visit his patron, a man of higher rank who he hopes will help him to success. He is his patron's client and as such will have to do him favors in return.

Between daybreak and the second hour (see the note at the end of the chapter), he presents himself at his patron's house. This morning greeting is called the *salūtātiō*. He hopes for a small present of money (*sportula*) or an invitation to dinner that evening. His patron might well insist that he accompanies him to the forum where business begins at the third hour. A Roman writer called Pliny complained about how many things there were to do there. 'I attended a coming-of-age ceremony,' he wrote, 'I went to an engagement or a wedding, one man called me to witness a will, another to give legal advice.' This may well be an exaggeration, but the morning was certainly the time for business, both political, legal and financial.

There would be a welcome interval after the sixth hour for lunch. This was a light meal consisting of fish, eggs or pork with vegetables, followed by fruit. After a rest, a tradition still kept up by the Italians with their siestas, our Roman would probably take some exercise.

He may well pay a visit to the Campus Martius (Plain of Mars). This broad plain, enclosed on its western side by a bend in the river Tiber, was the playground of ancient Rome. Its vast expanse of green was the perfect place for a stroll in the open; it was the ideal location for military training; and the young men of Rome gathered here to practise each and every sport. They ran, rode on horseback, drove chariots, wrestled and threw balls, javelins and the discus. The nearby river with its strong current gave the opportunity for an energetic swim. Roman sportsmen crowded the Campus Martius to such an extent that Julius Caesar thought of creating an even larger sports ground on the other side of the river.

Our Roman moves on at about the eighth hour to the public baths (*balnea*) for a refreshing wash. There were many of these in Rome and they were all extremely cheap. There were separate facilities in the biggest for men and women; different times could be set aside for the two sexes in the smaller ones.

The bather would start in the changing room (*apodȳtērium*). He would proceed from here to the warm room (*tepidārium*), where he would immerse himself in warm water in preparation for the hot room (*calidārium*). The water was heated by a system underneath the floor called a hypocaust. After a brief bath here, he was oiled with olive oil, which was then scraped off with a strigil (see illustration). Then he walked back through the warm room to the cold room (*frīgidārium*) where he leapt into cold water. He now dried himself with a towel and returned to the changing room.

An athlete scraping off oil with a strigil

Strigils and oil flask

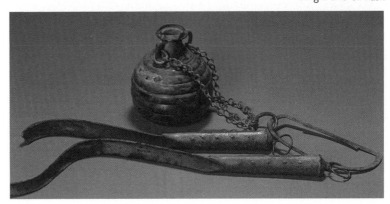

It was all a lively, ear-splitting business, and the writer Seneca vividly describes the drawbacks of living near the baths. The noise, he says, was appalling. Vigorous body-builders groaned and panted, masseurs energetically slapped their victims, and the scorer shouted out the totals at ball games. There was the noise of quarrelling, of a thief being arrested, probably as he ran off with somebody's clothes, and of the splashing caused by those who insisted on hurtling themselves into the water. Additional hazards were those who liked singing in the baths as well as the sellers of cakes, sausages and other foods, advertising their wares each with his own strident call.

Finally, dinner (*cēna*) was a big affair, starting at about the ninth hour in summer and the tenth in winter, and it was considered short if it lasted only three Roman hours. This is a long time to spend eating! But there was plenty of conversation and often some entertainment.

Roman food

Our Roman returns home nervously after dinner through the dark and narrow city streets, earnestly hoping that he will not be mugged.

PS (*post scrīptum*) There were twelve hours in a Roman day. Each hour was one-twelfth of the time from sunrise to sunset. Thus hours were longer in summer than in winter and varied between about $^3/_4$ and $1^1/_4$ modern hours.

> *The Roman poet Martial summed up – no doubt satirically – his day in the city:*
>
> > *The first and second hour wear down those greeting their patrons, and the third is business time for the husky-voiced lawyers. Rome prolongs its different employments to the fifth hour. The sixth offers rest for the exhausted and the seventh is the end of the working day. The eighth and some of the ninth see the couches filled with the reclining dinner guest.*
>
> *Tell us about your imaginary day at Rome, basing your schedule on Martial's timetable.*

haec nāvis longior est quam illa; haec nāvis longissima est.

hic canis maior est quam ille; hic canis maximus est.

numquam puellam amīciōrem vīdī quam Horātiam; Horātia amīcissima est.

numquam puerum cognōvī peiōrem quam Decimum; Decimus pessimus est.

What do **longior** and **longissimus** mean? And what does **longior quam** mean?

Vocabulary 24

verbs		*nouns*	
numerō, numerāre	I count	**victōria, -ae**, f.	victory
caveō, cavēre, cāvī	I beware of	**inimīcus, -ī**, m.	enemy
praetereō, praeterīre,		**praemium, -ī**, n.	reward
praeteriī	I go past, pass	**spectāculum, -ī**, n.	show
prōvideō, prōvidēre,		**cliēns, clientis**, m.	client, dependant
prōvīdī	I foresee	**ōrdō, ōrdinis**, m.	rank, line, order
vehō, vehere, vēxī	I carry	**spectātor, spectātōris**, m.	spectator
fīō, fīerī	I become	**genus, generis**, n.	race, kind, sort
		cōnspectus, cōnspectūs, m.	sight, view
adverbs			
dēnique	lastly, finally	*adjectives*	
magnopere	greatly	**superbus, -a, -um**	proud
quam	than	**crūdēlis, crūdēle**	cruel
		ferōx, ferōcis	fierce
conjunction			
quamquam	although		

What do the following English phrases mean, and from what Latin word is each of the adjectives in italics derived: a *ferocious* beast, a *dire* event, a *spectacular* sight, an *ordinal* number, a *client* kingdom, an *inimical* speech, *innumerable* ants?

Julius Caesar

Caesaris triumphī

tempus celeriter fūgit. Quīntus iam quīnque annōs Rōmae
mānserat. plūrēs amīcōs habēbat quam numerāre poterat; in diēs
laetior fīēbat. mēnse Quīntīlī C. Iūlius Caesar ab Africā Rōmam
tandem rediit. quattuor iam annōs bellum cīvīle per tōtum orbem
5 terrārum gesserat. omnēs inimīcōs vīcerat, tōtum imperium
Rōmānum regēbat. cōnstituit igitur triumphōs agere ob victōriās
quās reportāverat in Galliā, in Aegyptō, in Pontō, in Africā. fēriās
prōnūntiāvit quīndecim diērum. spectācula omnis generis ēdidit,
mūnera gladiātōria, vēnātiōnēs, lūdōs scaenicōs et tragicōs et
10 comicōs. nēmō umquam lūdōs splendidiōrēs ēdiderat quam illōs.
    prīmō diē fēriārum Quīntus māne surrēxit. patrem valēre
iussit festīnāvitque ad scholam Orbiliī, ubi amīcō cuidam, Pūbliō
nōmine, occurrit. sine morā ad forum contendērunt. ubi
advēnērunt, iam aderat ingēns multitūdō, virī, fēminae, puerī, et
15 cīvēs et servī; Quīntus numquam maiōrem turbam vīderat quam
illam. interdum senātor per mediam turbam cum comitātū

in diēs day by day
mēnse Quīntīlī in the month of July

triumphōs agere to hold triumphs
ob (+ acc.) because of
reportāverat he had won
fēriās holiday
prōnūntiāvit declared
ēdidit he gave
mūnera gladiātōria gladiatorial
    shows
vēnātiōnēs wild beast hunts
lūdōs scaenicōs dramatic shows
interdum from time to time
comitātū retinue

clientium perrūpit. interdum mulier nōbilis ad Capitōlium
prōcēdēbat lectīcā imposita, quam ferēbant octō servī. crustulāriī
botulāriīque per turbam ambulābant quī mercēs suās maximā
20 vōce venditābant. Quīntus ad botulārium praetereuntem accessit
plūrimōsque botulōs ēmit; in gradibus templī cum amīcō sēdit
botulōsque avidē dēvorāvit.

mox pompa triumphālis accēdēbat. Quīntus Pūbliusque
clāmōrēs plausūsque spectātōrum audīre poterant. in prīmum
25 ōrdinem sē trūsērunt pompamque accēdentem spectābant.
pompam dūxērunt legiōnāriī, armīs fulgentibus indūtī. deinde
plaustra innumerābilia praeteriērunt, quae spolia bellī vehēbant;
plaustra titulōs ferēbant quī nōmina urbium captārum exhibēbant.
plaustrum quod spolia Ponticī bellī vehēbat hunc titulum sōlum
30 exhibēbat: VENI, VIDI, VICI.

post plaustra captīvī contendēbant, catēnīs gravātī, inter quōs
erat Vercingetorix, Gallōrum fortissimus; nēmō Caesarī hostis
ferōcior fuerat quam ille; etiam nunc superbē sē gerēbat,
quamquam mortem crūdēlissimam mox obitūrus erat.

35 dēnique Caesar ipse in cōnspectum veniēbat. palūdāmentum
purpureum gerēbat et in capite corōnam lauream. currū
quadriiugō vectus manum dextram identidem tollēbat, turbam
spectātōrum salūtāns. currus Quīntum praeterībat cum subitō
axis frāctus est; Caesar ipse paene ad terram cecidit sed sine
40 morā surrēxit montemque Capitōlīnum pedibus ascendit inter
duōs ōrdinēs elephantōrum.

perrūpit burst through
lectīcā imposita lying on a litter
crustulāriī cake-sellers
botulāriī sausage-sellers
mercēs suās their wares
venditābant advertised
praetereuntem passing
avidē greedily
pompa triumphālis the triumphal
    procession
sē trūsērunt pushed (themselves)
legiōnāriī legionary soldiers
fulgentibus shining
indūtī dressed in, wearing
plaustra wagons; **spolia** spoils
titulōs notices; **captārum** captured
exhibēbant displayed
catēnīs gravātī weighed down by
    chains
sē gerēbat bore himself, behaved
obitūrus about to meet
palūdāmentum purpureum a
    purple cloak
corōnam lauream a laurel crown
currū quadriiugō four-horsed chariot
vectus carried by, riding in
dextram right
identidem again and again
axis axle; **frāctus** broken

Word-building

What do the following pairs of adjectives mean?

amīcus   inimīcus
cautus   incautus
certus   incertus
dignus   indignus
fēlīx   īnfēlīx
memor   immemor
nōtus   ignōtus

A Roman triumph

Quīntus fortūnam suam cognōscit

Translate the first paragraph of the following passage and answer the questions on the second

Quīntus Pūbliusque sē vertērunt et summā difficultāte per turbam sē trūsērunt. ad cūriam advēnerant cum anus dīvīna eīs obstetit. illa 'nōnne vultis, iuvenēs,' inquit, 'fortūnam vestram cognōscere? age, belle iuvenis, manum tuam mihi dā.' sīc dīxit et manum
5 Pūbliī prehendit. Pūblius invītus concessit. illa manum eius diū īnspexit. deinde 'iuvenis es summā virtūte quī mīles fortissimus fīēs. sed cavē, iuvenis, cavē Germāniam. nōlī in Germāniā mīlitāre. mortem prōvideō, mortem crūdēlissimam in silvīs Germāniae.' Pūblius manum suam āvulsit. rīsit et 'nōlō plūra
10 cognōscere,' inquit; 'age, Quīnte, tū fortūnam tuam cognōsce.'

    Quīntus invītus dīvīnam sīvit manum suam īnspicere. illa, ubi manum Quīntī īnspexit, eī arrīsit. 'fortūnam optimam tibi prōvideō,' inquit. 'es iuvenis summō ingeniō. poēta clārissimus fīēs prīncipumque comes. age, cārissime, fortūnam meliōrem
15 nēminī prōvīdī quam tibi; itaque praemium fortūnā tuā dignum mihi trāde.' Quīntus crumēnam ē sinū sūmpsit argentumque eī trādidit. continuō Pūblium valēre iussit domumque cucurrit. diū cōgitābat dē eīs quae dīvīna eī dīxerat sed nēminī rem rettulit, nē patrī quidem. tandem dīvīna illa ex memoriā eius cecidit, sed
20 paucīs post annīs verba eius in animum revocātūrus erat.

anus dīvīna an old fortune-teller	
eīs obstetit (+ dat.) stood in their way	
belle pretty, handsome	
prehendit seized; **concessit** gave in	
fīēs you will become	
āvulsit snatched away	
arrīsit (+ dat.) smiled at	
crumēnam his purse; **sinū** pocket	
argentum silver, money	
cōgitābat thought, reflected	
dē eīs quae about what (the things which)	
nē… quidem not even	
revocātūrus erat was going to recall	

1   What fortune does the old woman predict for Quintus?   [3]
2   Why does she claim a reward?   [2]
3   How does Quintus respond to her demand?   [2]
4   How seriously do you think he took the old woman's prophecy?   [2]
5   Why should he have recalled her words later?   [2]

THE ROMAN TRIUMPH

One of the most sensational events to be seen in ancient Rome was the triumph of a victorious general. This was not an honor which could easily be won. The *triumphātor* had to be dictator, a consul or a praetor. He must have conquered in person, and so completely that his troops could safely leave for Rome; he must have killed at least 5,000 of the enemy and added new territory to the empire.

    The day of triumph was a holiday for the whole city. Flowers bedecked the buildings and statues, and every altar blazed with fire. The people, wild with excitement, poured forth to line the streets.

    The *triumphātor* had spent the previous night with his troops on the Campus Martius. From here the vast triumphal procession entered the city by a special gate used only on these occasions, the *porta triumphālis.*

The city magistrates led the way, followed by trumpeters sounding the charge. After them came the plunder taken in the campaign, and pictures of the forts, cities, mountains, lakes and seas of the captured territory. Next priests walked, leading the richly adorned white oxen to the sacrifice. And then there were the captives, with the king and his family and chief nobles at their head. Behind them, musicians played and danced. It was a spectacular scene, greeted with deafening applause.

But the cheers redoubled when the *triumphātor* himself came into view, riding in a strange turret-shaped chariot drawn by four white horses. He was robed in gold and purple, his face was painted red, and he was crowned with a laurel wreath. He carried a laurel branch in his right hand and an ivory sceptre in his left. A public slave stood behind him on the chariot holding over his head the crown of Jupiter, an oak wreath made of gold and studded with jewels. The slave continually repeated the words 'Remember that you are a mortal,' amid the hysterical shouting. Since the *triumphātor* was the earthly representative of Capitoline Jupiter, he needed to be reminded that he was also a mere man.

The triumph of Caesar

The victorious soldiers came behind their general wearing olive wreaths, shouting '*Iō triumphe!*' (Behold the triumph!) and singing lively songs. The procession went through the Circus Maximus, round the Palatine, and then followed the Sacred Way to the forum. From there it climbed the Capitoline hill to the temple of Jupiter. Meanwhile the chief captives were being put to death in a prison next to the forum.

The oxen were sacrificed outside the temple and the *triumphātor* set his laurel wreath on the lap of the god. Afterwards there was a great banquet in his honour, and then, as evening approached, he went to his home accompanied by the music of flutes and pipes.

So ended a day in which the jubilant Romans celebrated with uncontrolled emotion the military qualities which had made their nation great.

Julius Caesar's triumphs in 46 BC

The triumphal procession of Julius Caesar described in this chapter was part of possibly the most spectacular series of triumphs in Roman history. Over the course of a month, Caesar held four triumphs in celebration of four great campaigns.

As well as staging these vast celebratory pageants, Caesar gave generous gifts to his veterans and to the people of Rome. Each of the former received a minimum of 24,000 sesterces and a grant of land; the latter were given two months' rations of grain and olive oil as well as 300 sesterces. In addition Caesar flung a vast public banquet at which 22,000 dining couches were laid out in the forum.

He put on a sensational series of public shows, a gladiatorial contest in the forum, plays in Greek and Latin in the four districts of Rome, chariot races, athletic competitions and a mock sea-battle with 4,000 oarsmen and 2,000 marines. He also staged wild beast hunts in a specially built wooden amphitheatre for four days running. And the entertainment ended with a battle between two armies in the Circus Maximus, each consisting of 500 infantry, 30 cavalry and 20 elephants.

So vast a crowd flocked to see these events that large numbers of visitors had to sleep in tents placed along the streets of the city and many of them were killed in the crush.

*What do you think were Caesar's motives in laying on these extravagant celebrations? (You may remember Juvenal's phrase '*pānem et circēnsēs*' from the background section of chapter 17.)*

Think of any great parade or procession that has taken place in modern times. In what ways, if any, is it like a Roman triumph?

Pūblius celerrimē cucurrit; nēmō celerius
currere potest quam ille.

Quīntus Homērum facillimē legit; nēmō
Homērum melius legit quam ille.

numquam puellam pulchriōrem vīdī quam
Iūliam; Iūlia pulcherrima est.

Horātia saltū (*dancing*) magnopere gaudet; nēmō
saltū magis gaudet quam illa.

Vocabulary 25

verbs		*adjectives*	
lūceō, lūcēre, lūxī	I shine	**brevis, breve**	short
sūmō, sūmere, sūmpsī	I take (up); I put on	**īnsignis, īnsigne**	outstanding, distinguished
		puerīlis, puerīle	of boys, childish
nouns		**virīlis, virīle**	of men, manly
dīligentia, -ae, f.	care, diligence	**toga virīlis**	the toga of manhood
litterae, -ārum, f. pl.	letters, literature		
campus, -ī, m.	plain, field	*adverb*	
facilitās, facilitātis, f.	ease, facility	**quam** + superlative, e.g. **quam**	
lēx, lēgis, f.	law	**celerrimē =** as quickly as possible	
multitūdō, multitūdinis, f.	multitude, crowd		
iūs, iūris, n.	right, justice		
tumultus, tumultūs, m.	riot, uproar		

List twelve English words derived from Latin words in this vocabulary.

Quīntus togam virīlem sūmit

Quīntus iam nōn puer erat sed iuvenis, togam virīlem sūmere
parātus. amīcōrum plūrimī ā lūdō Orbiliī discesserant et
rhētoricae studēbant. ipse nōlēbat diūtius in lūdō studēre;   **rhētoricae** rhetoric
cupiēbat lātiōrem campum inīre. hiems praeterierat, vēr iam
5   aderat. Quīntus in scholā sedēbat dum Orbilius dē poētā quōdam
vetere disserēbat; Quīntus nūllī poētae studuerat frīgidiōrī quam   **disserēbat** was lecturing
illī. Orbilium nōn audiēbat, sed carmen ipse scrībēbat; hōs versūs   **frīgidiōrī** more boring
iam fēcerat quī eī maximē placēbant:

diffūgērunt nivēs, redeunt iam grāmina campīs   **nivēs** the snows; **grāmina** (n. pl.)
10   arboribusque comae...   grass; **comae** leaves

Orbilius eum vīdit scrībentem. 'Quīnte,' inquit, 'quid
facis?' Quīntus respondit: 'ego, magister? nihil faciō. tē
audiō.' Orbilius 'nōn tibi crēdō, Quīnte,' inquit. 'venī hūc
et dā mihi illam tabulam.'

The goddess of flowers,
the embodiment of spring

Teacher and boy

15   Quīntus invītus magistrō pāruit. surrēxit tabulamque eī
trādidit. Orbilius īrātus erat, sed, ubi tabulam eius īnspexit, etiam
magis īrātus erat. nam in angulō tabulae Quīntus imāginem   **angulō** corner; **imāginem** picture
scrīpserat magistrī.
      ille Quīntum ferōciter īnspexit et maximā vōce 'quid?' inquit,
20   'quid? dum ego poētam optimum expōnō, tū imāginēs magistrī
scrībis et versūs pessimōs? vidē! hī versūs nē rēctī quidem sunt.   **nē ... quidem** not even
venī hūc.' haec dīxit et ferulam sūmpsit; sex plāgās Quīntō dedit,   **ferulam** cane; **plāgās** strokes
trēs quod magistrum nōn audīverat, trēs quod malōs versūs
scrīpserat. Quīntus ad sēdem rediit, et dolēns et īrātus.   **dolēns** smarting, in pain
25   Quīntus, ubi domum rediit, patrī omnia nārrāvit. Flaccus, ubi
omnia cognōvit, 'Quīnte,' inquit, 'paene quīnque annōs in lūdō
Orbiliī mānsistī; dīligentissimē studuistī. iam iuvenis es. tempus
est togam virīlem sūmere et studia puerīlia dēpōnere. iam dēbēs
ad rhētorem īre.' postrīdiē Quīntus, quī vīgintī annōs nātus erat,   **rhētorem** the rhetoric teacher
30   togam virīlem sūmpsit.   **vīgintī annōs nātus** twenty years old
      paucīs post diēbus Flaccus fīlium ad Hēliodōrum dūxit. ille
optimus erat rhētorum, quī iuvenēs ōrātiōnēs facere īnstituēbat ac **īnstituēbat** trained
multa docēbat dē iūre et lēgibus. discipulōrum eius plūrimī in
rēpūblicā īnsignēs fiēbant. Hēliodōrus pauca eum rogāvit;
35   Quīntus ad omnia facillimē respondit. ille Flaccō dīxit: 'iuvenis
est magnō ingeniō. paucōs libentius in numerum discipulōrum   **libentius** more gladly
meōrum accēpī.'

Respondē Latīnē

1   dum Orbilius dē poētā vetere disserēbat, quid faciēbat
    Quīntus?
2   ubi Orbilius Quīntum vīdit scrībentem, quid dīxit?
3   ubi Quīntus tabulam eī trādidit, cūr etiam magis īrātus
    erat Orbilius?
4   ubi Quīntus eī omnia nārrāvit, quid respondit pater?
5   quis erat Hēliodōrus?

Word-building

What do the following adjectives mean?
From what noun is each formed?

    labōriōsus, -a, -um
    perīculōsus, -a, -um
    glōriōsus, -a, -um
    fābulōsus, -a, -um
    ōtiōsus, -a, -um
    fōrmōsus, -a, -um

A Roman orator

Quīntus rhētoricae studet

Without translating answer the questions below the following
passage

cotīdiē Quīntus ad scholam Hēliodōrī ībat et cum iuvenibus
nōbilibus rhētoricae studēbat. ōrātiōnēs compōnere discēbat;
contrōversiīs intererat; plūrima dē iūre, plūrima dē lēgibus   **contrōversiīs** debates
cognōscēbat. studia longa et difficillima erant nec Quīntum
5 multum dēlectābant; mālēbat enim litterīs studēre, in prīmīs   **dēlectābant** pleased
poētīs Graecīs. nihilōminus summā dīligentiā studēbat quod patrī   **in prīmīs** above all
placēre cupiēbat.   **nihilōminus** nevertheless
    Idibus Martiīs Quīntus, ubi Hēliodōrus discipulōs dīmīsit,   **Idibus Martiīs** on 15 March
domum lentē redībat. illā nocte maxima tempestās fuerat, sed iam
10 diēs amoenus erat; sōl lūcēbat, aura lēnis per viās flābat. itaque   **amoenus** pleasant; **lēnis** gentle
Quīntus cōnstituit ad Campum Martium īre; volēbat enim in   **flābat** was blowing
flūmine Tiberī natāre. forum trānsiit et mox ad Viam   **natāre** to swim
Triumphālem advēnit. sed ubi ad theātrum Pompēī vēnit,
maximam turbam hominum vīdit prō theātrō stantem.

1 What did Quintus learn in the rhetorical school?   [2]
2 Why didn't he like these studies much? Why did he work hard?   [2+2]
3 Why did he decide to go to the Campus Martius?   [3]
4 What did he find on his way there?   [3]

INTO ADULTHOOD

The toga virīlis

While girls generally left their childhood behind on the eve of their marriage when they would dedicate their toys and dolls to the household gods (the Lares), a boy could come of age at any stage of his teens. He and his father would agree when this should happen. The ceremony regularly took place on 17 March, the festival of Liber and Libera. The youth laid his boy's tunic (the straight tunic – *tunica rēcta* – so called because it was woven straight) before the Lares and, in the case of a freedman's son such as Quintus, his leather collar with its amulet.* Instead of the purple-boardered *toga praetexta* he wore the white *toga pūra* or *toga virīlis* of adulthood. Escorted by family and friends, he went to the *tabulārium*, the Public Records Office, on the slopes of the Capitol. Here he was registered as a full citizen and enrolled in his tribe, one of the voting groups of ancient Rome.

A young man in a toga

An upper-class youth was now in a position to enter on public life and learn the ropes of public administration under the guidance of his father or some other distinguished individual. Here Cicero describes his own sixteenth year:

> When I had formally put on the *toga virīlis* I was taken by my father to the lawyer Quintus Mucius Scaevola. The idea was that – so far as was humanly possible – I should never leave the old man's sight. There were all manner of things that Scaevola used to talk about with intelligence and penetration. I formed the habit of memorizing all his epigrammatic remarks as a useful addition to my knowledge.

We have marked Quintus' journey into adulthood by sending him to the *rhētor*.

The rhētor

Rhetoric, or the art of speaking, was the basic tertiary or further education to which well-to-do boys proceeded on leaving the *grammaticus*. Philosophy was an optional extra which was taken by relatively few. Rhetoric had been developed as a teachable skill by the sophists, the travelling teachers of the Greek world, in Athens in the last quarter of the fifth century BC. They raised questions about beliefs which had been previously taken for granted – such as whether the gods had any effect on the world of men – and their weapon was argument. Thus one of the things they taught was the art of speaking.

Rhetoric, taught by the *rhētor*, involved learning how to argue a case clearly and elegantly, and it has been called the art of

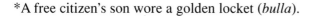

*A free citizen's son wore a golden locket (*bulla*).

persuasion. The whole study was reduced to a complex system with many technical terms and rules. Students studied model speeches, composed their own on set subjects, and took part in debates, often on imaginary law cases. The practical importance of rhetoric in a world without newspapers, television or radio can scarcely be exaggerated. The public speech was the only way of communicating with your fellow citizens in the mass and any Roman who hoped to make his mark had to strive to excel in this art.

In Horace's day, debates divided into (1) abstract, general themes such as 'Should one marry?' and (2) particular themes related to a situation, for example with the students imagining themselves as the young Hannibal in Carthage wondering, 'Should I cross the Alps to invade Italy?'

We have sent Quintus to the *rhētor* Heliodorus. The latter was a historical figure and a friend of Quintus who describes him as '*Graecōrum longē doctissimus*' ('by far the most learned of the Greeks'). But we do not know whether he in fact kept a rhetorical school at Rome, though it is quite likely that he did since most of the teachers of rhetoric were Greek.

When a youth had completed his rhetorical studies, he was ready to embark on a career in politics, which often began, as in Cicero's case, with practising at the bar, or in business, which many preferred to the hurly burly of politics, while others would go on to study philosophy as Quintus is to do.

A son banished from home studies medicine. When his father falls ill, and all the other doctors despair of saving him, he is summoned and says that he can cure him, if he drinks the medicine he gives him. The father, having drunk part of the medicine, says that he has been poisoned. The son drinks the rest, but the father dies, and the son is accused of parricide.

Present the case either for or against the accused.

Quīntus Iūlium Caesarem vīdit theātrum cum magistrātibus intrantem.

coniūrātī Caesarem circumstantēs eum undique oppugnāvērunt.

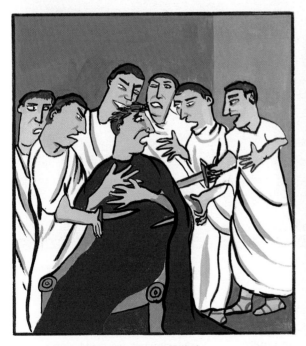

inter aliōs Caesar Brūtum vīdit in sē currentem.

coniūrātī Caesarem relīquērunt in terrā ante statuam Pompēiī iacentem.

Vocabulary 26

verbs			*nouns*	
ardeō, ardēre, arsī	I burn, am on fire		**causa, -ae,** f.	cause, reason
accidit, accidere, accidit	it happens		**gladius, -ī,** m.	sword
feriō, ferīre	I strike		**tyrannus, -ī,** m.	tyrant
perveniō, pervenīre, pervēnī	I arrive, reach		**theātrum, -ī,** n.	theatre
			pars, partis, f.	part
adverbs			**timor, timōris,** m.	fear
num?	surely not?		**caput, capitis,** n.	head
satis + gen.	enough			
			adjectives	
preposition			**armātus, -a, -um**	armed
prō + abl.	in front of; on behalf of, for		**quantus, -a, -um?**	how great?
			ultimus, -a, -um	furthest, last

What are: (1) an ardent lover, (2) an ordinal number, (3) a cautious advance, (4) an ultimate goal, (5) a capital city? From what Latin word is each English adjective derived?

A procession of senators

Idūs Martiae

Quīntus, ubi multitūdinem hominum vīdit prō theātrō Pompeī
stantem, cognōscere cupiit causam tantī conventūs. itaque per
turbam ad prīmum ōrdinem sē īnsinuāvit, unde omnia vidēre
poterat. plūrimī senātōrēs aliīque virī īnsignēs theātrum inībant.
5 deinde Quīntus vīdit Gāium Iūlium Caesarem cum magistrātibus

    conventūs gathering
    sē īnsinuāvit wormed his way

The killing of Caesar, a scene from Shakespeare's *Julius Caesar*

intrantem. togam purpuream gerēbat et in capite corōnam   **purpuream** purple
lauream. omnēs senātōrēs surrēxērunt Caesaremque salūtāvērunt.   **corōnam lauream** a laurel crown
    dum sēdet, multī senātōrēs eum circumstant. deinde senātor
quīdam eum aliquid rogat et togam eius manibus tenet. eō ipsō
10 tempore alter senātōrum eum pugiōne ferit; tertius brācchium   **pugiōne** with a dagger
vulnerat. Caesar surgere temptāvit, sed coniūrātī eum undique   **brācchium** his arm
oppugnābant.   **coniūrātī** the conspirators
    inter aliōs Caesar Brūtum vīdit amīcum suum intimum in sē   **intimum** closest
currentem; 'et tū, Brūte?' inquit. tum caput togā obvolvit et   **obvolvit** wrapped
15 dēcidit ad terram, tribus et vīgintī vulneribus cōnfossus.   **cōnfossus** pierced
    coniūrātī Caesarem relīquērunt in terrā iacentem ante statuam
Pompēiī. ē theātrō ērūpērunt et populō clāmāvērunt: 'mortuus est **ērūpērunt** burst out
tyrannus; populum Rōmānum līberāvimus.' sed omnēs tacitī
stābant, rē dīrā obstupefactī.   **obstupefactī** dumfounded
20 Quīntus sē vertit et domum cucurrit. ubi domum advēnit,
patrem vocāvit. Flaccus eum ānxius audīvit omnia nārrantem.
paulīsper tacuit. tandem 'quid iam futūrum est?' inquit;   **futūrum** going to happen
'rēspūblica in magnō perīculō est. sine dubiō tumultūs vidēbimus. **vidēbimus** we shall see
tū, Quīnte, cavēre dēbēs.'
25 quīntō diē post mortem Caesaris, ubi Quīntus ad forum
advēnit, ingentem turbam vīdit tōtum forum complentem. nōn   **complentem** filling
poterat pervenīre ad viam quae ad scholam Hēliodōrī ferēbat.
itaque in ultimā parte forī manēbat gradūsque templī ascendit,
unde omnia vidēre poterat.

The daggers, the cap of liberty
and the Ides of March

Word-building

Remember that **con-** either = 'together' or simply strengthens
the meaning of the uncompounded verb, e.g. **iaciō** = 'I throw',
coniciō = either 'I throw together' or 'I hurl'.
What is the meaning of the following compound verbs?

> **concurrō, conclāmō, cōnficiō, commoveō, convocō,
> compōnō, conveniō, conferō**

The prefix **per-** either means 'through', like the preposition, e.g.

percurrō	I run through
perrumpō	I break through

or gives the notion of completeness, e.g.

faciō	I do	**perficiō**	I carry through, complete
suādeō	I persuade	**persuādeō**	I (completely) persuade
veniō	I come	**perveniō**	I come all the way, I reach

This prefix is attached to some adjectives, e.g.

facilis	easy	**perfacilis**	extremely easy
dūrus	hard	**perdūrus**	extremely hard

The prefix **dī-/dis-** means 'in different directions', e.g.

dīmittō	I send in different directions, I dismiss
dispōnō	I put in different places, I arrange
diffugiō	(I) flee in different directions, scatter
discurrō	(I) run in different directions, run about

The preposition **circum** + acc. = 'around'; it is found
prefixed to many verbs, e.g.

circumveniō	I surround
circumvolō	I fly around
circumeō	I go around
circumdūcō	I lead around

Caesaris fūnus

fūnus funeral

Translate the first paragraph and answer the questions below on the second

Quīntus in gradibus templī stāns magnam pompam cōnspexit in
forum prōcēdentem. magistrātūs feretrum ferēbant, in quō
iacēbat corpus Caesaris. in medium forum prōcessērunt
feretrumque prō rōstrīs dēposuērunt. Marcus Antōnius, Caesaris
5 amīcus, rōstra ascendit et ōrātiōnem ad populum habuit.
Caesarem laudāvit, coniūrātōs vehementer accūsāvit, populum ad
furōrem excitāvit.

    ubi Antōnius ōrātiōnem cōnfēcit dēscenditque dē rōstrīs,
hominēs ubīque clāmābant et furēbant. duo hominēs, quī prope
10 rōstra stābant, gladiīs armātī facēsque manibus tenentēs, ad
feretrum accessērunt. feretrum facibus accendērunt. aliī
accurrērunt et virgulta in flammās iēcērunt; aliī subsellia
rapuērunt et imposuērunt. mox ingēns pyra ardēbat et corpus
Caesaris flammīs cremātum erat. deinde manūs hominum ē forō
15 cucurrērunt coniūrātōs quaerentium, certī mortem Caesaris
vindicāre.

feretrum bier
corpus body
rōstrīs the Rostra

vehementer violently
furōrem madness

furēbant ran mad
facēs torches

virgulta (n. pl.) brushwood
subsellia (n. pl.) benches
cremātum burnt; **manūs** bands, gangs; **certī** resolved
vindicāre to avenge

1 What was the effect of Antony's speech on the crowd? [2]
2 What did the two men standing near the platform do? [2]
3 How did other members of the crowd react? [4]
4 What did the men who ran from the forum intend to do? [2]

THE END OF THE REPUBLIC

A key moment in the long drawn-out death of the Roman
republic occurred in 60 BC. As we saw in chapter 21, the three
most powerful men of the time, Julius Caesar, Gnaeus Pompey
and Marcus Licinius Crassus, joined in an alliance known as the
First Triumvirate. They made it clear that nothing would stand in
their way and, when he became consul in 59 BC, Caesar made
sure that nothing did. The Triumvirate was supported by the
army, the knights and the people, and so the senate was unable to
oppose it. Nobody paid any attention to Cicero's frantic appeals
to save the republic.

    Over the next decade Caesar fought his famous and brilliant
campaigns in Gaul (France, Holland and Belgium), through
which he established a justified reputation as one of the greatest
generals in the history of the world. He ensured that his military
genius gained a wide circulation by writing his own history of his
campaigns in the seven books of his *Commentaries of the War in
Gaul*. These show him not only as a great general but as a fine
war correspondent. They are direct and plain in style but always
exciting. His two raids on Britain (in 55 and 54 BC) proved of

Mark Antony

little lasting value but had all the glamour of perilous journeys into the unknown. However, the situation at Rome was less happy for him. The alliance between Pompey, Crassus and himself, all of them ruthlessly ambitious, lasted a surprisingly long time; it threatened to dissolve in 56 BC, but the three met and patched things up. Crassus, however, was killed in Parthia in 53 BC (see the end of chapter 21), and Pompey became more and more closely allied to the senate. Caesar and Pompey were being driven further apart, and the senate voted on 1 January 49 BC that Caesar, who was still in Gaul, should lay down his command.

Caesar's response came on 10 January, when he brought his army into Italy. This was really a declaration of civil war since it was treason for a general to enter Italy at the head of an army. Caesar fully realized the great significance of what he was doing. He spent one hour in solitary thought. Then he crossed the river Rubicon, which marked the frontier between Gaul and Italy, and exclaimed '*iacta ālea est*!' ('The die is cast!')

Pompey and most of the senate withdrew across the Adriatic to Greece. Caesar defeated Pompey's supporters in Spain, then followed him to Greece and in 48 BC won a great victory over him at Pharsalus. Pompey fled on horseback and succeeded in escaping to Egypt, but was stabbed to death as he landed. Ptolemy, the boy king of Egypt, sent his head to Caesar, hoping to win favor with him, but the victor was revolted and distressed by this grisly gift.

Other wars were to follow – including the lightning campaign in Pontus in Asa when he polished off his opponents there with the celebrated boast '*vēnī, vīdī, vīcī*' ('I came, I saw, I conquered'). He had a notorious love affair with Cleopatra, the irresistible Egyptian queen. He was by now the most powerful man in the Western world, and, great statesman that he was, he embarked on a series of major reforms and a vast building program. Yet many worried that he was taking so much power into his hands. He was appointed dictator, first in 49 BC and then for life in February 44 BC. Though he refused the title *rēx* (king), he put on the purple robe worn by the Tarquins, and his supreme power struck many as intolerable. A conspiracy to assassinate him led by Marcus Brutus and Gaius Cassius succeeded in 44 BC. His mutilated body fell at the foot of the statue of his great opponent Pompey, as you have read.

It was now the task of his friend Marcus Antonius and of his great-nephew and heir Octavian to avenge his death.

Write a paragraph describing Julius Caesar's thoughts as he sat by the Rubicon.

Octavian

Quīntus iānuam diū pulsat. tandem Hēliodōrus ē
fenestrā prōspicit.

Quīntus Hēliodōrum valēre iubet; nam mox
Athēnās nāvigābit.

ille 'cum Athēnās advēneris,' inquit, 'hanc
epistolam amīcō meō trāde; ille tē iuvābit.'

Quīntus grātiās eī agit et 'cum Athēnās advēnerō,'
inquit, 'epistolam tibi mittam.'

These captions introduce two new tenses; what time do they express?

Vocabulary 27

verbs		*nouns*	
vexō, vexāre, vexāvī	I worry, annoy	**philosophia, -ae**, f.	philosophy
augeō, augēre, auxī	I increase	**exitium, -ī**, n.	destruction
accendō, accendere,		**imperium Rōmānum**, n.	the Roman empire
accendī	I set fire to	**ōtium, -ī**, n.	leisure
colligō, colligere,		**orbis, orbis**, m.	circle, globe
collēgī	I collect, gather	**orbis terrārum**	the globe, the world
ruō, ruere, ruī	I rush	**potestās, potestātis**, f.	power
		portus, portūs, m.	port
adjectives			
benignus, -a, -um	kind	*adverbs*	
plēnus, -a, -um + abl.	full (of)	**crās**	tomorrow
scelestus, -a, -um	wicked, criminal	**ergō**	and so
ūllus, -a, -um	any	**māne**	early (in the morning)
cīvīlis, cīvīle	of citizens, civil		
prūdēns, prūdentis	prudent, sensible, wise		

Form English words from the following Latin words and make up an English sentence to illustrate the meaning of each: **augeō**, **cīvīlis**, **imperium**, **orbis**, **benignus**.

Quīntus Athēnās nāvigāre parat

Quīntus domum cucurrit territus et omnia patrī nārrāvit. ille caput dēmīsit oculōsque manibus operuit. tandem 'Quīnte,' inquit, 'bellum cīvīle prōvideō. cīvēs furunt. magistrātūs urbem regere nōn possunt. Rōmā discēdere dēbēmus. tū, Quīnte, dēbēs Athēnās nāvigāre et philosophiae studēre; ego Venusiam redībō et mātrem tuam sorōremque cūrābō.'

    postrīdiē Quīntus māne ad scholam Hēliodōrī festīnābat. iter difficillimum erat quod multae manūs scelestōrum per viās errābant; rēs rapiēbant, aedēs accendēbant. Quīntus tandem ad scholam advēnit; iānua clausa erat; Quīntus iānuam pulsāvit sed nēmō aperuit. ad aedēs igitur Hēliodōrī cucurrit, quae nōn longē aberant. diū iānuam pulsābat. tandem Hēliodōrus fenestram aperuit et prōspexit. Quīntum vīdit; dēscendit iānuamque aperuit. 'intrā celeriter,' inquit, et ubi Quīntus intrāvit, iānuam iterum clausit.

    Quīntus tōtam rem eī exposuit. Hēliodōrus respondit: 'pater tuus vēra dīcit; vir prūdentissimus est. urbs in maximō perīculō est. ducēs enim nec pācem nec lēgēs cūrant; nihil cupiunt nisi suam potestātem augēre. bella cīvīlia prōvideō et proelia tōtum per orbem terrārum redintegrāta; cīvēs cum cīvibus pugnābunt, patrēs cum fīliīs. numquamne pācem vidēbimus et ōtium? quis deus, quis homō rempūblicam servāre poterit? tōtum imperium Rōmānum in exitium ruit.'

Marginal glosses:

dēmīsit lowered; **operuit** covered
furunt are running mad

clausa shut; **pulsāvit** knocked on

fenestram window

redintegrāta renewed

25 nōn poterat plūra dīcere; oculī lacrimīs plēnī erant. paulīsper
tacēbat, deinde 'ergō tū, Quīnte,' inquit, 'Athēnās ībis
philosophiaeque ibi studēbis? euge! iuvenis es magnō ingeniō, et
sī dīligenter studueris, multa discēs et valdē doctus fīēs. sed   **doctus** learned
manē; ego epistolam scrībam ad amīcum meum quī in Acadēmīā
scholās habet.'   **scholās habet** gives lectures

30 in tablīnum exiit; mox revēnit epistolamque Quīntō trādidit.
'cum Athēnās advēneris,' inquit, 'hanc epistolam Theomnēstō
trāde; vir est summā ērudītiōne, vetus meus amīcus. ille tē   **ērudītiōne** learning
benignē accipiet et tua studia cūrābit. deī tē servābunt. valē.'
Quīntus grātiās eī ēgit domumque festīnāvit.

Word-building

Learn the following compounds of **speciō** *(which is only used in compounds):*

aspiciō (= **ad-spiciō**), **aspicere**, **aspexī**	I look at
cōnspiciō, **cōnspicere**, **cōnspexī**	I catch sight of
dēspiciō, **dēspicere**, **dēspexī**	I look down at
īnspiciō, **īnspicere**, **īnspexī**	I look at, inspect
prōspiciō, **prōspicere**, **prōspexī**	I look forward, look out
respiciō, **respicere**, **respexī**	I look back at

Quīntus Rōmā discēdit

Translate the first paragraph and answer the questions on the rest

Quīntus ubi domum rediit patrem invēnit rēs compōnentem. ille
'age, Quīnte,' inquit; 'nōlī cessāre; sine morā ad portum ībimus
nāvemque quaerēmus quae ad Graeciam tē feret. nōlō diūtius in
urbe manēre; melius est statim discēdere.'

5 Quīntus librōs et vestīmenta collēgit et mox parātus erat. pater
fīliusque statim in viam exiērunt festīnābantque ad portum.

A Roman merchant ship
in the harbor at Ostia

vesper aderat cum ad Ostia advēnērunt. Flaccus 'sēra hōra est,'
inquit; 'noctem in caupōnā manēbimus; crās māne ad portum
ībimus nāvemque quaerēmus.'

10   prīmā lūce surrēxērunt et festīnāvērunt ad portum. plūrimās
nāvēs prope lītus vīdērunt, et magnās et parvās. ex aliīs nautae
frūmentum ferēbant ad horrea; ex aliīs servī, catēnīs vīnctī,
exībant. ubīque clāmōrēs et tumultus. Flaccus fīliusque
secundum lītus ambulābant nāvem idōneam quaerentēs. tandem
15   parvam nāvem invēnērunt quae illō ipsō diē ad Graeciam
nāvigātūra erat. magister eōs benignē accēpit et viāticum
modicum rogāvit.

Ostia (n. pl.) Ostia, the port of Rome	
sēra hōra late	
caupōnā inn	
horrea (n. pl.) granaries	
catēnīs vīnctī bound with chains	
secundum (+ acc.) along	
idōneam suitable	
nāvigātūra about to sail	
viāticum modicum a modest fare	

1   How did Quintus prepare for his journey?   [2]
2   When they got to the port of Rome, why did they stay in an inn? [2]
3   What did they see in the port the next morning?   [4]
4   How did the captain of the ship receive them?   [2]

Fābella: Idūs Martiae

Persōnae: Iūlius Caesar, Calpurnia (uxor eius), Decimus Brūtus

> *Caesar post noctem turbulentam ad senātum īre parat.*   **turbulentam** wild

Caesar: quanta tempestās tōtam per noctem furēbat!
Calpurnia, dum dormit, ter exclāmāvit: 'succurrite!   **ter** three times
5   Caesarem trucīdant.'   **trucīdant** they are murdering

> *intrat Calpurnia.*

Calpurnia: quid facis, Caesar? num in animō habēs ad senātum
īre? nōlī hodiē ex aedibus exīre.
Caesar: quid dīcis? certē ad senātum ībō. nūlla causa timōris
10   est.
Calpurnia: Caesar, prōdigia numquam magnī fēcī, sed nunc   **prōdigia** (n. pl.) portents
multa mē terrent. leaina, ut dīcunt, in viīs peperit;   **magnī fēcī** I have valued much
mortuī ē sepulcrīs surgunt; caelum sanguine ardet.   **leaina** a lioness; **ut** as, so
omnia mortem tuam praedīcunt.   **peperit** has given birth
**   sanguine** with blood
15 **Caesar:**   hominēs ea vītāre nōn possunt quae deī dēcernunt   **praedīcunt** foretell
omnipotentēs. ībō ad senātum. nam haec prōdigia   **vītāre** to avoid; **dēcernunt** decree
nōn ad mē attinent sed ad hominēs ūniversōs.   **attinent** concern, point to
Calpurnia: cum pauperēs pereunt, nūlla prōdigia in caelō   **praedīcit** foretells
vidēmus; sed mortem prīncipum praedīcit caelum   **exardēscēns** flaming
20   ipsum, ignibus exardēscēns.   **ōmina** (n. pl.) omens
Caesar: ōmina nihilī faciō. ad senātum ībō.   **nihilī faciō** I count for nothing
Calpurnia: Caesar, nōlī hodiē exīre. Marcum Antōnium ad   **tē aegrum esse** that you are sick
senātum mitte, quī dīcet tē aegrum esse. tibi   **supplicō** (+ dat.) I beg
supplicō; fac sīcut tē moneō.
25 **Caesar:**   nōlī tē vexāre, uxor cārissima. domī manēbō.

> *intrat Decimus Brūtus.*

Caesar:	ecce! adest Decimus Brūtus. ille hunc nūntium ad senātum feret.	
Decimus:	salvē, Caesar. vīsne mēcum ad senātum venīre? senātōrēs tē exspectant.	
Caesar:	salvē, Decime; temporī vēnistī. senātōribus salūtem dā et haec eīs dīc: 'Caesar ad senātum hodiē venīre nōn vult.'	**temporī** in good time
Calpurnia:	dīc eum aegrum esse.	
Caesar:	nōlī haec dīcere, Decime. dīc: 'Caesar ad senātum venīre nōn vult.' id satis est.	
Decimus:	sed, Caesar, cūr īre nōn vīs? dīc mihi causam. senātōrēs mē rīdēbunt, sī nūllam causam dīxerō.	
Caesar:	nōlō venīre; id satis est senātōribus. sed hoc tibi dīcam sōlī, quod amīcus es fīdus: Calpurnia, et propter somnium dīrum quod nocte vīdit et propter prōdigia quaedam quae eam terrent, mē domī manēre iubet.	**sōlī** (dat.) alone; **fīdus** faithful **propter somnium dīrum** because of a terrible dream
Decimus:	num prōdigia vāna et somnia Caesar timet? senātōrēs tē rīdēbunt sī haec cognōverint. omnēs tē exspectant. venī mēcum.	**vāna** empty
Caesar:	bene mē monēs, Decime. Calpurnia, timōrēs tuī vānī sunt. nōlī somnia et prōdigia timēre. togam prōfer; ad senātum ībō.	

Line numbers: 30, 35, 40, 45

Trajan's harbor, Ostia

TRADE BY WATER

As the hub of a great empire, Rome was the center of a vast trading network extending from the Baltic coast to southern Arabia, India and China. A Greek of the second century AD wrote:

The Markets of Trajan, Rome

> From every land and sea is imported everything that the seasons bring forth, everything that all the countries, the rivers, the lakes and the skills of Greeks and barbarians produce. And so if anyone wants to see all these things he must either travel over all the world to look at them or must come to Rome. For all that each nation produces and manufactures is here in abundance. So many merchant ships come here carrying their cargoes from every corner of the earth in every season of the year and with each return of harvest, that the city is like a common workshop of the world. You can see so many cargoes from India and if you wish from Arabia Felix too that you may guess that the trees have been left permanently bare for the inhabitants and if they need anything they must come here to beg for their own products... Egypt, Sicily and Rome's empire in Libya are her farms... Everything comes together here, trade, shipping, farming, metallurgy, all the crafts that are and have ever been, everything that is bred and grown. What one cannot see in Rome simply does not exist.

Luxury goods abounded, but the main imports were olive oil, wine and grain. Something like 200,000 tons of this grain had to be imported annually to keep Rome's huge population fed.

The Roman empire was criss-crossed with a vast and supremely efficient road system, which will be discussed in Part III, chapter 44. However, most of the trade came by sea – which made larger loads possible and took less time than land travel, but carried considerable risks. Trimalchio, the fictitious multi-millionaire from a novel by Petronius, makes this very clear:

> I built five ships, I loaded them up with wine – which was then worth its weight in gold – and I sent them to Rome. But all the ships were wrecked. That's fact, not fiction. Neptune gulped down three million sesterces in a single day.

But he also stresses the vast financial rewards when things went well:

> Do you think I gave up?... I built more ships, bigger, better and luckier ones... and I loaded them up again with wine, bacon, beans, perfume and slaves... On one voyage I rounded off a million sesterces.

At the time at which our course is set, Rome's harbor was the port at Ostia where the Tiber flowed into the sea. This was not suitable for large cargo ships (*nāvēs onerāriae*), and these had to dock at Puteoli on the bay of Naples, some hundred and fifty miles

to the south.* From here smaller ships would take the cargoes up
the coast to Ostia. Here they were unloaded into a kind of barge
(*nāvis cōdicāria*) to be carried up the Tiber to Rome.

These barges had flat keels and ample holds and their mainmast
was equipped with a beam which could be used as a crane to lift
merchandise. They were tied to teams of oxen which were driven
up the right bank of the river to the city's port area on the Tiber, to
the south-west of the Aventine hill, where they were tied up to the
pairs of mooring rings which can still be seen in the retaining walls
of the Tiber. Here the merchandise would be stored in vast
warehouses before being taken off to Rome's numerous markets to
be sold.

*Draw a picture of a barge being unloaded at the city port
in Rome.*

* Over the course of the next two centuries, the emperors
Claudius and Trajan had larger and deeper harbors dredged out
near Ostia, to avoid the extra transportation from Puteoli.

Chapter 28 — Quintus ad Graeciam navigat

magister, cui Flaccus argentum trādiderat, Quīntum in nāvem vocāvit.

Flaccus, cuius oculī lacrimīs plēnī erant, Quīntum valēre iussit.

nautae, quibus magister signum dederat, nāvem solvērunt.

Quīntus, quī in puppe (*stern*) nāvis stābat, ad lītus respiciēbat.

Vocabulary 28

verbs		adjectives	
crēscō, crēscere, crēvī	I grow, increase	**dexter, dextra, dextrum**	right
edō, ēsse, ēdī	I eat	**dextrā (manū)**	on the right (hand)
solvō, solvere, solvī	I loose, untie, cast off	**sinister, sinistra, sinistrum**	left
		sinistrā (manū)	on the left (hand)
nouns		**reliquus, -a, -um**	remaining
lūna, -ae, f.	moon	**vīvus, -a, -um**	alive, living
argentum, -ī, n.	silver, money		
nūbēs, nūbis, f.	cloud	adverbs	
viātor, viātōris, m.	traveller	**inde**	thence, from there
		cum prīmum	as soon as

Explain the meaning of the following English phrases with reference to the Latin roots of the words in italics: a *lunar* month, a *crescent* moon, an *edible* fungus, a *vexatious* problem, a *vivid* picture.

Quīntus ad Graeciam nāvigat

magister, cui Flaccus viāticum iam trādiderat, Quīntum in nāvem vocāvit. Flaccus, cuius oculī lacrimīs plēnī erant, ad Quīntum sē vertit; 'valē, fīlī cārissime,' inquit; 'cum prīmum ad Graeciam advēneris, epistolam ad nōs scrībe. deī tē servābunt; nam puer
5 bonō ingeniō es.' Quīntus, patrem complexū tenēns, 'valē, cāre pater,' inquit; 'hoc prōmittō; cum prīmum ad Graeciam advēnerō, epistolam longissimam vōbīs scrībam in quā omnia nārrābō dē itinere. et tū, cum Venusiam redieris, mātrī et Horātiae et Argō salūtem plūrimam dā. sī deīs placēbit, vōs omnēs mox vidēbō.'
10   Flaccus sē vertit et sine morā ē portū festīnāvit. Quīntus eum spectābat abeuntem. deinde nāvem cōnscendit. nautae, quibus magister signum dederat, nāvem solvērunt. ubi ad apertum mare advēnērunt, vēla sustulērunt. Quīntus, quī in puppe nāvis stābat, ad lītus respiciēbat, futūrōrum īnscius; nec patrem nec mātrem
15 nec sorōrem umquam posteā vīsūrus erat.
    iter quod Quīntus inībat longum et difficile fuit. tōtum lītus Italiae praetervectī, tandem ad Siciliam advēnērunt et per fretum Siciliēnse nāvigāvērunt; ibi ā dextrā habitāverat Scylla, quae comitēs Ulixis rapuerat vīvōsque ēderat; ā sinistrā Charybdis
20 fuerat, vertex terribilis, quī Ulixem ipsum paene dēvōrāverat. Quīntus montem Aetnam procul cōnspexit flammās in caelum prōicientem; Aenēam Trōiānōsque in animum revocāvit, quōs Cyclōps paene cēperat.
    inde per apertum mare ad Graeciam nāvigābant; nūlla terra
25 iam in cōnspectū erat; ubīque caelum, ubīque mare. subitō ventī crēscunt; undae māiōrēs fīunt; nūbēs caelum obscūrant. nāvis maximō in perīculō erat; viātōrēs flēbant deōsque ōrābant. nautae ipsī dēspērābant mortemque timēbant.

viāticum fare

complexū in his embrace

vēla (n. pl.) sails
sustulērunt raised; **puppe** stern
futūrōrum of the future
īnscius ignorant
vīsūrus going to see
praetervectī having sailed past
fretum Siciliēnse the straits of Messina; **vertex** whirlpool
dēvōrāverat had swallowed down

sed magister, quī prōram in tempestātem vertit, nāvem
30 servāvit. mox ventī cadunt undaeque minōrēs fīunt. omnēs grātiās
deīs reddidērunt quod ē tempestāte incolumēs ēvāserant.

reliquum iter sine perīculō cōnfēcērunt decimōque diē ad
Pīraeum, portum Athēnārum, advēnērunt.

prōram prow

Respondē Latīnē

1 ubi Quīntus patrem valēre iussit, quid eī prōmīsit?
2 ubi per fretum Siciliēnse nāvigāvērunt, quid vīdit Quīntus?
3 in apertō marī, cūr nāvis maximō in perīculō erat?
4 in hōc perīculō, quid fēcērunt viātōrēs? quid fēcit magister?

Word-building

*The present participles of some verbs are used
as ordinary adjectives (with ablative -ī).
What is the meaning of the following?*

amāns, amantis
ardēns, ardentis
intellegēns, intellegentis
neglegēns, neglegentis
placēns, placentis

Piraeus

Quīntus Athēnās advenit

*Translate the first paragraph and answer the
questions on the letter*

nāvis tandem ad mōlem religāta est; Quīntus in terram exiit
festīnāvitque ad urbem, cupiēns ante noctem eō advenīre. vesper
iam aderat cum ad agoram advēnit, sed lūna lūcēbat, quae
Acropolim illūminābat. diū omnia spectābat; Parthenōna vidēre
5 poterat, templum nōbilissimum deae Athēnae, et multa alia
monumenta dē quibus in librīs saepe lēgerat.

tandem ad caupōnam rediit et epistolam scrīpsit, sīcut patrī
prōmīserat:

mōlem pier; **religāta** moored

agoram the agora (city center)
Acropolim (acc.) Acropolis
Parthenōna (acc.) Parthenon

sīcut just as

Quīntus patrī mātrīque cārissimīs Horātiaeque salūtem
10   plūrimam dat.

hodiē Athēnās advēnī. iter longissimum fuit nec sine
perīculō, sed tandem decimō diē incolumēs ad portum
advēnimus. ego statim in mediam urbem festīnāvī et
monumenta illa nōbilia, dē quibus totiēns lēgī, spectāvī.

15   et vōs, cārissimī, quid agitis? omnia cupiō audīre quae
domī fīunt. segetēsne bonae sunt? Argusne valet? epistolam
statim ad mē scrībite. mox epistolam longiōrem ad vōs
scrībam. intereā cūrāte ut valeātis.

totiēns so often
quid agitis? how are you?
segetēs crops; **valet** is well

cūrāte ut valeātis take care that you
    keep well

The Parthenon, Athens

1 What does Quintus say about the journey?   [3]
2 What news does he want to hear?   [4]
3 What does he promise to do?   [2]

GREECE

From the dark age to the golden age

Troy fell in about 1,250 BC, but the Achaeans' triumph was short-lived. Soon tribes of Greeks living to the north destroyed their civilization and Greece was plunged into a dark age. However, very gradually it emerged from the darkness. Homer, who lived during the second half of the eighth century BC, was a triumphant example of the rebirth of the arts, and writing had been rediscovered by the end of that century.

The reborn Greek civilization was at its height in the fifth century BC. It is in Athens above all that we can find evidence of its glories. In that city democracy was invented in 507 BC by Cleisthenes. This may be the greatest of the gifts which the Greeks have bequeathed to the modern world. It was in Athens also that drama, philosophy and science flourished, and it was there that the great buildings which Quintus admires were built at the inspiration of the outstanding Athenian statesman Pericles. The most famous of these is the Parthenon, the temple of the virgin goddess Athene, built on the top of Athens' precipitous citadel, the Acropolis. Inside stood Pheidias' monumental statue of Athene, thirty-nine feet high and made from gold and ivory.

The tragedy underlying the greatness of the Greek achievement was that the numerous city states of Greece found it impossible to unite with each other. They did this once when in 480 BC a great Persian army and fleet invaded their country and found itself opposed and driven out in a series of famous battles. The names of Thermopylae and Salamis live on and you may wish to investigate them. But the end of this glorious century was marked by a long and bloody conflict between Athens and her allies and her leading Greek opponent Sparta and her allies. In 404 BC, after nearly thirty years of war, Athens lost.

From Macedonia to Rome

Over the course of the next century the Greek states achieved a delicate balance. None was supreme and there was no unity. It was a situation that enabled Philip, king of the northerly state of Macedonia, to gain power over the rest of Greece. The great Athenian orator Demosthenes tried in his speeches to urge his fellow countrymen to resist Philip. However, Athens and her allies were defeated by the Macedonians in 338 BC.

Philip II
of Macedonia

Philip united the Greek states under his leadership and planned to invade Persia. However, he was assassinated in 336 BC on the eve of his departure. He was succeeded by his twenty-year-old son Alexander. The latter's vast eastern conquests justly gave him the title 'the Great'. He won the huge Persian empire as well as Egypt where he founded the important city of Alexandria. He marched into India but here his troops cried 'enough'. In 323 BC he died of a fever at the age of thirty-two.

After the death of Alexander, his three leading generals carved up his empire between them. Antigonus took the old kingdom of Macedonia, Seleucus took Syria and all Alexander's conquests as far as Afghanistan and India, and Ptolemy took Egypt. The cultural center of the Greek world shifted from Athens to Alexandria in Egypt, Ptolemy's capital. We call the period from Alexander's death in 323 BC to that of Cleopatra, Queen of Egypt, in 30 BC the Hellenistic age.

Alexander the Great

In the second war which Rome waged with Carthage, the war against Hannibal, Macedonia came in on the side of Carthage. Rome defeated Macedonia and thus became involved in the politics of the eastern Mediterranean. She found herself fighting a war with Macedonia and Syria from which she emerged victorious. Afterwards Rome was indisputably the center of the Mediterranean world; the Hellenistic kingdoms, the legacy of Alexander, one after another became part of the Roman empire, ruled by Roman governors. This was the situation in Greece, now the Roman province of Achaea, when Quintus arrived at Athens. The city's days of political independence were long past.

What impression do you gain from the above of the strengths and weaknesses of the Greeks?

Chapter 29   Academia

Theomnēstus ad mēnsam sēdēbat librum legēns.

Quīntus ad portās redībat cum intrāvērunt duo iuvenēs rīdentēs et magnā vōce colloquentēs.

Marcus sē vertit et 'dī immortālēs!' inquit; 'nōnne Quīntum videō? oculīs crēdere vix possum.'

mox in tabernā sēdēbant vīnum bibentēs.

Vocabulary 29

verbs
condō, condere, condidī   I found, establish
cōnfīdō, cōnfīdere + dat.   I trust

nouns
scholam habeō   I give a lecture
vīta, -ae, f.   life
negōtium, -ī, n.   business
adventus, adventūs, m.   arrival

adjectives
doctus, -a, -um   learned
grātus, -a, -um   pleasing, welcome; grateful
hūmānus, -a, -um   human; humane, kind
iūcundus, -a, -um   pleasant, delightful
dulcis, dulce   sweet

adverbs
libenter   gladly
quandō?   when?

pronouns
alter, altera, alterum   one or the other
                   (of two); second
uter, utra, utrum?   which? (of two)
utrum...an?   whether...or?
quisquam, quicquam   anyone, anything
                   (after a negative)

prepositions
propter + acc.   on account of,
                because of
super + acc.   above, over

conjunctions
nisi   unless; except
ut   as, when
sīcut   just as, like

Explain the following English phrases by reference to the Latin roots of the words in italics:
a *legal* requirement, *civil* war, an *intelligent* pupil, a *popular* demonstration,
a *gradual* improvement, *juvenile* crime, a *tumultuous* reception, a *vital* decision.

Acadēmīa

postrīdiē Quīntus māne surrēxit festīnāvitque ad Acadēmīam,
epistolam ferēns quam Hēliodōrus ad Theomnēstum scrīpserat.
ille prīnceps erat scholae quam Platō trecentīs ante annīs   **prīnceps** chief, principal
condiderat; nūlla schola per tōtum orbem terrārum nōbilior erat
5 nec melior quam illa. Quīntus, ubi intrāvit, duōs iuvenēs vīdit in
ātriō colloquentēs. accessit ad alterum et 'Theomnēstum quaerō'   **colloquentēs** chatting
inquit. 'vīsne mē ad eum dūcere?' ille respondit: 'venī mēcum. ad
eum tē dūcam.' Quīntum per porticum longissimam ad   **porticum** (f.) colonnade
Theomnēstī tablīnum dūxit. Quīntus eī grātiās reddidit
10 iānuamque pulsāvit.
     Theomnēstus ad mēnsam sedēbat, librum legēns. vir gravis
erat et venerābilis; barbam longissimam habēbat vultumque   **venerābilis** venerable
sevērissimum. Quīntum īnspexit et 'quid cupis, iuvenis?' inquit.   **barbam** beard
Quīntus respondit: 'discipulus tibi fīerī cupiō.' ille 'utrum rē vērā
15 studēre cupis' inquit 'an lūdere?' Quīntus respondit: 'epistolam
ferō quam Hēliodōrus ad tē scrīpsit.' ille epistolam accēpit; ubi
eam lēgit, Quīntō arrīsit. 'tū iuvenis es optimō ingeniō, ut dīcit   **arrīsit** (+ dat.) smiled at
Hēliodōrus, neque quisquam discipulōrum dīligentius studet.

The Academy

libenter igitur tē in numerum discipulōrum meōrum accipiam. abī
20 nunc. crās ad theātrum redī et scholam meam audī.'

    Quīntus laetissimus ad ātrium rediit. ad portās accēdēbat cum
intrāvērunt duo iuvenēs rīdentēs et magnā vōce colloquentēs.
alterum Quīntus agnōvit; oculīs suīs crēdere vix poterat: Marcus   **agnōvit** recognized
Cicerō aderat. Quīntus eum vocāvit. ille sē vertit et 'dī   **dī immortālēs!** immortal gods!
25 immortālēs!' inquit, 'nōnne Quīntum videō? nēmō mihi grātior
Rōmā vēnit quam tū. venī mēcum; in urbem ībimus et aliquid vīnī   **aliquid vīnī** some wine
bibēmus.'

    Quīntum in urbem dūxit et mox in tabernā sēdēbant vīnum
bibentēs. 'age, Quīnte,' inquit, 'omnia mihi nārrā. quandō Athēnās
30 advēnistī? quid Rōmae fit? quid audīvistī dē patre meō? utrum in
perīculō manet an in ōtium recessit?' Quīntus omnia eī nārrāvit dē
studiīs suīs, dē morte Caesaris, dē perīculīs urbis. Marcus 'vēra
dīcis, Quīnte. tempora numquam difficiliōra fuērunt. propter eam
causam pater mē Athēnās mīsit, quod ipse maximō in perīculō est.
35 itaque in Lycēō studeō. sed haec studia mihi nōn placent; scholās   **Lycēō** the Lyceum
Cratippī vix intellegō et librī philosophōrum frīgidī sunt. praetereā   **frīgidī** boring
in angustiās quāsdam incidī. nam omne argentum quod pater mihi   **angustiās** (f. pl.) difficulty
dedit iam cōnsūmpsī. pater plūs argentī mihi nōn mittet nisi   **cōnsūmpsī** I have used up
meliōrem fāmam dē mē audīverit. quid faciam?'

Respondē Latīnē

1 quid faciēbat Theomnēstus cum Quīntus tablīnum eius intrāvit?
2 cūr volēbat Theomnēstus Quīntum in numerum discipulōrum suōrum accipere?
3 ubi ad ātrium rediit Quīntus, cui occurrit?
4 cūr Marcī pater eum Athēnās mīserat?
5 quōmodo Marcus in angustiās quāsdam inciderat?

Word-building

What is the meaning of the following groups of words?

mīles, mīlitis, *m.*; mīlitō, mīlitāre; mīlitāris, -e; mīlitia, -ae, *f.*
mors, mortis, *f.*; mortuus, -a, -um; mortālis, -e, immortālis, -e.
numerus, -ī, *m.*; numerō, numerāre; numerōsus, -a, -um; numerābilis, -e; innumerābilis, -e.

Marcus epistolam ad Tīrōnem scrībit

Translate the first two paragraphs and answer the questions on Marcus' letter without translating

Quīntus paulīsper cōgitābat; deinde 'Marce,' inquit, 'utrum ad patrem scrībere dēbēs an ad Tīrōnem? nōnne pater tuus Tīrōnī maximē cōnfīdit? sī ille dē tē bene dīxerit, sine dubiō pater plūs argentī tibi mittet.'

5   Marcus 'Quīnte,' inquit, 'mē optimē monēs. epistolam nūper ā Tīrōne accēpī. statim ad eum rescrībam.' ad mēnsam sēdit et hanc epistolam ad Tīrōnem scrīpsit:

    Cicerō fīlius Tīrōnī suō dulcissimō salūtem dat.
    tabellārium cotīdiē valdē exspectābam: tandem vēnit
10 quadrāgēsimō diē postquam ā vōbīs discessit. eius adventus mihi fuit grātissimus; nam et maximam cēpī laetitiam ex epistolā cārissimī patris, et tua iūcundissima epistola summum gaudium mihi attulit.

    gaudeō quod grātōs rūmōrēs dē mē accēpistī, mī dulcissime
15 Tīrō, et hōs rūmōrēs aliīs refers. errāta enim aetātis meae maximum mihi attulērunt dolōrem. iam nūntium tibi grātissimum referam: Cratippō nōn sōlum optimus discipulus sum sed etiam velut fīlius. nam eum libenter audiō; sum tōtōs diēs cum eō et saepissimē ille mēcum cēnat.

20   librārium, sī vīs, mihi quam celerrimē mitte, quī mihi hypomnēmata exscrībet. cūrā ut valeās.

cōgitābat reflected

nūper lately
ad mēnsam at the table

tabellārium postman
quadrāgēsimō fortieth

errāta aetātis meae the errors of my youth

velut like

librārium copyist, secretary
hypomnēmata my lecture notes

1 How long did it take the mail to get from Rome to Athens? [1]
2 Why was Marcus so pleased by his mail? [3]
3 What reports did he ask Tiro to pass on to others? Why do you think he was so anxious for Tiro to do this? [4]
4 How does he describe his relations with his tutor, Cratippus? [4]
5 What was his final request to Tiro? Why do you think he asked Tiro to do this? [3]

STOIC AND EPICUREAN

What is a philosopher? The literal meaning of the word is a 'lover of wisdom'. Philosophers try to discover the truth about the world we live in. They suggest ways in which we can lead our lives for the best. They tell us about the nature of good and evil, and about what sort of behaviour is best for us both as individuals and as members of a society. The most important question for Greek philosophers was 'What is the greatest good?' Their teaching was highly valued by men of action in the ancient world. Marcus Cicero's teacher Cratippus was made a Roman citizen by Julius Caesar. Cratippus was the head of the Lyceum, the philosophical school founded by the famous Greek thinker Aristotle who was tutor to Alexander the Great.

Aristotle

The founder of the Academy, of which Theomnestus was head when Horace arrived in Athens, was Aristotle's teacher, Plato, who lived from about 429 to 347 BC. He was the greatest of the Greek philosophers. His works are still studied by philosophers today, and the most famous of them is the *Republic*. We call this book a 'dialogue', a conversation between two or more people, because Plato presents his views through an imaginary discussion led by his own teacher Socrates. The *Republic* sets forth the view that the ideal state should be governed by philosophers since they know best what is good and what is bad.

As time passed, new schools were founded, notably the Stoic and the Epicurean, the two philosophies which dominated the Roman world in Quintus' day. The Stoics preached that to be virtuous was the only good and not to be virtuous the only evil. Man must always act in accordance with reason. He should accept whatever happens to him with calm, giving way neither to intense joy nor to excessive grief. Thus he will come into harmony not only with the universal brotherhood of man but also with God. Brutus, the assassin of Julius Caesar, seemed to many to display the Stoic qualities at their noblest.

Plato

The Stoic school was founded by Zeno of Cyprus (335–263 BC) who came to Athens early in life and taught there in the Painted Porch (Stoa) from which the philosophy took its name. It had a greater effect on Roman life than any other philosophy, lasting from its introduction to Rome in the second century BC until the third century AD. It proved a humane influence in the treatment of slaves whom Stoics believed to be equal with other men because all alike are the sons of God. The Stoic emperor Antoninus (86–161 AD)

87

wrote, 'My city and my country, so far as I am Antoninus, is Rome, but so far as I am a man, it is the world' and 'Men exist for the sake of one another.'

The Stoics involved themselves in the real world of politics and war, but the followers of Epicurus (341–270 BC), who had founded the other main philosophy of the age, tried to avoid such disturbing pursuits. Epicurus' main purpose was to lead men to a happy life. This did not mean that they should always aim at the most obvious pleasures. After all, an evening of drinking is followed by a hangover. Their ideal was peace of mind. The fear of death, for example, could be overcome by the belief that the soul dies with the body and that there is no danger of survival. The great Roman poet Lucretius (94–55 BC) gives twenty-eight proofs that the soul is mortal. The Epicureans recommended withdrawal from the turmoil and confusion of the active life into the study of philosophy. This is celebrated by Lucretius in the following passage:

Epicurus

> It is sweet, when the winds are lashing the waves on the high seas, to view from the land the great struggles of someone else. But nothing is sweeter than to dwell in the serene temples built on the teaching of the wise, from where you can look down on others and see them wandering this way and that and going astray while they seek the path of life, as they strive to outdo each other in their ability and their claims to noble birth, struggling night and day by supreme efforts to rise to the height of power and gain dominion over the world.

If you had lived in Roman times, would you have been a Stoic or an Epicurean? Give the reasons for your choice. (You may be interested to know that Quintus became an Epicurean.)

Horātia ā mātre excitāta surgit.

Scintilla Horātiam excitātam ad nūptiās sē parāre iubet.

Horātia ad nūptiās parāta Decimum salūtat.

Decimus Horātiam ad novam domum ductam super līmen tollit.

Vocabulary 30

NB From this chapter on, a fourth part (the *supine*) of each verb is given. See the Grammar, p. 140.

verbs

dēlectō, dēlectāre, dēlectāvī, dēlectātum	I please, delight
supplicō, supplicāre, supplicāvī, supplicātum + dat.	I pray to, beg
arcessō, arcessere, arcessīvī, arcessītum	I summon
mē gerō	I behave myself
rem gerō	I conduct a matter
nūbō, nūbere, nūpsī, nūptum + dat.	I marry
nūptiae, -ārum, f. pl.	wedding
nūptiālis, nūptiāle	of a wedding, nuptial
tollō, tollere, sustulī, sublātum	I raise, lift
pereō, perīre, periī, peritum	I perish, die
sentiō, sentīre, sēnsī, sēnsum	I feel, realize

adverbs

herī	yesterday
nūper	lately

nouns

chorus, -ī, m.	chorus
dōnum, -ī, n.	gift
līmen, līminis, n.	threshold
lūmen, lūminis, n.	light
mōs, mōris, m.	custom
mōs maiōrum	the custom of our ancestors
sōl, sōlis, m.	sun

adjectives

aequus, -a, -um	equal, fair
aequē	equally, fairly
antīquus, -a, -um	old, ancient
dubius, -a, -um	doubtful
sine dubiō	without doubt
dīves, dīvitis	rich
potēns, potentis	powerful

What are: a *solar* eclipse,
a *choral* song,
an *illuminating* lecture,
a *nuptial* celebration,
a *sensitive* remark?

A Roman marriage ceremony

Horātiae nūptiae

cotīdiē Quīntus, māne excitātus, surrēxit et festīnāvit ad
Acadēmīam. dīligenter studēbat et multīs scholīs aderat
Theomnēstī aliōrumque doctōrum. mox plūrimōs amīcōs habēbat
inter iuvenēs quī in Acadēmīā studēbant.

5   quondam in tabernā cum amīcō quōdam sēdēbat cum
tabellārius epistolam eī trādidit ā patre scrīptam. ille epistolam
summō gaudiō acceptam continuō lēgit:

Flaccus Scintillaque fīliō cārissimō salūtem plūrimam dant.
tuam epistolam accēpimus et gaudēmus quod incolumis
10   Athēnās advēnistī et in Acadēmīā studēs. omnēs Venusiae
valēmus. nūntium magnī mōmentī tibi mittimus.
pater Decimī, veteris amīcī tuī, nūper vēnit ad mē et 'fīlius
meus' inquit 'fīliam tuam adamāvit et amōre eius perit, ut dīcit.
itaque vīsne tū eam Decimō spondēre, sī illa eum accipiet?' hoc
15   nōbīs maximē placuit. nam vir dīves est probātusque ab
omnibus. itaque dē dōte disserēbāmus; ille rem aequē gessit, et
mox pactum cōnfēcerāmus. Horātiam igitur arcessītam rogāvī
quid sentīret dē hōc mātrimōniō; illa Decimum bene cognōvit
et eī nūbere cupiēbat. paucīs post diēbus spōnsālia cōnfēcimus.
20   multī cognātī amīcīque ad epulās vocātī testēs erant pactī.
Decimus Horātiae ānulum dedit quem illa in tertium digitum
imposuit.
herī nūptiās perfēcimus. prīmā lūce Horātia, ā mātre
excitāta, sē parābat. pūpās et cētera puerīlia mātrī trādita valēre
25   iussit. deinde vestīmenta nūptiālia induit, tunicam candidam et
pallam lūteam; postrēmō flammeum in capite induit
corōnamque flōrum. numquam virginem pulchriōrem vīdī
quam eam.
iam aderat Decimus ipse novam togam indūtus plūrimīs
30   cum amīcīs. mox auspicēs advēnērunt et auspicia bona
prōnūntiāvērunt. Horātia Decimusque dextrās manūs rīte
cōnseruērunt. omnēs Iūnōnī supplicāvērunt et conclāmāvērunt
'bene verruncet!' deinde cēnam sūmptuōsam ā mātre tuā
parātam ēdimus.
35   tandem Hesperus aderat. tempus erat Horātiae domum suam
relinquere. mātrem valēre iussit nōn sine plūrimīs lacrimīs.
deinde Decimus eam ad novam domum dūxit. tībīcinēs
pompam dūxērunt iuvenēsque facēs in manibus tenentēs.
chorus puerōrum puellārumque carmen solitum canēbant:
40   'Hymen ō Hymenaee,* Hymen ades ō Hymenaee!' ubi ad
Decimī aedēs pervēnērunt, Decimus Horātiam super līmen
sustulit dōnaque eī obtulit, ignem et aquam, quod iam Horātia
domina facta erat familiae. sīc omnia secundum mōrem
maiōrum cōnfēcerāmus.
45   hic nūntius sine dubiō tē summō gaudiō afficiet. scrībe
igitur ad Horātiam grātulātiōnemque eī mitte optimī
mātrimōniī. cūrā ut valeās.

doctōrum of teachers

quondam once
tabellārius postman

magnī mōmentī of great importance

adamāvit has fallen in love with
amōre eius with love for her
spondēre to betroth
probātus respected; dōte dowry
disserēbāmus we discussed
pactum an agreement
quid sentīret what she felt
spōnsālia (n. pl.) engagement party
cognātī relations; epulās (f. pl.) feast
testēs witnesses; ānulum a ring
digitum finger
pūpās dolls

pallam lūteam yellow robe
flammeum bridal veil
corōnam garland
virginem maiden, bride
indūtus wearing
auspicēs the augurs
auspicia the auspices
rīte duly, according to custom
cōnseruērunt joined
Iūnōnī Juno, goddess of marriage
bene verruncet good luck!
sūmptuōsam sumptuous
Hesperus the evening star
tībīcinēs flute players
facēs torches; solitum customary
ades be present! = come!

facta erat had become
secundum (+ acc.) according to

* **Hymen, ō Hymenaee**: *Hymen* was the god of marriage; *Hymenaeus* means the wedding song. The poet Catullus wrote a wedding song in which these words are used as a refrain at the end of each verse. He starts by setting the scene: the wedding feast is coming to an end, the evening star (*Vesper*) is rising in the sky (*Olympō*); the young men who form the choir tell each other to get up, leave the rich feast (*pinguēs mēnsās*), and prepare to sing the wedding song when the bride (*virgō*) appears:

> Vesper adest, iuvenēs, cōnsurgite: Vesper Olympō
> exspectāta diū vix tandem lūmina tollit.
> surgere iam tempus, iam pinguēs linquere mēnsās,
> iam veniet virgō, iam dīcētur hymenaeus.
> Hymen ō Hymenaee, Hymen ades ō Hymenaee.

tempus (supply **est**) it is time
linquere = relinquere
dīcētur will be sung

A marriage scene

Word-building

1   Perfect passive participles are often used as ordinary adjectives, like those you have already met, e.g.

parātus, -a, -um (from **parō**) having been prepared, i.e. ready
territus, -a, -um (from **terreō**) having been terrified, i.e. terrified

So also:

doctus, -a, -um (from **doceō**) learned (having been taught)
nōtus, -a, -um (from **nōscō**) known (having been learned)
nūptus, -a, -um (from **nūbō**) married; **nūpta, -ae**, *f.* a bride, a wife

2   The neuter of the perfect passive participle is often used as a noun, e.g.

dictum, -ī, *n.* a saying (a thing having been said)
factum, -ī, *n.* a deed (a thing having been done)
iussum, -ī, *n.* an order (a thing having been ordered)
prōmissum, -ī, *n.* a promise (a thing having been promised)
scrīptum, -ī, *n.* a writing (a thing having been written)

Rēspūblica in perīculum venit

Without translating answer the questions on the following passage

Quīntus hāc epistolā dēlectātus statim Horātiae scrīpsit.
Decimum bene meminerat; in lūdō Flāviī molestus fuerat
Quīntumque saepe vexāverat, sed iam adultus erat et sine dubiō
melius sē gerēbat. hāc spē adductus grātulātiōnem Horātiae mīsit.

5   intereā rēspūblica, morte Caesaris commōta, cotīdiē maius in
perīculum veniēbat. Antōnius, Caesaris amīcus, potestātem suam
augēre temptābat. Octāviānus, iuvenis ā Caesare in testāmentō
adoptātus, Rōmam advēnerat; nōmen Caesaris assūmpserat,
argentum mīlitibus distribuēbat, in diēs potentior fīēbat.

10 senātōrēs, ab Antōniō territī, Octāviānum in suās partēs addūcere
temptābant. multī bellum cīvīle praedīcēbant.

hae rēs Athēnās relātae summā ānxietāte omnēs affēcērunt.
Marcus in prīmīs prō patre timēbat, quod ille rempūblicam
dēfendere temptābat senātōrēsque in Antōnium excitātōs dūcēbat.

meminerat remembered
molestus tiresome
adultus grown up

testāmentō in his will
assūmpserat had assumed, taken on
in diēs daily
partēs (political) party
praedīcēbant predicted

in prīmīs especially

1   What did Quintus feel about Decimus?   [4]
2   Why was the political situation so dangerous?   [8]
3   Why was Marcus especially afraid for his father?   [3]

Fābella: Horātia ad nūptiās sē parat

Persōnae: Horātia, Scintilla, prōnuba, Flaccus

prōnuba matron-of-honor

Scintilla prīmā lūce Horātiam excitat.

Scintilla: surge, cārissima. tempus est tē parāre. ecce, sōl nūptiīs
tuīs arrīdet.

arrīdet (+ dat.) smiles on

5 **Horātia:** ō māter, nōlō surgere. sine mē paulō diūtius dormīre.
Scintilla: age, cārissima. nōn licet tibi diūtius dormīre. mox
veniet prōnuba.

paulō a little
age come on!
nōn licet tibi you may not

Horātia invīta surgit.

Horātia: quid nunc?
10 **Scintilla:** nunc dēbēs pūpās et cētera puerīlia mihi trādere.
Horātia: ō māter, nōlō pūpās meās valēre iubēre.
Scintilla: fīlia cārissima, mox mātrōna eris. tālibus nōn opus est
tibi. age, omnia mihi trāde.

pūpās dolls
mātrōnā married woman
tālibus nōn opus est tibi you have
no need of such things

Horātia pūpās invīta trādit.

15 **Scintilla:** iam dēbēs vestīmenta nūptiālia induere. ecce, adest
prōnuba; illa tē iuvābit.
prōnuba: salvē, Horātia. tempus est ad nūptiās tē ōrnāre. mox
aderit Decimus plūrimīs cum amīcīs. age, prīmum
hanc tunicam candidissimam indue; euge! et nunc
20   hanc pallam lūteam.
Horātia: quam gravis est haec palla! vix stāre possum.

ōrnāre to deck, adorn

pallam lūteam yellow robe
quam gravis how heavy!

Scintilla: nōlī tē vexāre, cārissima. palla pulcherrima est; crēde mihi, tē valdē decet.

decet it suits

prōnuba: postrēmō caput tuum flammeō involvam. ecce, iam parāta es.

flammeō (red) veil
involvam I will wrap

25

intrat Flaccus. Horātiam bāsiat.

Flaccus: salvē, cārissima. quam fōrmōsa es! numquam virginem vīdī pulchriōrem. sed festīnā; iam adsunt Decimus amīcīque eius. omnēs tē exspectant.

fōrmōsa beautiful

30 **Scintilla:** manē! hanc corōnam flōrum capitī tuō impōne. ecce! nunc tē spectā in hōc speculō. nōnne tibi placēs?

speculō mirror

Horātia imāginem suam diū spectat; corōnam pallamque corrigit.

imāginem image, reflection
corrigit straightens

Horātia: nisi speculum mē fallit, optimē ōrnātā sum. dūc mē ad Decimum.

fallit deceives

35

WEDDINGS

We now draw together from our story the details of a Roman wedding

A girl was considered eligible for marriage at about the age of fourteen. When the two families had come to an agreement, an engagement would take place and the future bride and groom would exchange gifts, above all a ring which the bride-to-be would wear on the third finger of her left hand. An engagement party would be held in celebration of the match.

The favored time for weddings was the second half of June, a time when ill-omened days could be most easily avoided. On the eve of the wedding the bride dedicated her child-hood dolls and toys to the Lares. She put on her marriage dress, the vertically woven straight tunic (*tunica rēcta*) and a flame-colored veil. Then she went to bed.

A Roman bride preparing for her wedding

On the wedding day the door and doorposts of her father's house would be festooned with flowers, evergreen branches and colored ribbons, and carpets would be spread at the entrance. The bride would prepare for the ceremony. Her hair was arranged in an old-fashioned manner with six strands parted using a bent iron spearhead. Her head was crowned with a garland of flowers and the flame-colored veil. Her plain white tunic, which stretched to the ground, was held by a belt fastened with a special knot and she wore saffron-colored shoes. The guests and the bridegroom arrived, the auspices (the prophetic signs) were taken and the marriage contract signed in the presence of ten witnesses. A married woman (*prōnuba*) would join the bride and groom's right hands. This solemn moment, with its silent exchange of vows between the couple, was the heart of the ceremony. The company prayed to the gods and goddesses of weddings, particularly to Juno, goddess of marriage, and then a sacrifice was made to Jupiter. The guests now cried out 'Good luck!' and the bride's parents hosted the wedding feast.

In the evening the ritual started up again. Just as she was about to leave with the groom, the bride would take refuge in her mother's arms and the groom would tear her away from them. This looks back to the early days of Rome when its early inhabitants seized the women of a neighboring tribe, the Sabines, to ensure that their race continued. Flute-players and torch-bearers escorted the procession to the groom's house, and a noisy crowd followed shouting the marriage cry (*talasse* or *talassiō*) and bawdy jokes. In one of his poems about weddings, Catullus evokes this part of the proceedings:

Boys, lift up your torches:
I see the veil approaching.
Come, sing in the proper way
the joyous song to Hymen,
god of marriage.

The bride carried three small coins, one for her bridegroom, one for his household gods and one for the gods of the crossroads. She also carried a distaff and a spindle, and ahead of her went a boy brandishing a hawthorn torch lit at the hearth of her former home, while two other boys held her hands. The groom would scatter nuts and small coins to the children who would scramble to get hold of them.

At her new house the bride smeared the doorposts with pig's fat and oil and garlanded them with wool. Now her groom stood on the threshold of his house and asked her her name. She replied with the words '*ubi tū Gāius, ego Gāia*' (where you are Gaius, I am Gaia).* Her companions then carried her over the threshold in case she might provide a bad omen by slipping, and the groom, signifying that she was mistress of the house, presented her with fire and water. Finally, seated in her new home, she spoke the ritual prayers to its god.

The ceremony was now over and the guests went off home.

Find five similarities and five dissimilarities between this and a modern wedding.

* In fact she kept her name.

omnēs iuvenēs ad theātrum ā Theomnēstō
vocātī erant; Quīntus locum vacuum invenīre
vix poterat.

Theomnēstus, quī dē officiīs disserēbat, ā
iuvenibus intentē audītus est.

iuvenēs, quī valdē commōtī sunt, ā Brūtō
salūtātī sunt.

Brūtus, cui maximus datus est plausus
(*applause*), ē theātrō ā comitibus ductus est.

Vocabulary 31

verbs

mīlitō, mīlitāre, mīlitāvī,
  mīlitātum   I campaign, serve as a soldier
valeō, valēre,
  valuī, valitum   I am strong, I am well
disserō, disserere, disseruī,
  dissertum   I discuss
expellō, expellere, expulī,
  expulsum   I drive out
opprimō, opprimere, oppressī,
  oppressum   I oppress

nouns

officium, -ī, n.   duty
eques, equitis, m.   horseman
  equitēs, equitum, m. pl. cavalry
fīnis, fīnis, m.   end, finish
  fīnēs, fīnium, m. pl.   boundaries, territory
lībertās, lībertātis, f.   liberty

adjectives

īdem, eadem, idem   the same (= **is, ea, id** + suffix **-dem**)

nōnnūllī, -ae, -a   some
hilaris, hilare   cheerful
immortālis, immortāle   immortal
senior, seniōris   older
vehemēns, vehementis   violent

The following political terms consist entirely of words derived from Latin roots.
Using a dictionary, if necessary, find out what these roots are: *prime minister*, *local elections*, *urban councillor*, *universal suffrage*, *the Conservative party*, *the Labour party*, *the Liberal party*, *the Communist candidate*. What do the Latin roots of *conservative*, *labor*, *liberal* and *communist* tell you about the political principles of these parties?

Brūtus Athēnās advenit

paucīs post diēbus Quīntus, dum agoram trānsit, ab aliquō   **agoram** city center
vocātus est; sē vertit et Marcum vīdit ad sē currentem. 'venī hūc,
Quīnte,' inquit; 'rem magnī mōmentī volō tibi referre.' dum in   **mōmentī** of importance
tabernā sedent, Marcus 'vidē,' inquit; 'epistolam accēpī ā Tīrōne
5 missam. pater Athēnās venit; cupit mē vidēre. paucīs diēbus
aderit. dī immortālēs! nunc dēbeō omnibus scholīs adesse et
Cratippum ad cēnam invītāre. ō mē miserum! quid faciam?'   **mē miserum!** poor me!
    Quīntus rīsit; 'cūr tam commōtus es?' inquit; 'nōnne Cratippō
optimus discipulus es? nōnne eum libenter audīs et saepissimē ad
10 cēnam vocās? sīc enim ad Tīrōnem scrīpsistī, quī sine dubiō
eadem patrī tuō rettulit.'
    hīs verbīs Marcus minimē dēlectātus est. 'nōlī mē rīdēre,   **minimē** very little, not at all
Quīnte,' inquit. 'veniam tēcum ad agoram et librum nēscioquem   **librum nēscioquem**: some book or
emam. deinde ad Lycēum redībō et scholam Cratippī audiam. ō   other
15 diem nigrum!'   **nigrum** black
    postrīdiē Quīntus eī occurrit in eādem tabernā bibentī.
Quīntus numquam eum hilariōrem vīderat. ille 'ecce, Quīnte,'
inquit, 'alteram epistolam ā patre scrīptam accēpī. Athēnās nōn
veniet. rēbus maximī mōmentī Rōmae retentus est. dī mē

20 servāvērunt. nunc est bibendum.' Quīntus rīsit Marcumque **est bibendum** (we) must drink
relīquit vīnum bibentem. ad Acadēmīam recurrit; scholam enim
Theomnēstī audīre cupiēbat.

ad Acadēmīam reversus, multitūdinem iuvenum invēnit **reversus** having returned
theātrum frequentantium. omnēs valdē commōtī sunt. causam **frequentantium** crowding
25 tantī tumultūs mox cognōvit. vix enim sēderat cum plērīque **plērīque** several
seniōrēs theātrum intrāvērunt ā Brūtō ductī. Quīntus attonitus est;
Brūtus ipse, patriae līberātor, ad Acadēmīam vēnerat.

continuō intrāvit Theomnēstus; ā discipulīs salūtātus est
tribūnalque ascendit. paulīsper audītōrēs tacitus īnspiciēbat; **tribūnal** (n.) platform
30 deinde scholam incēpit. dē officiīs disseruit. hanc quaestiōnem **quaestiōnem** question
prōposuit: 'quid facere dēbet vir bonus, sī tyrannus rempūblicam
opprimit lībertātemque cīvium praecīdit?' exemplum revocāvit **praecīdit** cuts off
Harmodiī et Aristogeitōnis, quī quīngentīs ante annīs tyrannum **quīngentīs ante annīs** five
Athēnārum occīderant lībertātemque populō redidderant. illī ab hundred years before
35 omnibus laudātī erant glōriamque immortālem sibi pepererant. **pepererant** had won

Theomnēstus ab omnibus intentē audītus est; ubi schola ad
fīnem perducta est, iuvenēs ad Brūtum sē vertērunt et vehementer
plausērunt. ille manūs sustulit eōs salūtāns, deinde sine verbō ē **plausērunt** applauded
theātrō exiit.

Brutus

Respondē Latīnē

1 cūr tam commōtus erat Marcus?
2 cūr patrem suum vidēre nōlēbat?
3 postrīdiē cūr hilaris erat?
4 ubi Quīntus ad Acadēmīam rediit,
   quid invēnit?
5 quam quaestiōnem Theomnēstus
   iuvenibus prōposuit?

Harmodius and Aristogeiton

Word-building

Three types of noun are formed from the supines of many verbs,
e.g. from **moneō** (I warn, I remind), supine **monit-um**:

1 **monit-or**, **monitōris**, *m.* a reminder (someone who reminds)
   (masculine 3rd declension nouns ending **-or** in the nominative
   denote the person who performs the action of the verb);

2 **monit-us**, **monitūs**, *m.* a reminder, a warning
   (4th declension nouns ending **-us** denote the action of the verb);

3 **monit-iō**, **monitiōnis**, *f.* a reminding, warning
   (3rd declension feminine nouns with nominative **-iō** also
   denote the action of the verb).

What do the following nouns mean?

	supine	*nouns*
currō	cursum	cursor, cursōris, *m.*
		cursus, cursūs, *m.*
audiō	audītum	audītor, audītōris, *m.*
		audītiō, audītiōnis, *f.*
inveniō	inventum	inventor, inventōris, *m.*
		inventiō, inventiōnis, *f.*

Marcus Brūtō sē coniungit

Without translating answer the questions below this passage

postquam Brūtus ē theātrō exiit, omnēs iuvenēs circumstābant
inter sē colloquentēs. verbīs enim Theomnēstī commōtī
lībertātem populī Rōmānī ā Caesare Antōniōque oppugnātam
dēfendere cupiēbant. Brūtī abavum in animum revocāvērunt, ā
5 quō Tarquinius Superbus Rōmā expulsus erat. Caesaris caedem
probābant, quod ille tyrannus fierī temptāverat.

    Brūtus multōs diēs Athēnīs manēbat; scholīs saepe aderat;
cum iuvenibus sedēbat doctōrēs audiēns. nōnnūllōs ad cēnam
vocāvit. tandem Athēnīs in Macedoniam discessit ubi exercitus
10 parātus erat. multōs iuvenum sēcum dūxit, quī in exercitū eius
mīlitāre volēbant. inter aliōs Marcus Cicerō cum Brūtō discessit
et mox ālae equitum praefectus est.

sē coniungit joins

colloquentēs talking

abavum ancestor
caedem the murder
probābant they approved of

ālae squadron; **praefectus est** (+
dat.) was put in command of

1 How did the students react to Theomnestus' lecture? [2]
2 What historical event did they recall? [3]
3 What did Brutus do in Athens? [3]
4 Why did he go to Macedonia? [2]
5 What happened to Marcus Cicero? [2]

ANTONY, OCTAVIAN AND THE SENATE

When Caesar was assassinated in 44 BC, his fellow consul was Mark Antony. He was born in 82 BC and had been a wild young man whom Cicero called a gambler; but he was a popular and capable soldier. He managed affairs with great skill after Caesar's death. The killers had been given a frosty reception by the Roman mob, but Antony pretended to make peace with them and a tense quiet fell upon the city.

Caesar, however, in his will had left his fine gardens beyond the Tiber to the Roman people and declared that every Roman citizen was to receive 300 sesterces. When Antony delivered Caesar's funeral oration, he inflamed the emotions of the mob by talking of the generosity of his will and displaying his corpse and blood-stained toga. Shakespeare has given a memorable portrayal of this in *Julius Caesar*. Antony's speech proved so powerful that Brutus and Cassius were forced to flee from Rome. Two months after Caesar's death, Antony was in control and Cicero complained that 'at times one could wish Caesar back'. The assassins' dream of the return of the republic had been an empty one. The power would continue to be in the hands of individuals.

However, one major setback to Antony during this time was the discovery that Caesar had named as his chief heir not Antony but his great-nephew and adopted son Octavian. This eighteen-year-old, called the 'boy' by those who under-estimated him, was to receive three quarters of Caesar's estate. Antony was full of bitter feelings towards him, and when Octavian arrived in Rome in April 44 BC, the relationship between them proved difficult. But there was as yet no open quarrel.

Cicero delivered the first of his speeches against Antony in September, calling him among other things a drunkard who had wasted a fortune. Later his onslaughts were even more vitriolic. Here he attacks Antony for his disgusting behavior in the morning, at a time of day when a true Roman noble would be conducting his business in a dignified fashion:

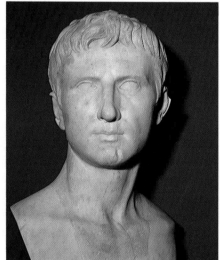

Octavian

> Down those jaws of yours, down those lungs, with that physical stamina worthy of a gladiator, you sank so much wine at Hippias' wedding that you had to vomit in full view of the people of Rome the morning after. It was a revolting sight – it was revolting even to hear about it. If this had happened at a dinner party when you drain your notoriously huge goblets, it would still have seemed disgusting. But in an assembly of the Roman people, you, a man holding public office, a Master of the Horse – from whom even a belch would have been deplorable – you, I say, filled your lap and the whole platform as you threw up chunks of food stinking of wine.

Lion hunt mosaic from Pella, the capital of King Philip of Macedon

Cicero called his attacks on Antony his *Philippics*, bringing to mind the speeches of the great Athenian orator Demosthenes against Philip of Macedon (see p. 82). They proved equally futile in the long run but, under their inspiration, the senate turned to Octavian for support. Octavian and Antony, the one apparently the champion of the republic and the senate, the other their opponent, found themselves locked in battle with each other in a conflict in which Octavian proved the victor.

Antony was humiliated, and the senate now tried to brush the young Octavian aside and to put its authority behind Caesar's murderers. Octavian would have none of this. He controlled eight legions and, in a pattern of events familiar in the history of this time, he marched on Rome, demanding the consulship. He gained it, as well as the legal right to refer to himself as Caesar.

Julius Caesar's murderers were outlawed. Octavian decided to come to terms with Antony. The senate was powerless. The diplomacy of Cicero and the violent action of Brutus and Cassius had been in vain. The republic was dead.

In February 43 BC, Cicero wrote a letter to Cassius which starts, 'I wish you had invited me to your dinner on the Ides of March. If you had, there would have been nothing left over.'

What did he mean by this? Do you think it would have made much difference to the survival of the republic if nothing had been left over?

Scintilla Flaccum ad tabernam piscātōriam dūcēbat. (Flaccus ā Scintillā ad tabernam piscātōriam dūcēbātur.)

Scintilla 'quantī' inquit 'vendis illōs piscēs?' piscātor respondet: 'hōs piscēs ūnō dēnāriō vendō'. ('quantī venduntur illī piscēs?' 'hī piscēs ūnō dēnāriō venduntur.')

Flaccus 'dī immortālēs,' inquit, 'piscātor tē fraudat, Scintilla.' ('ā piscātōre fraudāris, Scintilla.')

Scintilla 'tacē, Flacce,' inquit. argentum piscātōrī trādit piscēsque accipit. (argentum trāditur ā Scintillā piscēsque accipiuntur.)

Vocabulary 32

verbs

comparō, comparāre, comparāvī, comparātum	I acquire, get
occupō, occupāre, occupāvī, occupātum	I seize, occupy
cōgō, cōgere, coēgī, coāctum	I compel
cōnsistō, cōnsistere, cōnstitī, cōnstitum	I halt, stand still
dīvidō, dīvidere, dīvīdī, dīvīsum	I divide
ēvertō, ēvertere, ēvertī, ēversum	I overturn
corripiō, corripere, corripuī, correptum	I seize, steal
praeficiō, praeficere, praefēcī, praefectum	I put x (acc.) in command of y (dat.)
recipiō, recipere, recēpī, receptum	I take back
mē recipiō, recipere, recēpī, receptum	I take myself back, retreat
praesum, praeesse, praefuī + dat.	I am in command of

nouns

bona, -ōrum, n. pl.	goods	
cōpiae, -ārum, f. pl.	forces	
vīlla, -ae, f.	villa, country house	
lēgātus, -ī, m.	deputy, officer, envoy	
ferrum, -ī, n.	iron; sword	
partēs, partium, f. pl.	political party	
tot (indeclinable)	so many	
totiēns	so often	

adjective

adversus, -a, -um   contrary, opposed

adverb

clam   secretly

conjunction

atque   and

What do the following English words mean? Show how their meaning is related to their Latin roots: prefect, patriotic, partial, inimical, adversity.

Bellum cīvīle

paucīs post diēbus Quīntus ubi ad Acadēmīam advēnit, epistolam invēnit ā Marcō scrīptam:

    Marcus Cicerō Quīntō suō salūtem dat.

      nōn diūtius Athēnīs manēbō, scholās audiēns quās
5   intellegere vix possum. tū scholās audīs dē officiīs, ego
    officium meum perficiam. lībertās populī Rōmānī ab Antōniō
    oppugnātur. ego in Macedoniam prōcēdō; in exercitū Brūtī
    mīlitābō. tū, sī vir bonus es et fortis, idem faciēs. mox, ut
    spērō, tē in Macedoniā vidēbō; summō gaudiō ā mē ibi
10   accipiēris. intereā cūrā ut valeās.

    Quīntus hāc epistolā valdē commovētur. intereā nūntiī semper peiōrēs Rōmā afferuntur. Antōnius Octāviānusque inimīcī fīunt. Octāviānus ā Cicerōne laudātur et in partēs senātōrum addūcitur. exercitus ab Octāviānō comparātur. dēnique Antōnius cōpiās suās
15 in Galliam dūcit atque ad bellum sē parat. senātōrēs, ā Cicerōne excitātī, Antōnium hostem populī Rōmānī dēclārāvērunt; et cōnsulēs et Octāviānum contrā eum mīsērunt. ubi proeliō

accipiēris   you will be received

cūrā ut valeās   see that you keep well

concurrērunt, Antōnius victus est et in Galliam Ulteriōrem sē
recēpit, sed ambō cōnsulēs in proeliō occīsī sunt.

20   Octāviānus igitur tōtī exercituī praeerat. ambitiōne adductus,
lēgātōs Rōmam mīsit; senātum iussit sē cōnsulem creāre. ubi
senātus hoc facere nōluit, Octāviānus exercitum suum in Italiam
dūxit et Rōmam celerrimē contendit. senātōrēs, adventū eius
territī, invītī eī concessērunt. Cicerō dē rēpūblicā dēspērāns in
25 vīllam rūsticam sē recēpit.

    intereā Octāviānus Rōmā discesserat exercitumque velut in
Antōnium dūcēbat. proelium maximum ab omnibus
exspectābātur. sed ubi Octāviānus propius accessit, cōnstitit
lēgātōsque ad Antōnium mīsit; dūcēs cōnstituērunt rem
30 compōnere nōn ferrō sed verbīs. Antōnius et Octāviānus et tertius
dux, nōmine Lepidus, clam convēnērunt. foedus faciunt;
imperium Rōmānum inter sē dīvidunt. lēgātī Rōmam mittuntur
quī senātōrēs iubent hunc triumvirātum lēge cōnstituere.

    deinde triumvirī Rōmam prōcēdunt. urbs occupātur, senātōrēs
35 cōguntur omnia facere quae illī cupiunt. inimīcī triumvirōrum
prōscrībuntur; plūrimī occīduntur bonaque eōrum corripiuntur.

ambō both

concessērunt gave in to

velut as though

compōnere to settle

triumvirātum triumvirate
cōnstituere to establish

prōscrībuntur are proscribed, outlawed

Word-building

What is the meaning of the following words?

1 dēfendō, dēfendere; dēfēnsor, dēfēnsōris, *m.*;
   dēfēnsiō, dēfēnsiōnis, *f.*
2 ōrō, ōrāre; ōrātor, ōrātōris, *m.*;
   ōrātiō, ōrātiōnis, *f.*
3 lūdus, -ī, *m.*; lūdō, lūdere; lūsor, lūsōris, *m.*;
   lūsus, -ūs, *m.*
4 laus, laudis, *f.*; laudō, laudāre; laudātor,
   laudātōris, *m.*; laudātiō, laudātiōnis, *f.*
5 nāvis, nāvis, *f.*; nauta, -ae, *m.* (= nāvita);
   nāvigō, nāvigāre; nāvigātor, nāvigātōris, *m.*;
   nāvigātiō, nāvigātiōnis, *f.*

The Rostra

Mors Cicerōnis

Without translating, answer the questions below

nēmō Antōnium vehementius oppugnāverat quam Cicerō.
Antōnius ipse manum mīlitum mīsit quī iussī sunt eum occīdere.
ille in vīllā manēbat prope mare; ubi dē adventū mīlitum
cognōvit, temptāvit in nāve effugere. ventīs tamen adversīs
5 repellēbātur. tandem ad vīllam redīre cōnstituit; 'mortem obībō'   **obībō** I shall meet
inquit 'in patriā quam saepe servāvī.'

    in lectīcā ad vīllam ferēbātur, cum mīlitēs advēnērunt. nōn   **lectīcā** a litter
restitit sed cervīcem ē lectīcā extendit. illī caput gladiō   **cervīcem** his neck
praecīdunt. tum manūs quoque praecīdērunt, quae tot ōrātiōnēs in   **extendit** stretched out
10 Antōnium scrīpserant. caput eius ad Antōnium relātum inter duās   **praecīdunt** they cut off
manūs in eīs rōstrīs affīxum est in quibus Antōnium tantā   **rōstrīs** the speaker's platform
ēloquentiā totiēns oppugnāverat.

1   Why did Antony himself send soldiers to kill Cicero?   [3]
2   Where was Cicero staying when the soldiers came
    and what did he try to do?   [4]
3   Why did he not succeed?   [2]
4   What were his last words?   [5]
5   What did Cicero do when the soldiers found him?   [3]
6   How did the soldiers mutilate his body?   [2]
7   What did Antony do with the parts the soldiers had
    cut off? Why did this seem to him appropriate?   [4]
8   Write a character sketch of Cicero based on what you
    have read about him so far.   [10]

THE SECOND TRIUMVIRATE

The triumvirate referred to in the Latin narrative, and known by
historians as the Second Triumvirate, was formed when Octavian
met with Antony and another leading politician called Lepidus, a
former lieutenant of Caesar's, in 43 BC on a small island in a
river in Cisalpine Gaul. After marching on Rome, they arranged
that they should hold power for five years, make laws and
nominate magistrates and governors. Thus the single dictator
Caesar was replaced by three dictators. Realizing the inevitability
of war with Caesar's avengers, Brutus and Cassius were now
with their legions in the East. The triumvirs carved up the
western provinces of the Roman empire between them, and, to
cement the alliance, Octavian married Antony's step-daughter.

    They wished to dispose of their many political enemies and,
even more importantly, to raise money, and so they reintroduced
the grim practice of proscription. They would publish a list of
names. Whoever killed a man named on the list would receive a
reward and the state would get the dead man's property. Some

Octavian

Mark
Antony

105

Lepidus

300 senators and 2,000 knights were proscribed in this way. A reign of terror followed. Shakespeare in his *Julius Caesar* includes a chilling scene in which the triumvirs sit round a table listing their enemies:

Antony: These many, then, shall die; their names are prick'd [i.e. marked off].

Octavian (*to Lepidus*): Your brother too must die; consent you, Lepidus?

Lepidus: I do consent, –

Octavian: Prick him down, Antony.

Lepidus: Upon condition Publius shall not live, Who is your sister's son, Mark Antony.

Antony: He shall not live; look, with a spot I damn him.

Many who were named in the proscription lists fled and later returned with a pardon. Cicero was not so lucky, as you have seen in this chapter. He met his grisly end in 43 BC, and proved that he had meant what he said in his speeches against Mark Antony: 'As a young man, I defended the republic: I shall not desert it in my old age.' Cicero's tragedy was that the republic had long been past saving.

It may seem strange that Octavian agreed to the proscription of Cicero, a man who had given him much support. But Octavian was implacably determined to take revenge on all the conspirators who had killed Julius Caesar and while Cicero had not been a member of the conspiracy, he had rejoiced, even gloated over Caesar's assassination. This, joined with Cicero's rash pronouncement that Octavian was a young man to be made use of and then cast aside, may well have stopped Octavian stepping in to save him.

Octavian and Antony took twenty-eight legions to Greece in 42 BC to fight with Brutus and Cassius. They were to meet at Philippi.

Cicero's tomb

What do you think of Cicero both as a man and a politician?

Scintilla epistolam ad Quīntum scrībit.

Vocabulary 33

verbs

adiuvō, adiuvāre, adiūvī, adiūtum	I help
administrō, administrāre, administrāvī, administrātum	I manage, administer
immineō, imminēre + dat.	I hang over, threaten
valeō, valēre, valuī, valitum	I am strong, I am well
committō, committere, commīsī, commissum	I entrust
aliquem certiōrem faciō	I make someone more certain, I inform someone

adjectives

cautus, -a, -um	cautious
certus, -a, -um	certain; resolved
honestus, -a, -um	honorable
ōtiōsus, -a, -um	at leisure, idle
sollicitus, -a, -um	anxious

nouns

fīliolus, -ī, m.	a little son
dolor, dolōris, m.	pain, grief
īnfāns, īnfantis, c.	baby
mēnsis, mēnsis, m.	month

The following is the opening of an article in *The Independent* of 18 April 1995:

> If the unions are to be credible, they must heal their divisions and curb the militants. As the teachers' unions embark this week on a series of uncoordinated plans for action over class sizes next term, their failure to serve ordinary union members and children in schools has never been more apparent.

These two sentences include ten words derived from Latin roots. List those you recognize and say what Latin word each is derived from.

Scintilla epistolam ad Quīntum scrībit

Read and understand the following pasage; answer the questions below without translating

paucīs post mēnsibus Quīntus epistolam accēpit Venusiā missam. Scintilla ad eum scrīpserat:

> Scintilla fīliō cārissimō salūtem plūrimam dat.
> nūntium optimum tibi referō: Horātia nūper fīliolum
> peperit. partus nōn facilis erat; Horātia magnum dolōrem   **peperit** has given birth to
> subiit. Lūcīnae ānxiē supplicābāmus; tandem tamen omnia   **partus** the birth
> bene ēvēnērunt; et māter et īnfāns valent. omnēs gaudēmus, in   **Lūcīnae** Lucina, goddess of
> prīmīs Decimus. īnfāns dulcissimus est, quī iam mātrem   childbirth; **in prīmīs** especially
> cognōscit rīsūque salūtat.   **rīsū** with a smile
>
> Horātia ipsa ad tē mox scrībet, sed nōn ōtiōsa est; nam nōn
> modo īnfantem cūrat sed magnae familiae domina facta est.
> omnēs rēs domesticae eī ā Decimō commissae sunt; ille enim   **rēs domesticae** domestic affairs
> multīs rēbus occupātus est; nōn modo rūra sua administrat sed   **rūra** estates
> etiam candidātus est in comitiīs quae mox Venusiae fīent.   **comitiīs** elections
>
> pater tuus valet; dē rēbus tamen pūblicīs valdē sollicitus
> est. cotīdiē nūntiī pessimī Rōmā afferuntur. rēspūblica in
> maximum perīculum, ut dīcit, addūcitur; Octāviānus
> Antōniusque pactum cōnfēcērunt inimīcōsque oppugnant;   **pactum** an agreement
> multī virī honestī prōscrībuntur. Cicerō ipse, pater amīcī tuī,   **prōscrībuntur** are being proscribed,
> occīsus est ab Antōniī mīlitibus. quae omnia nōs summā   outlawed
> ānxietāte afficiunt. quīn etiam Brūtus ad Graeciam fūgit   **quae omnia** all these things
> exercitumque ibi parat.   **quīn etiam** what is more
>
> quid tū Athēnīs audīvistī? Brūtōne occurristī? multōs
> iuvenēs quī Athēnīs student, ut dīcunt, in exercitum
> cōnscrīpsit. bellum cīvīle reīpūblicae imminet. cautus estō, mī   **cōnscrīpsit** he has enrolled
> Quīnte; nōlī Brūtī illecebrās audīre; Athēnīs manē; dīligenter   **illecebrās** enticements
> studē; mox domum redī patremque adiuvā.
>
> statim nōbīs epistolam scrībe. Horātiae grātulātiōnem mitte
> nōsque certiōrēs fac tē incolumem esse. cūrā ut valeās.   **tē incolumem esse** that you are safe

Line numbers: 5, 10, 15, 20, 25

A woman giving birth

1 What news does Scintilla send Quintus?   [2]
2 Why is Horatia so busy?   [3]
3 What is Decimus doing?   [3]
4 What is worrying Flaccus?   [4]
5 What is especially worrying Scintilla?   [3]

Word-building

From some nouns diminutives are formed, e.g.

fīliolus, -ī, m. (from **fīlius**) a little son
fīliola, -ae, f. (from **fīlia**) a little daughter
agellus, -ī, m. (from **ager**) a little field
libellus, -ī, m. (from **liber**) a little book
homunculus, -ī, m. (from **homō**) a little man
rēgulus, -ī, m. (from **rēx, rēgis**) a petty king

Although the basic significance of the diminutive form is
smallness, diminutives can also express affection (e.g. **fīliolus** can
mean 'a dear little son') or contempt (e.g. **homunculus** can mean 'a
silly little man'), according to the context in which they occur.

BIRTH AND CHILDHOOD

Childbirth carried a high element of risk in the ancient world.
Miscarriages were common, as was infant and child mortality.
Julius Caesar's daughter suffered a miscarriage and when she
died in childbirth, her child died too. Among the poor, the deaths
of mothers and babies were made more common by malnutrition
and lack of medical attention. And when poor parents could not
afford to bring their children up, they were likely to expose them

(i.e. abandon them to die or to be picked up by anyone who wanted them).

Two ceremonies followed a child's birth. First the father took it up in his arms to acknowledge that it was legitimate. Then on the eighth day in the case of a girl and the ninth in the case of a boy came the day of purification when the child was named. Children would be given small presents strung together as a necklace. These would be small models of everyday objects (swords, axes, etc.), and would serve as a sort of charm. Children would also be given a *bulla* to wear over their tunics; this was a gold, bronze or leather locket containing a lucky charm or mascot.

Roman children played with terracotta dolls and kept mice, caged birds and dogs as pets. Pliny tells the story of Regulus whose extravagant show of grief at his son's death led him to a grisly display:

> Regulus has lost his son and now that he is lost, he mourns him insanely. The boy had lots of ponies, some of them pairs, he had dogs both great and small, and nightingales, parrots and blackbirds. All of these Regulus slaughtered at his son's funeral pyre.

As for games, Quintus himself writes in one of his poems of those that adults must leave behind as part of the process of growing up: 'building toy houses, harnessing mice to a little cart, playing odds and evens, riding a long stick'. If the cart was big enough to hold a child, it would be drawn by a sheep, a goat, a dog or even another child. In odds and evens children would hold some pebbles or nuts in their closed fist and challenge their companion to say whether the number was odd or even. *Capita et nāvia* was the Roman equivalent of 'heads and tails' – would the

A Roman boy at play

coin fall with the head side or the ship side uppermost? They spun tops with strings or whips and bowled hoops with sticks. (The best hoops were decorated with bells and rings, and jingled merrily as they ran.) They rode hobby horses, and used knucklebones as dice, which they would throw for nuts as the stake. They would also play at being grown ups, enacting legal cases, and assuming the roles of soldiers, gladiators, charioteers and kings. And they would pretend to be magistrates and lictors holding model fasces and axes.

It is possible that relations between parents and children may have frequently been more distant than is usually the case in the modern world. The high rate of infant mortality may have caused parents to harden their hearts against loss, and the slaves who had responsibility for the children, from the wet nurses who suckled them to the nannies and the *paidagōgī*, may have inspired more love than the parents, as is indicated by many a gravestone set up for such slaves. However, other gravestones reveal a very strong love between parents and children. One of them reads:

> To the departed spirit of Eucopio, who lived for six months and three days. He was the sweetest and most charming of infants and although he could not yet speak he was utterly delightful.

And the epitaph of a little girl called Politta reads:

> A good plant from a holy root – citizens, weep for me. I was pleasing to all, blameless in my mother's eyes, faultless in my father's. I lived five years.

The Roman poets also convey a strong sense of family love. Here is Lucretius, writing of what death takes away from us:

> No longer now will your happy house welcome you, and your best of wives and your sweet children will no longer run to meet you to snatch your kisses; no longer will they touch your heart with silent joy.

Here is Virgil's vision of a happy family in a country setting:

> Meanwhile the farmer's sweet children hang about his lips and his pure home preserves its decency.

And Catullus expresses a delightful wish:

> May tiny Torquatus stretch out his delicate hands from his mother's breast and give his father a delightful laugh from half-open lips.

How big a part do you feel that mothers played in the upbringing of their children in Roman times?

Grammar and exercises

Chapter 17

Tenses

Verbs in Latin alter their endings to indicate different *tenses*, i.e. the time at which an action or event takes place. So far all the stories have been told in the *present tense*; this is used when the action of the verb is happening now or happens regularly, e.g.

> **Flaccus in agrō labōrat.** Flaccus is working in the field (now)
> *or* Flaccus works in the field (every day).

(Latin does not have separate tenses to indicate these different meanings.)

We now introduce two *past tenses*:

1 The imperfect tense

This tense is used when an action in the past is *continuous*, *repeated* or *incomplete*, e.g.

> **Flaccus in agrō diū labōrābat.**
> Flaccus was working in the field for a long time.
> **Quīntus ad lūdum cotīdiē ambulābat.**
> Quintus used to walk to school every day.
> **Horātia iānuam claudēbat, cum māter 'nōlī' inquit 'iānuam claudere.'**
> Horatia was shutting the door when her mother said 'Don't shut the door.'

Note that English does not always indicate time so precisely, e.g.

> Flaccus *worked* in the field a long time: but Latin will say **labōrābat**, since the action is continuous.
> Quintus *walked* to school every day: but Latin will say **ambulābat**, since the action is repeated.

The imperfect tense is formed by adding the following endings to the present stem:

		compare person endings
-bam	I	[**par-ō**]
-bās	you (*singular*)	**par-ās**
-bat	he/she	**par-at**
-bāmus	we	**par-āmus**
-bātis	you (*plural*)	**par-ātis**
-bant	they	**par-ant**

So:

	1st conj.	2nd conj.	3rd conj.	4th conj.
stem:	parā-	monē-	reg-	audi-
	parā-bam	monē-bam	reg-ē-bam	audi-ē-bam
	(I was preparing)	(I was warning)	(I was ruling)	(I was hearing)
	parā-bās	monē-bās	reg-ē-bās	audi-ē-bās
	parā-bat	monē-bat	reg-ē-bat	audi-ē-bat
	parā-bāmus	monē-bāmus	reg-ē-bāmus	audi-ē-bāmus
	parā-bātis	monē-bātis	reg-ē-bātis	audi-ē-bātis
	parā-bant	monē-bant	reg-ē-bant	audi-ē-bant

NB 1 3rd and 4th conjugation verbs insert **-ē-** after the stem before the imperfect person endings.

2 3rd conjugation **-iō** verbs form imperfects like **audiō: capi-ē-bam** etc.

3 The imperfect of **sum** is:

eram	I was
erās	you (sing.) were
erat	he/she was
erāmus	we were
erātis	you (pl.) were
erant	they were

Exercise 17.1

Translate

1 litterās cotīdiē (*every day*) scrībēbāmus.
2 urbem fortiter dēfendēbant.
3 in agrīs errābam.
4 fīlium diū quaerēbat.
5 in casā quiēscēbās.
6 fessī erāmus.
7 ad forum ambulābant.
8 magistrum nōn audiēbātis.
9 domum fugiēbam.
10 in forō diū manēbant.

2 The perfect tense

The *perfect tense* is most often used to express completed past action, e.g.

Flaccus ad agrum ambulāvit. Flaccus *walked* to the field.
Flaccus ad agrum nōn ambulāvit. Flaccus *did* not *walk* to the field.
nōnne Flaccus ad agrum ambulāvit? *Didn't* Flaccus *walk* to the field?

The perfect person endings are the same for every conjugation:

singular	**-ī**	I		*plural*	**-imus**	we
	-istī	you (sing.)			**-istis**	you (pl.)
	-it	he/she			**-ērunt**	they

These endings are attached to the perfect stem:

1st conjugation	**parāv-**
2nd conjugation	**monu-**
3rd conjugation, e.g.	**rēx-**
4th conjugation	**audīv-**

1 -a- verbs perfect stem **parāv-**		2 -e- verbs perfect stem **monu-**	
parāv-ī	I prepared	**monu-ī**	I warned
parāv-istī	you (*sing.*) prepared	**monu-istī**	you (*sing.*) warned
parāv-it	he/she prepared	**monu-it**	he/she warned
parāv-imus	we prepared	**monu-imus**	we warned
parāv-istis	you (*pl.*) prepared	**monu-istis**	you (*pl.*) warned
parāv-ērunt	they prepared	**monu-ērunt**	they warned

3 consonant verbs perfect stem, e.g. **rēx- (regs-)**		4 -i- verbs perfect stem **audīv-**	
rēx-ī	I ruled	**audīv-ī**	I heard
rēx-istī	you (*sing.*) ruled	**audīv-istī**	you (*sing.*) heard
rēx-it	he/she ruled	**audīv-it**	he/she heard
rēx-imus	we ruled	**audīv-imus**	we heard
rēx-istis	you (*pl.*) ruled	**audīv-istis**	you (*pl.*) heard
rēx-ērunt	they ruled	**audīv-ērunt**	they heard

The perfect stem is formed in various ways:

1 Regular verbs of the 1st, 2nd and 4th conjugations form perfects as follows:

The suffix **-v** or **-u** is added to the verb stem, e.g.

1st **para-**,	perfect **parā-v-ī**
2nd **mone-**,	perfect **mon-u-ī** (the **e** of the stem drops out)
4th **audi-**,	perfect **audī-v-ī**

Exercise 17.2

Form the imperfect and perfect (1st person singular) of the following verbs

dormiō, salūtō, habeō, labōrō, exerceō, custōdiō

2 3rd conjugation verbs, the stems of which end in a consonant or in **u**, follow various patterns:

(1) The suffix **-s** is added to the verb stem, e.g.

reg-ō, reg-ere:	perfect **rēx-ī** (for **rēg-s-ī**)
dīc-ō, dīc-ere: ✓	perfect **dīx-ī** (for **dīc-s-ī**)

(2) The verb stem is unchanged, e.g.

contend-ō, contendere: ✓	perfect **contend-ī**
cōnstitu-ō, cōnstituere: ✓	perfect **cōnstitu-ī**

(3) The vowel of the present stem is lengthened, e.g.

leg-ō, leg-ere: ✓	perfect **lēg-ī**
em-ō, em-ere:	perfect **ēm-ī**

(4) The present stem is reduplicated (i.e. the first syllable is doubled), e.g.

cad-ō, cad-ere: ╱	perfect **ce-cid-ī**
curr-ō, curr-ere: ✓	perfect **cu-curr-ī**

(5) The suffix **-v/īv** or **-u** is added to the stem, e.g.

sin-ō, sin-ere:	perfect **sīvī**
pet-ō, pet-ere:✓	perfect **petīvī**
pōn-ō, pōn-ere: ✓	perfect **posuī**

These rules will enable you to recognize most perfect forms in your reading.

At present only *learn the following*, which add the suffix **-s** to the present stem:

scrīb-ō, scrīb-ere, scrīp-sī ✓	I write
dīc-ō, dīc-ere, dīx-ī ✓	I say
dūc-ō, dūc-ere, dūx-ī ✓	I lead
reg-ō, reg-ere, rēx-ī	I rule
claud-ō, claud-ere, claus-ī	I close
ēvād-ō, ēvād-ere, ēvās-ī	I escape
cēd-ō, cēd-ere, ces-sī ✓	I yield, I go
lūd-ō, lūd-ere, lūs-ī ✓	I play
mitt-ō, mitt-ere, mīs-ī ✓	I send
surg-ō, surg-ere, surrēx-ī ✓	I get up, rise
ger-ō, ger-ere, ges-sī ✓	I carry, wear

NB 1 When **-s** is added to the consonant in which the present stem ends, certain changes of spelling occur, e.g. **c + s = x** (**dīc-si** becomes **dīxī**); **d** drops out (**claud-si** becomes **clausī**), etc.

2 The perfect of compound verbs is usually the same as that of the simple, e.g.

dūcō, dūxī; **re-dūcō, re-dūxī**
cēdō, cessī; **ac-cēdō, ac-cessī**
mittō, mīsī; **re-mittō, re-mīsī**

3 A few 2nd conjugation verbs also form the perfect by adding suffix **-s**; *learn the following*

augeō, augēre, auxī	I increase
iubeō, iubēre, iussī ✓	I order
maneō, manēre, mānsī ✓	I remain, stay
persuādeō, persuādēre, persuāsī + dat.	I persuade
rīdeō, rīdēre, rīsī	I laugh

4 The perfect stem of **sum** is **fu-:** ⭐

fu-ī	I was
fu-istī	you (*sing.*) were
fu-it	he/she was
fu-imus	we were
fu-istis	you (*pl.*) were
fu-ērunt	they were

Exercise 17.3

Put the following verb forms into (a) the imperfect (b) the perfect

1	monet	**6**	custōdiunt	**11**	manēmus
2	dormiō	**7**	dūcō	**12**	dīcitis
3	superant	**8**	mittimus	**13**	ēvādunt
4	dēbēmus	**9**	claudis	**14**	amat
5	clāmātis	**10**	iubeō	**15**	exerceō

Exercise 17.4

Translate

1 ad urbem ambulāvimus.
2 Quīntus nōn dormīvit.
3 mihi omnia dīxistī.
4 mīlitēs prope castra sē exercuērunt.
5 mē cūrāvistis.
6 fīlium ad agrum dūxī.
7 Flaccus puerum ad agrum mīsit.
8 eum iussit in agrō labōrāre.
9 cūr iānuam nōn clausistī?
10 puellae litterās bene scrīpsērunt.

Exercise 17.5

Translate the following verb forms

1 spectā	7 dūcēbās	13 dormīre	19 monuērunt
2 spectābam	8 dūcere	14 dormīte	20 monēbat
3 spectat	9 dūcunt	15 dormiēbant	21 monēre
4 spectāvī	10 dūxistis	16 dormiō	22 monēte
5 spectāre	11 dūc	17 dormīvistī	23 monuimus
6 spectāvērunt	12 dūxit	18 dormiēbāmus	24 monuit

Exercise 17.6

In the following sentences put each verb in parentheses into the appropriate tense (imperfect or perfect) and translate the whole sentence. For example:

Horātia Quīntusque in hortō (lūdere), cum Scintilla eōs (vocāre).
    lūdēbant; vocāvit.
Horatia and Quintus were playing in the garden when Scintilla called them.

1 Scintilla Quīntum Horātiamque (vocāre); ad agrum eōs (mittere).
2 puerī ad agrum (ambulāre); cēnam ad patrem (portāre).
3 nōn (festīnāre) sed in viā diū (lūdere).   *manserunt*
4 tandem ubi agrum (intrāre), Horātia patrem (vocāre).   *reduerunt*
5 ille fīliam nōn (audīre); sub arbore (dormīre); nam fessus (esse).
6 Horātia frātrem (monēre); 'nōlī patrem excitāre,' inquit; 'fessus (esse).'
7 sed ille (ēvigilāre) puerōsque (salūtāre).
⑧ puerī in agrō diū (manēre); tandem Quīntus Horātiam domum (redūcere).   *returned*

Exercise 17.7

stayed   manerunt   reducerunt

Translate into Latin
    Q et H ad ludum Festinabant
1 Quintus and Horatia were hurrying to school.
2 But on the way they stayed and played with a friend, who was exercising his dog.
3 When they approached the school, the master was standing near the door.
4 He watched them and said, 'Why are you coming late?'
5 Quintus laughed and said, 'We are not coming late.'
6 The master was angry. He told (= ordered) them to go in at once.
7 When he dismissed the other children, he told them to stay and write their letters again.

Chapter 18

Perfect stems of verbs (cont.)

Learn the following 3rd conjugation verbs, which have the same stem for present and perfect:

ascend-ō, ascend-ere, ascend-ī	I climb
contend-ō, contend-ere, contend-ī	I march, hasten
dēfend-ō, dēfend-ere, dēfend-ī	I defend
dēscend-ō, dēscend-ere, dēscend-ī	I descend
incend-ō, incend-ere, incend-ī	I set on fire
ostend-ō, ostend-ere, ostend-ī	I show, point out
vert-ō, vert-ere, vert-ī	I turn
cōnstitu-ō, cōnstitu-ere, cōnstitu-ī	I decide

Note that the 3rd person singular and 1st person plural have identical forms for present and perfect, e.g.

dēfendit = either 'he defends' or 'he defended'; **vertimus** = either 'we turn' or 'we turned'.

The context will show which meaning is intended.

Note also:

respondeō, respondēre, respondī	I answer

Exercise 18.1

Put the following verb forms into corresponding forms of the perfect

1	dēfendimus	3	vertit	5	incendis	7	augeō	9	persuādet
2	cōnstituunt	4	ostendō	6	dīcunt	8	sumus	10	lūdunt

Exercise 18.2

Translate

1 ad agrum contendēbāmus; in viā Gāium vīdimus.
2 Gāius arborem ascendēbat; ubi eum vocāvī, celeriter dēscendit.
3 Gāius nōbīscum contendit; ubi agrum intrāvimus, ego patrem eī ostendī.
4 pater nōs audīvit; sē vertit Gāiumque salūtāvit.
5 omnēs in agrō diū labōrābāmus.
6 tandem fessī erāmus; cōnstituimus domum redīre.

Note: the stem of **eō** is **i-**; hence infinitive **ī-re**, imperfect **ī-bam**, perfect **i-ī**. This verb is most commonly found in compounds.

Exercise 18.3

Translate the following verb forms

1	ībāmus	5	redīre	9	exeunt
2	īte	6	redībant	10	exībās
3	iērunt	7	redī	11	exiit
4	iit	8	rediimus	12	exit

Numerals

Learn the following

cardinals			ordinals	
ūnus, ūna, ūnum	I	one	**prīmus, -a, -um**	first
duo, duae, duo	II	two	**secundus, -a, -um**	second

117

	III	three		
trēs, tria	III	three	**tertius, -a, -um**	third
quattuor	IV	four	**quārtus, -a, -um**	fourth
quīnque	V	five	**quīntus, -a, -um**	fifth
sex	VI	six	**sextus, -a, -um**	sixth
septem	VII	seven	**septimus, -a, -um**	seventh
octō	VIII	eight	**octāvus, -a, -um**	eighth
novem	IX	nine	**nōnus, -a, -um**	ninth
decem	X	ten	**decimus, -a, -um**	tenth

The *ordinal* numbers (first, second, third, etc.) all decline like **bonus, bona, bonum.** Numerals 4 (**quattuor**) to 100 (**centum**) do not decline. For numerals 11–1,000 see Reference grammar, p. 155.

The Romans wrote their numerals I, II, III, etc. How does IX come to mean 9? They had no sign for zero; what problems would this cause in arithmetic?

	m.	*f.*	*n.*
nom.	ūnus	ūna	ūnum
gen.	ūnīus	ūnīus	ūnīus
dat.	ūnī	ūnī	ūnī
acc.	ūnum	ūnam	ūnum
abl.	ūnō	ūnā	ūnō

	m. f.	*n.*
nom.	trēs	tria
gen.	trium	trium
dat.	tribus	tribus
acc.	trēs	tria
abl.	tribus	tribus

	m.	*f.*	*n.*
nom.	duo	duae	duo
gen.	duōrum	duārum	duōrum
dat.	duōbus	duābus	duōbus
acc.	duo/duōs	duās	duo
abl.	duōbus	duābus	duōbus

ūnus declines like **ille** in gen. and dat. sing.; **trēs** declines like the plural of **omnis.**

Learn **vīgintī** = 20

30, 40, etc. are easily recognized by the termination **-gintā: trī-gintā, quadrā-gintā,** etc.

Learn **centum** = 100

200, 300, etc. are easily recognized by the termination **-centī: du-centī, -ae, -a; tre-centī, -ae, -a,** etc.; these decline like the plural of **bonus.**

Learn **mīlle** = 1,000

duo mīlia = 2,000, **tria mīlia** = 3,000, etc.

NB **mīlle** is an indeclinable adjective, e.g. **mīlle passūs** = '1,000 paces' = one mile.

But **mīlia** is a neuter plural noun, e.g. **duo mīlia passuum** = '2,000 of paces' = two miles.

Expressions of time

Duration of time, saying *how long* an action or event lasts, is expressed by the *accusative* case, e.g.

trēs hōrās ambulābāmus. We were walking *for three hours.*
sex annōs manēbāmus. We stayed *for six years.*

Time when, saying *at what time* an action or event took place, is expressed by the *ablative* case, e.g.

prīmā lūce domō discessērunt. They left home *at dawn.*
septimō annō domum rediimus. *In the seventh year* we returned home.

The ablative is also used to express the time *within which* something happens, e.g.

> **tribus hōrīs domum rediit.** He returned home *within three hours.*

In the following exercises we shall use **diēs** = 'day'; this noun belongs to the fifth or **-e-** declension (see chapter 21): acc. sing. **diem**, abl. sing. **diē**, acc. plural **diēs**, abl. plural **diēbus**.

Exercise 18.4

Translate

1 Quīntus paterque trēs diēs ad iter sē parābant; quārtō diē discessērunt.
2 prīmā lūce Flaccus surrēxit Quīntumque excitāvit. *[handwritten: @ dawn ~ the first day of spring, Flaccus got up and woke up quintus.]*
3 tertiā hōrā Scintillam Horātiamque valēre iussērunt iterque iniērunt.
4 novem diēs in viā Appiā contendēbant; decem diēbus urbem Rōmam adiērunt.
5 posterō (*the next*) diē ad forum festīnāvērunt et trēs hōrās ibi manēbant.

The meanings of the perfect tense

parāvī usually means 'I prepared' (*simple past time*) but it can also mean 'I have prepared'. This we call the *perfect with have* or the *true perfect*.

There is nothing in the verb form to tell you which meaning is intended, but the context will usually make this clear, since the *perfect with have* occurs only in present contexts, e.g.

> **quīnque diēs contendērunt sed Rōma adhūc longē abest.**
> They have walked for five days but Rome is still far away.
>
> **nōlī timēre, fīlī; lupus abiit.**   Don't be afraid, son; the wolf has gone away.

Exercise 18.5

Translate the following, making sure that you translate all perfect tenses appropriately, choosing between the two possible meanings

1 in viā Appiā ambulābam; subitō lupum vīdī.
2 pater dīxit: 'nōlī timēre, fīlī; lupus abiit.'
3 novem diēs contendēbāmus; decimō diē urbem intrāvimus.
4 pater 'gaudē, fīlī,' inquit; 'iter cōnfectum est.'
5 Flaccus epistolam (*a letter*) ad Scintillam scrīpsit: 'incolumēs sumus. Rōmam intrāvimus; lūdum Orbiliī spectāvimus.'
6 māter ānxia erat; nam fīlius domō aberat. 'ānxia sum,' inquit; 'trēs hōrās fīlium exspectāvī, sed ille domum nōn rediit.'
7 tandem quīntā hōrā noctis puer rediit. māter īrāta erat.
8 'ō fīlī,' inquit, 'cūr tam sērō rediistī? quattuor hōrās tē exspectāvī. quīntā hōrā tandem rediistī.'
9 puer respondit: 'cum amīcīs duās hōrās lūdēbam. deinde domum festīnāvī.
10 ecce! tertiā hōrā noctis rediī. nōlī tē vexāre.'

Exercise 18.6

Match up the English translations below with the following Latin verb forms

1	studuit	4	trānsīre	7	erāmus	10	dīcēbas	13	contendī
2	mānsistī	5	dīc	8	dēfendistī	11	mīsit	14	prōmīsistī
3	monuimus	6	possunt	9	dīxērunt	12	mittit	15	cōnstituērunt

we were, he/she sent, I marched, they have decided, he/she studied, to cross, he/she sends, you defended, we warned, you promised, say!, they can, they said, you have stayed, you used to say

Exercise 18.7

Translate into Latin

1 Quintus stayed in the forum for three hours; he was waiting for Gaius,
2 At the fourth hour he decided to return home; but when he turned round, he caught sight of Gaius.
3 Gaius was hurrying through the street; he crossed the forum and approached Quintus.
4 Quintus greeted him and said, 'I have waited for you for three hours. Why have you come (*veniō, venīre, vēnī*) so late?'
5 Gaius replied: 'On the way I saw a friend, who showed me his dog.
6 We played with the dog. Then we climbed a tree. Don't be angry. I have arrived at last.'

Chapter 19

Perfect stems of verbs (cont.)

Many verbs lengthen the vowel of the present stem to form the perfect. Learn the following:

1st conjugation:	**iuvō, iuvāre, iūvī**	I help
	lavō, lavāre, lāvī	I wash
2nd conjugation:	**sedeō, sedēre, sēdī**	I sit
	videō, vidēre, vīdī	I see
3rd conjugation:	**agō, agere, ēgī**	I do, I drive
	emō, emere, ēmī	I buy
	legō, legere, lēgī	I read
	frangō, frangere, frēgī	I break
	vincō, vincere, vīcī	I conquer
	relinquō, relinquere, relīquī	I leave behind
3rd conjugation -iō:	**capiō, capere, cēpī**	I take
	(also **accipiō, accēpī**; **recipiō, recēpī**, etc.)	
	faciō, facere, fēcī	I do, make
	iaciō, iacere, iēcī	I throw
	fugiō, fugere, fūgī	I flee
4th conjugation:	**veniō, venīre, vēnī**	I come

Exercise 19.1

Translate the following verb forms

1	lavāmus	6	relinquunt	11	sēdimus	16	cēpērunt
2	lāvimus	7	relīquērunt	12	sedēmus	17	iēcistī
3	vēnit	8	vidēmus	13	vīcistī	18	fugit
4	venit	9	vīdimus	14	lēgī	19	fūgimus
5	ēmistis	10	sedēbāmus	15	legō	20	fēcī

The pluperfect tense

e.g. **parāv-eram** = I had prepared.

The tense is used to represent a past action or event which precedes another past action or event, e.g.

> **nox iam <u>vēnerat</u> cum Rōmam intrāvērunt**. Night <u>had come</u> already when they entered Rome.
> (Both events are in the past but night had fallen before they entered Rome.)

> **ubi Horātia domum rediit, Scintilla ad forum iam <u>prōcesserat</u>.**
> When Horatia returned home, Scintilla had already gone on to the forum.

The tense is formed by adding the following endings to the perfect stem:

-eram	I had	**-erāmus** we had	(these endings are the same as
-erās	you (*sing*.) had	**-erātis** you (*pl*.) had	those of the imperfect of **sum**)
-erat	he/she had	**-erant** they had	

	1st **parō**	2nd **moneō**	3rd **regō**	3rd **-iō capiō**	4th **audiō**	**sum**
perfect stem	parāv-	monu-	rēx-	cēp-	audīv-	fu-
pluperfect	parāv-eram	monu-eram	rēx-eram	cēp-eram	audīv-eram	fu-eram

Exercise 19.2

Give the pluperfect of **dīcō** *(all persons) and translate each form*

Exercise 19.3

Match up the following verb forms to the translations below

> ēmerant, vīcimus, prōmitte, lēgerāmus, discessit, abesse, flēbat, relīquit, init, studuimus, iniit, frēgistī, ēgimus, clauserātis, relinquit

> he/she entered, we have conquered, we did, to be absent, they had bought, he/she left, we studied, he/she was weeping, he/she is entering, you had shut, promise!, we had read, he/she departed, you broke, he/she leaves

Note the following idioms

> **media urbs** = the middle of the city (literally: 'the middle city')
> **summus mōns** = the top of the mountain (literally: 'the highest mountain')

Exercise 19.4

Translate

1   Flaccus in summō colle stābat cum moenia Rōmae vīdit.
2   nox iam vēnerat cum Flaccus Quīntum in urbem dūxit.
3   ubi ad mediam urbem vēnērunt, in forō diū manēbant; aedificia tam splendida numquam vīderant.
4   Flaccus tabellārium (*the postman*) quaerēbat; epistolam ad Scintillam scrīpserat.
5   Scintilla laeta erat; tandem Flaccus epistolam mīserat.
6   māter Horātiam vocāvit, quae in hortum exierat.

Expressions of place

> **ad urbem** festīnāvērunt. They hurried <u>to the city</u>.
> But **Rōmam** festīnāvērunt. They hurried <u>to Rome</u>.
>
> **ab urbe** discessērunt. They went away <u>from the city</u>.
> But **Rōmā** discessērunt. They went away <u>from Rome</u>.

The names of cities and towns do not have a preposition in expressions of *motion to* or *from* a place. The *accusative* case is used to express *motion towards* and the *ablative* to express *motion from*.

The same applies to **domus**:

> **domum** rediērunt. They returned (to) home.
> **domō** discessērunt. They left (from) home.

Note that prepositions are only omitted with the names of *towns* and the word **domus**. Names of countries require prepositions, e.g.

> **ille senex ad Italiam nāvigāvit Rōmamque festīnāvit.**
> That old man sailed to Italy and hurried to Rome.
>
> **Quīntus ad Graeciam nāvigāvit, Flaccus Venusiam rediit.**
> Quintus sailed to Greece, Flaccus returned to Venusia.

The locative case

You have met **dom-ī** = 'at home'. This is called the *locative* case, expressing *place where*, e.g. **domī manēbat**; **domī** tells you where he stayed.

All names of towns and cities can form a locative case.

The names of places have various forms, singular and plural, e.g.

nominative		*locative*	
Rōma	(1st decl. sing.)	**Rōmae**	at/in Rome
Athēnae	(1st decl. plural)	**Athēnīs**	at/in Athens
Corinthus	(2nd decl. sing.)	**Corinthī**	at/in Corinth
Londinium	(2nd decl. n. sing.)	**Londiniī**	at/in London
Puteolī	(2nd decl. plural)	**Puteolīs**	at Puteoli

(The locative is the same in form as the genitive for place names of the 1st and 2nd declensions singular, the same as the ablative for those which are plural.)

A few place names are 3rd declension and have locatives ablative in form whether singular or plural:

Carthāgō	(3rd decl. sing.)	**Carthāgine**	at Carthage
Gādēs	(3rd decl. plural)	**Gādibus**	at Cadiz

Exercise 19.5

In the following sentences translate the names of the towns only into the correct Latin case

1 We stayed a week in Capua.
2 We then travelled to Cumae.
3 We stayed two nights in Cumae.
4 On the next day we departed from Cumae.
5 We stayed in Antium a few days.
6 Finally we returned to Rome.

Exercise 19.6

Translate

1 Aenēās Trōiae nātus est (*was born*).
2 ubi Graecī Trōiānōs vīcērunt, comitēs ad Siciliam dūxit.
3 Trōiānī ad Italiam nāvigābant cum tempestās eōs ad Libyam ēgit.
4 Aenēās diū Carthāgine cum Dīdōne manēbat.
5 tandem Iuppiter eum iussit ad Italiam nāvigāre.
6 itaque Carthāgine discessit comitēsque Puteolōs dūxit.

Exercise 19.7

Translate into Latin

1 Flaccus and Quintus left home, but Scintilla and Horatia stayed in Venusia.
2 Father and son marched to Rome; within ten days they had reached (**perveniō ad**) the city.
3 The journey had been long and difficult.
4 They stayed in Rome for seven years; then Flaccus decided to return home.
5 Flaccus returned to Venusia; Quintus left Italy and sailed to Athens.
6 Quintus stayed in Athens for a long time.

Chapter 20

Perfect stems of verbs (cont.)

Verbs with reduplicated perfects form their perfect by putting before the present stem either the first letter of the stem + **e** (e.g. **dō, de-dī**) or the first syllable of the stem (e.g. **currō, cu-currī**).

Learn the following verbs:

cadō, cadere, ce-cidī	I fall
canō, canere, ce-cinī	I sing
currō, currere, cu-currī	I run
dō, dare, de-dī	I give
pellō, pellere, pe-pulī	I drive
stō, stāre, ste-tī	I stand

Most verbs drop reduplication in compounds, e.g.

incidō, incidere, incidī	I fall into
incurrō, incurrere, incurrī	I run into, run against

But compounds of **dō** and **stō** keep reduplication, e.g.

reddō, reddere, reddidī	I give back
instō, instāre, institī	I threaten, pursue

Exercise 20.1

Translate the following verb forms

1	dābant	6	crēde	11	currēbant
2	dedī	7	crēdidimus	12	cucurristī
3	dā	8	crēdēbam	13	currite
4	dederant	9	crēdō	14	currimus
5	dare	10	crēdiderat	15	cucurrerātis

Exercise 20.2

Translate the following sentences

1 Horātia per silvam ambulābat; Argus domō discesserat; Horātia eum quaerēbat.
2 Terentius ab agrō redībat, cum puellae occurrit.
3 Terentius 'quid facis, Horātia?' inquit; 'cūr domō discessistī?'
4 Horātia 'māter' inquit 'mē mīsit. nam Argus in silvam cucurrit. diū eum quaerō.'
5 Terentius 'nōlī tē vexāre,' inquit; 'sine dubiō Argus iam domum rediit.'
6 domum ambulābant cum Horātia lāpsāvit (*slipped*) ceciditque ad terram.
7 puella clāmāvit; Argus eam audīvit cucurritque ē silvīs.
8 puella canem laeta salūtāvit sed 'Arge,' inquit, 'cūr domō abiistī? malus canis es. mē valdē vexāvistī.'

Exercise 20.3

Put the verbs in parentheses into the correct forms and translate the sentences

1 Quīntus paterque ā forō iam (discēdere) et (prōcēdere) ad Subūram.
2 viae sordidae (esse); ubīque hominēs hūc illūc (currere).
3 Quīntus patrem (rogāre): 'quō (īre)? ubi domicilium quaerere dēbēmus?'
4 pater respondit: 'nōlī dēspērāre, fīlī. ad Subūram paene (advenīre). illīc sine dubiō domicilium invenīre (posse).'
5 mox Quīntus īnsulam (vidēre) cuius (*of which*) porta aperta (esse).
6 Flaccus fīlium in īnsulam (dūcere) iānitōremque (vocāre).
7 tandem iānitōrem (invenīre); ille (dormīre); ēbrius erat; nam multum vīnum (bibere).
8 Flaccus eum (excitāre); ille 'nūllum domicilium' inquit '(habēre) vacuum.'

Exercise 20.4

Translate into Latin

1 Flaccus led Quintus to the school of Orbilius.
2 Orbilius was sitting in the courtyard (**aula, -ae**, f.).
3 Flaccus greeted him and said, 'I have brought (= led) my son to you.'
4 Orbilius asked Quintus many things; Quintus could answer easily.
5 The other boys had now arrived and were playing near the door.
6 Orbilius was angry. 'Why are you playing?' he said; 'Why have you not entered the schoolroom (**schola, -ae**, f.)?'

4th declension

Nouns of the 4th declension have stems in **-u**; they decline very like 3rd declension nouns, but **u** appears in all cases except the dative and ablative plural:

	singular	*plural*
nom.	gradu-s	gradū-s
gen.	gradū-s	gradu-um
dat.	gradu-ī	grad-ibus
acc.	gradu-m	gradū-s
abl.	gradū	grad-ibus
voc.	gradu-s	gradū-s

Note the following 4th declension nouns:

exercitus, exercitūs, m.	army
gradus, gradūs, m.	step
cursus, cursūs, m.	course, race
magistrātus, magistrātūs, m.	magistrate
versus, versūs, m.	verse
vultus, vultūs, m.	face, expression
tumultus, tumultūs, m.	riot
manus, manūs, f.	hand

NB 1 Nearly all nouns of this declension are masculine; but **manus** is feminine, and there are a very few neuter nouns, e.g. **cornū** (= horn; for its declension, see Reference grammar, p. 153).

2 Nominative, vocative and genitive singular, and nominative, vocative and accusative plural all end **-us**; in the nominative and vocative singular **u** sounds short, but in the other cases it is long: **ū**.

3 Most 2nd declension masculine nouns, some 3rd declension nouns, and most 4th declension nouns all end **-us** in the nominative singular, but their genitives show which declension they belong to, e.g.

domin-us, domin-ī, m.	2nd declension
tempus, tempor-is, n.	3rd declension
versu-s, vers-ūs, m.	4th declension

Exercise 20.5

Decline in all cases, in the singular: **vultus sevērus**
and in the plural: **omnēs gradūs**

Exercise 20.6

Translate

1 cīvēs clāmābant tumultumque facere parābant.
2 cōnsul in gradibus templī stetit.
3 multī magistrātūs aderant, quī cīvium īram timēbant.
4 cōnsul cīvēs vultū sevērō spectābat.
5 tandem manūs sustulit* ōrātiōnemque ad populum habuit.
6 cīvēs tumultū dēstitērunt (*ceased from*) cōnsulemque audiēbant.

   *****sustulit**: perfect of **tollō** = I raise.

Exercise 20.7

Translate into Latin

1 Quintus was hurrying to school with his father.
2 Flaccus was carrying his son's books in his hands.
3 When they reached the school, Orbilius was waiting for them outside the door on the steps.
4 He looked at them with a severe expression.
5 'Why have you arrived late, Quintus?' he said. 'You must write fifty verses.'

Chapter 21

Perfect stems of verbs (cont.)

A few verbs form perfects in **-vī/īvī** or **-uī**.

Learn the following 3rd conjugation verbs:

sinō, sinere, sīvī	I allow
petō, petere, petīvī	I seek, ask, pursue
quaerō, quaerere, quaesīvī	I look for, ask
arcessō, arcessere, arcessīvī	I summon
colō, colere, coluī	I cultivate
pōnō, pōnere, posuī	I place

3rd conjugation **-iō**:

    cupiō, **cupere**, **cupīvī**   I desire
    rapiō, **rapere**, **rapuī**   I seize

4th conjugation:

    aperiō, **aperīre**, **aperuī**   I open

Exercise 21.1

Match the following verb Latin forms with the translations below

1	cecidit	6	posuerant	11	mōvistī
2	coluimus	7	ēgērunt	12	auxistis
3	mānsimus	8	iusserant	13	arcessīvit
4	lēgerat	9	quaesīvistis	14	rediimus
5	prōmīsistī	10	trādiderant	15	reddidimus

you looked for, you increased, he/she fell, we stayed, they had handed over, you promised, he/she summoned, they had ordered, we cultivated, they had placed, you moved, he/she had read, we returned (= went back), they did, we gave back

The 5th (and last) declension

This declension is formed from nouns with stems in **-e**, e.g.
rēs = thing, affair, matter, property.

	singular	*plural*
nom.	rē-s	rē-s
gen.	re-ī	rē-rum
dat.	re-ī	rē-bus
acc.	re-m	rē-s
abl.	rē	rē-bus
voc.	rē-s	rē-s

All 5th declension nouns are feminine except for **diēs**, **diēī**, *m.* = day

Learn **rēspūblica** = public affairs, politics, the state; both halves decline, **rēs** as a 5th declension noun, **pūblica** as a 1st:

nom.	rēspūblica
gen.	reīpūblicae
dat.	reīpūblicae
acc.	rempūblicam
abl.	rēpūblicā

Learn also **spēs**, **spēī**, *f.* hope.

(You have now learned all five declensions.
The Reference grammar, pp. 152–3, shows them all tabulated together.)

Exercise 21.2

Change the following phrases into (1) the genitive (2) the ablative

1 *singular*:   omnis rēs; prīma lūx; illud tempus; malus versus; nūlla spēs
2 *plural*:   omnēs diēs, longae nāvēs, altī gradūs, hominēs trīstēs, flūmina alta

Exercise 21.3

Translate

1 Quīntus iam multōs diēs in lūdō Orbiliī studuerat.
2 diē quōdam, ubi Orbilius puerōs dīmīsit, Marcus eum iussit domum sēcum venīre.
3 ubi Marcus Quīntum in tablīnum dūxit, pater eius epistolam scrībēbat dē rēbus pūblicīs.
4 Cicerō valdē ānxius erat dē rēpūblicā epistolāsque cotīdiē ad Atticum mittēbat.
5 Cicerō rempūblicam dēfendere semper temptāverat sed iam spem paene dēposuerat (*had given up*).

Exercise 21.4

Translate into Latin

1 Every day Flaccus used to tell his son many things about Roman history (= Roman affairs).
2 He used to praise the leaders of the old (**vetus, veteris**) republic.
3 'The leaders' he said 'used to love the republic and cared for the citizens.
4 Today the leaders don't care for the people; they want nothing except (**nisi**) to increase their own glory.
5 Who can have hope about the future (**futūra, -ōrum**, n. pl.)?'

Chapter 22

Perfect stems of verbs (concluded)

A few verbs add the suffix -sc- to the verb stem in the present, future and imperfect;
this suffix is dropped in the perfect, e.g.

cognō-sc-ō, cognō-sc-ere, cognō-vī	I get to know, learn
crē-sc-ō, crē-sc-ere, crē-vī	I grow
quiē-sc-ō, quiē-sc-ere, quiē-vī	I rest

Exercise 22.1

Decline in all cases, in the singular: **haec rēs**   *in the plural*: **illī diēs**

Exercise 22.2

Give the correct Latin form for the English verbs in parentheses and translate the sentences

1 diē quōdam Scintilla Horātiam māne (*woke*); nūndinae (*market day*) erant.
2 'ēvigilā,' inquit; 'tempus est ad forum (*to hurry*).'
3 Horātia mātrī (*obeyed*) et celeriter (*got up*).
4 ubi ad forum (*they arrived*), plūrimī hominēs iam (*were there*).
5 in gradibus templī (*they stood*) et rēs suās (*they put out*).
6 mox omnēs rēs (*they had sold*) domumque (*to return*) parābant.
7 per forum lentē ambulābant amīcīsque (*met*) quī ipsī rēs (*were selling*).
8 sed nihil (*they bought*); nam pauperēs (*they were*).

Uses of the ablative case

The ablative has a wide variety of meanings: *by, with, from, at, in, on*. We here summarize the commonest usages, which are already familiar to you:

1 from: the ablative can express *separation from* a place or thing, usually with a preposition, e.g.

ab urbe vēnit	he came from the city
ē silvā cucurrit	he ran out of the forest
dē monte dēscendit	he came down from the mountain
Rōmā discessit	he departed from Rome
domō festīnāvit	he hurried from home
forō longē aberat	he was a long way from the forum

So after some verbs and adjectives expressing *separation from*, e.g.

mē cūrā līberāvit	he freed me from care
fēminae līberae cūrā	women free from care
moenia dēfēnsōribus vacua	walls empty of defenders

2 at/in/on: the ablative can express *place where*, usually with a preposition, e.g.

in forō stābat	he was standing in the forum
sub arbore dormiēbat	she was sleeping under a tree
terrā marīque pugnābant	they fought on land and sea

3 at/on: the ablative is used to express *time when*, e.g.

prīmā lūce discessērunt	they departed at dawn
quīntō diē rediērunt	they returned on the fifth day

and *time within which*, e.g.

tribus diēbus rediit	he returned within three days

Note also:

multīs post annīs	many years after (literally: 'afterwards by many years')
paucīs ante diēbus	a few days before

Exercise 22.3

Translate

1 ubi Quīntus Flaccusque domō discessērunt, Scintilla Horātiaque Venusiae manēbant.
2 cotīdiē prīmā hōrā diēī surgēbant diūque in agrō labōrābant; vespere domum rediērunt, valdē fessae.
3 Scintilla rārō (*rarely*) cūrīs lībera erat sed numquam spem dēposuit.
4 paucīs post diēbus ab agrō redierat et in casā quiēscēbat cum tabellārius (*the postman*) epistolam eī trādidit.
5 Flaccus enim tandem epistolam Rōmā mīserat. Rōmam cum fīliō sine cāsū advēnerat. haec epistola Scintillam magnā ānxietāte līberāvit.

Chapter 23

ferō

Learn the verb **ferō, ferre, tulī** = I carry, bear.

The present is irregular:	**ferō, fers, fert, ferimus, fertis, ferunt**
imperatives:	**fer, ferte**
infinitive:	**ferre**

It has no perfect; it uses forms from another stem (**tul-**).

Exercise 23.1

Translate the following verb forms

1	fūgerant	6	fēcerātis	11	quaesīvimus
2	iaciēbat	7	fer	12	sīverāmus
3	tulistī	8	cupīvit	13	posuērunt
4	cēpī	9	tulerat	14	arcessīvistī
5	ferre	10	fertis	15	petīverat

Further uses of the ablative case

1 with/by: the ablative can express the *means* or *instrument* with or by which something is done:

mē gladiō vulnerāvit	he wounded me with a sword
pilīs lūdēbant	they were playing with balls
ad urbem pedibus ībant	they were going on foot (by feet) to the city

This use is very common in such phrases as: **equō vectus** carried by (= riding on) a horse; **gladiō armātus** armed with a sword.

2 with: the ablative can express the *manner* in which something is done, e.g.

summā celeritāte rediit	he returned with the greatest speed
magnā vōce clāmāvit	he shouted in (with) a loud voice

3 with/of: the ablative is used in describing *qualities*, e.g.

est puer magnō ingeniō	he is a boy of great talent
puella summā virtūte	a girl of the greatest courage
vir parvā prūdentiā	a man of little prudence

4 Some adjectives take the ablative where English has a genitive, e.g.

iuvenis dignus est laude	the young man is worthy of praise
urna aquā plēna erat	the pot was full of water

Exercise 23.2

Translate

1 prīmā lūce Horātia ā fonte domum redībat; urnam gravem manibus ferēbat.
2 Scintilla eam magnā vōce vocāvit; 'redī, Horātia,' inquit, 'mēque celeriter iuvā.'
3 Horātia urnam in terrā dēposuit summāque celeritāte ad mātrem recurrit.
4 illa ē iānuā cucurrit et 'ecce, fīlia,' inquit, 'ardet (*is on fire*) casa.'
5 Horātia urnam aquā plēnam tulit flammāsque celeriter exstīnxit (*put out*).
6 Scintilla fīliam laudāvit: 'puella es maximā virtūte, Horātia, summāque laude digna.'

Exercise 23.3

Put the phrases in parentheses into the correct case and translate the sentences

1 (prīma lūx) Quīntus cum (pater) (domus) discessit.
2 lūdus Orbiliī (forum) nōn longē aberat. (breve tempus) ad lūdum advēnerant.
3 amīcī, ubi Quīntum cōnspēxērunt, (magna vōx) eum vocāvērunt.
4 magister, (clāmōrēs) puerōrum commōtus, ē (lūdus) exiit puerōsque (vultus sevērus) spectāvit.
5 'nōlīte, puerī,' inquit 'tōtam urbem (tantī clāmōrēs) excitāre; celeriter intrāte.'

Exercise 23.4

Translate into Latin

1 One day (on a certain day) Quintus was hurrying to school.
2 He was crossing the forum when (**cum**) someone called him in a loud voice.
3 He turned round and saw Marcus, who was running at top speed towards him through the crowd.
4 'Quintus,' he said, 'you are a boy of great industry (**industria**) but you must not go to school today. Come with me to the races.'
5 Marcus led him from the forum to the Circus Maximus, which was full of men and women.

Exercise 23.5

In the following sentences change verb forms to the perfect and translate

1 iānuam aperit.
2 urnam frangis.
3 aquam ferō.
4 Rōmam contendimus.
5 domī manent.

6 canem quaerō.
7 pecūniam trādis.
8 togam emit.
9 omnia cognōscunt.
10 in casā quiēscimus.

Chapter 24

The comparison of adjectives

Both English and Latin adjectives have three degrees of comparison, e.g.

	positive	*comparative*	*superlative*
English	brave	braver	bravest, very brave
Latin	**fortis**	**fortior**	**fortissimus**

The comparative is often used in comparing one thing with another, e.g.

The girl is braver than the boy.
puella fortior est quam puer. (Notice **quam** = than.)

Most adjectives form the comparative by adding **-ior** and the superlative by adding **-issimus** to the stem, e.g.

long-us,   **long-ior,**   **long-issimus**
long,   longer,   longest, very long

trīst-is,   **trīst-ior,**   **trīst-issimus**
sad,   sadder,   saddest, very sad

Exercise 24.1

Form the comparative and superlative of the following adjectives

laetus, gravis, ingēns (*stem*: ingent-), altus

The comparative is a 3rd declension adjective (consonant stem: **-ior-**):

	singular		plural	
	m. & f.	*n.*	*m. & f.*	*n.*
nom.	fortior	fortius	fortiōrēs	fortiōra
gen.	fortiōris	fortiōris	fortiōrum	fortiōrum
dat.	fortiōrī	fortiōrī	fortiōribus	fortiōribus
acc.	fortiōrem	fortius	fortiōrēs	fortiōra
abl.	fortiōre	fortiōre	fortiōribus	fortiōribus

The superlative adjective declines like **bonus: fortissim-us, fortissim-a, fortissim-um**

A few common adjectives have irregular comparison; learn:

bonus	good	**melior**	better	**optimus**	best, very good
malus	bad	**peior**	worse	**pessimus**	worst, very bad
magnus	big	**maior**	bigger	**maximus**	biggest, very big
multus	much, many	**plūs***	more	**plūrimus**	most, very many
parvus	small	**minor**	smaller	**minimus**	smallest, very small

*****plūs** in the singular is a neuter *noun*, declining: **plūs, plūs, plūris, plūrī, plūre**; so **plūs vīnī** = more (of) wine.

In the plural it is a 3rd declension *adjective* (consonant stem: **plūr-**); so **plūrēs fēminae** = more women.

The use of quam = than

Marcus fortior est quam Quīntus. Marcus is stronger than Quintus.

numquam iuvenem fortiōrem vīdī quam Marcum. I have never seen a young man stronger than Marcus.

When **quam** is used, the two things compared are in the same case.

Exercise 24.2

Translate

1 numquam puellam prūdentiōrem vīdī quam Horātiam.
2 ego multīs puellīs occurrī prūdentiōribus quam Horātiae.
3 errās; Horātia multō (*much*) prūdentior est quam cēterae.
4 nēmō fortior fuit quam Achillēs.
5 nōn tibi crēdō; multōs virōs vīdī fortiōrēs quam Achillem.
6 errās; Achillēs fortissimus erat omnium hērōum.

Exercise 24.3

Translate into Latin

1 I am making a very long journey. I am looking for a bigger ship than this.
2 This ship is very good; you cannot find a better ship in all the harbor (**portus, -ūs**, *m.*).
3 The traveller (**viātor**) boarded the ship unwilling(ly). When they reached the open sea, he was very afraid.
4 The ship was very small; the waves were very big.
5 When they reached land, 'I have never made' he said 'a worse journey than this.'

Chapter 25

Irregular superlatives

Adjectives ending -er in the nominative double the **r** to form the superlative, e.g.

    celer, celerior, celerrimus   miser, miserior, miserrimus   pulcher, pulchrior, pulcherrimus

The following adjectives ending **-ilis** double the **l** to form the superlative:

    facilis, facilior, facillimus   difficilis, difficilior, difficillimus

The comparison of adverbs

fortiter	bravely
fortius	more bravely
fortissimē	very bravely

The accusative neuter of the comparative adjective is used as the comparative adverb:

    fortior = braver; **fortius** = more bravely.

The superlative adverb is formed by changing the ending of the superlative adjective **-us** to **-ē**:

    fortissimus = very brave; **fortissimē** = very bravely.

Exercise 25.1

Form adverbs from the following adjectives and give their comparative and superlative

    lentus, longus, bonus, facilis (*adverb*: facile), miser

Irregular comparison

	adverb	comparative adverb	superlative adverb
multus	multum	plūs	plūrimum
magnus	magnopere	magis	maximē

Note the comparison of the following adverbs:

    diū, diūtius, diūtissimē
    saepe, saepius, saepissimē.

Note also the use of **quam** with the superlative:

    quam celerrimē = as quickly as possible; **quam maximus** = as large as possible;
    quam prīmum = as soon as possible.

Exercise 25.2

Translate

1 petauristae (*acrobats*) Venusiam advēnerant; Scintilla Horātiam iussit sē quam celerrimē parāre.
2 ubi ad forum pervēnērunt, plūrimī hominēs iam concurrēbant. Scintilla locum vacuum difficillimē quaerēbat.
3 'festīnā, Horātia,' inquit, 'ad templī gradūs; optimum locum videō unde omnia melius vidēre possumus.'
4 templī gradūs ascendērunt unde petauristās clārissimē vidēre poterant.
5 petauristae optimī erant; aliī per circulōs ardentēs (*burning hoops*) saliēbant, aliī per fūnēs (*ropes*) altōs ambulābant.
6 Scintilla 'nihil spectāre mālō' inquit 'quam petauristās.'

7 Horātia 'nēmō' inquit 'fortior est quam ille petaurista, quī per fūnem altissimum ambulāvit.'
8 diūtissimē petauristās spectābant. Scintilla 'numquam' inquit 'melius spectāculum vīdī quam hoc.'
9 Horātia 'cūr nōn saepius' inquit 'Venusiam veniunt petauristae?'
10 tandem vesper aderat; discessērunt hominēs. Horātia miserrima erat quod lūdī cōnfectī sunt.

Exercise 25.3

Translate into Latin

1 Quintus no longer enjoyed his studies.
2 He was very miserable and very often wished to leave school.
3 At last his father said, 'Quintus, why aren't you enjoying your studies more?'
4 Quintus replied: 'All my friends have left school. I want to leave as soon as possible.'
5 Flaccus said, 'My son, you are no longer a boy, but a young man now. You must leave school and put on the toga of manhood.'

Exercise 25.4

Translate the following verb forms

1	cecidit	4	redīte	7	fuistī	10	fac	13	iēcimus
2	ferre	5	rettulistī	8	legimus	11	posuerat	14	volumus
3	reddiderant	6	posse	9	lēgimus	12	potuimus	15	quaesīvērunt

Chapter 26

The present participle

The present participle has often occurred in the narratives.

coniūrātī Caesarem relīquērunt in terrā <u>iacentem</u>.
The conspirators left Caesar lying on the ground.

Orbilius puerōs spectāvit lūdum <u>intrantēs</u>.
Orbilius watched the boys entering the school.

Participles are *verbal adjectives*; they decline like **ingēns** (except for the ablative singular which ends **-e**, not **-ī**). As *adjectives* they always agree with a noun or pronoun in case, gender and number, e.g. in the first example above **iacentem** agrees with **Caesarem**, accusative masculine singular. As verbs they can take an object, e.g. in the second example, **intrantēs** agrees with **puerōs**, the object of **spectāvit**, but it has itself an object – **lūdum**.

The present participles from the five conjugations are:

	1 **parā-**	2 **monē-**	3 **reg-**	3 **-iō capi-**	4 **audi-**
nom.	**parāns**	**monēns**	**regēns**	**capiēns**	**audiēns**
gen.	**parantis**	**monentis**	**regentis**	**capientis**	**audientis**
	preparing	warning	ruling	taking	hearing

The present participles of all verbs are formed regularly except for **eō**, which has nominative singular **iēns** but all other cases starting **e**: **euntis, euntī, euntem, eunte**, etc.

Exercise 26.1

In the following sentences say what noun or pronoun the participle agrees with and translate the whole sentence

1 Quīntus ad lūdum festīnāns forum trānsībat.
2 subitō aliquem vīdit ad sē currentem.
3 Quīntus Marcō occurrit ad circum prōcēdentī.
4 plūrimōs hominēs spectābant ad circum convenientēs.
5 Quīntus Marcusque circum intrantēs per turbam sē trūsērunt (*pushed*).
6 plūrimōs spectātōrēs vīdimus prope theātrum Pompēiī stantēs.
7 Quīntus coniūrātōs vīdit Caesarem oppugnantēs.
8 coniūrātī Caesarem mortuum relīquērunt in terrā iacentem.
9 turba hominum per viās discurrēbat magnā vōce clāmantium.
10 Quīntus patrī occurrit domum festīnantī.

NB Sometimes the Latin participle may be translated by a clause in English, e.g.

Horātia ad mātrem accessit in hortō quiēscentem.
Horatia approached her mother (while she was/who was) resting in the garden.

mihi haec rogantī pater nihil respondit.
When I asked this my father made no reply. (Literally: 'To me asking this my father replied nothing.')

Exercise 26.2

Translate the following sentences using clauses to translate the participles

1 Horātia ab agrō sōla rediēns iuvenī occurrit quī eam salūtāvit.
2 iuvenis Horātiae nōn nōtus erat; illa igitur festīnāvit eīque accēdentī nihil respondit.
3 eō ipsō tempore Horātia amīcum vīdit ad colōniam redeuntem.
4 ille Horātiae succurrit eamque domum ambulantem dēdūxit (*escorted*).
5 Horātia, ubi domum advēnit, omnia mātrī nārrāvit in casā sedentī.

Exercise 26.3

In the following sentences put the verbs in parentheses into the correct form of the present participle and then translate the whole sentence, e.g.

Horātia mātrem spectābat cēnam (parāre).
parantem: Horatia watched her mother preparing supper.

(To get the right answer, first ask yourself what the present participle means; **parāns** = preparing. Then ask 'Who was preparing supper?' Answer: **mātrem**; so the participle must agree with **mātrem** – accusative, feminine, singular.)

1 puerī in scholā (sedēre) dīligenter labōrābant.
2 sed Quīntus magistrum dē poētā vetere (dīcere) nōn audiēbat.
3 Orbilius eum vīdit aliquid in tabulā (scrībere).
4 magister eum vultū sevērō (īnspicere) rogāvit: 'quid facis, Quīnte?'
5 ille magistrō haec (rogāre) respondit: 'nihil faciō, magister. tē audiō.'
6 sed magister Quīntō haec (dīcere) nōn crēdidit.
7 Quīntus magistrātūs vīdit theātrum Pompēiī (intrāre).
8 Caesarem (sedēre) multī senātōrēs circumstābant.
9 Caesar Brūtum vīdit in sē (currere).
10 Brūtō in sē (currere) Caesar dīxit: 'et tū, Brūte?'

Exercise 26.4

Translate the following verb forms

1	date	6	fert	11	movet	16	discite
2	dabam	7	ferre	12	mōvit	17	discēbās
3	dedit	8	ferimus	13	movēte	18	didicī
4	dantem	9	ferentēs	14	mōverātis	19	discēns
5	dederat	10	tulerant	15	movēbant	20	didicerant

Chapter 27

The future tense

The future tenses of verbs of the 1st and 2nd conjugations go as follows:

1 **parā-**	2 **monē-**
parā-bō (I shall prepare)	monē-bō (I shall warn)
parā-bis	monē-bis
parā-bit	monē-bit
parā-bimus	monē-bimus
parā-bitis	monē-bitis
parā-bunt	monē-bunt

The future of verbs of 3rd and 4th conjugations and mixed conjugation goes as follows:

3 **reg-**	3rd **-iō capi-**	4 **audi-**	
reg-am (I shall rule)	capi-am (I shall take)	audi-am (I shall hear)	
reg-ēs	capi-ēs	audi-ēs	
reg-et	capi-et	audi-et	
reg-ēmus	capi-ēmus	audi-ēmus	
reg-ētis	capi-ētis	audi-ētis	Learn both sets of
reg-ent	capi-ent	audi-ent	endings carefully.

The future of **sum** is: **erō, eris, erit, erimus, eritis, erunt**   I shall be, etc.

Exercise 27.1

Translate the following verb forms

1	rogābimus	4	dīcunt	7	mittet	10	scrībēmus
2	docēbit	5	dormiam	8	mittit	11	pugnābunt
3	dīcent	6	eris	9	poterit	12	monēbitis

Exercise 27.2

Translate into Latin

1	We shall come	4	He/she will lead	7	They will flee	10	We shall climb
2	They will sail	5	I shall run	8	He/she is playing	11	We are climbing
3	I shall laugh	6	You (*sing.*) will come	9	He/she will play	12	You (*pl.*) will love

Exercise 27.3

Translate

1 Quīntus domum curret patrīque omnia nārrābit.
2 Flaccus 'in magnō perīculō erimus,' inquit. 'Rōmā discēdēmus.
3 ego Venusiam redībō, tū ad Graeciam nāvigābis.'
4 Quīntus 'ad Hēliodōrum festīnābō' inquit 'eumque valēre iubēbō.'
5 Flaccus 'festīnā, Quīnte,' inquit; 'crās ad portum contendēmus et nāvem inveniēmus quae tē ad Graeciam feret.'

The future perfect tense

By now Quintus will have reached Athens. **iam Quīntus Athēnās advēnerit**.

This tense, rare in English, is used to indicate an action completed in the future. It is commonly used in Latin in sentences such as:

cum Athēnās advēneris, in Acadēmiā studēbis. When you arrive/When you have arrived
(i.e. will have arrived) in Athens, you will study in the Academy.

sī patrem meum vīderis, omnia eī nārrā. If you see (i.e. will have seen) my father,
tell him everything.

The tense is formed by adding the following endings to the perfect stem:

-erō   -erimus
-eris   -eritis
-erit   -erint

1	2	3	3rd **-iō**	4
parāv-erō	monu-erō	rēx-erō	cēp-erō	audīv-erō
etc.	etc.	etc.	etc.	etc.
I shall have prepared	I shall have warned	I shall have ruled	I shall have taken	I shall have heard

Exercise 27.4

Translate

1 cum Athēnās advēneris, hanc epistolam Theomnēstō dā.
2 cum ad portum vēnerimus, multās nāvēs vidēbimus.
3 cum magister signum dederit, nautae nāvēs solvent.
4 sī magister prūdēns fuerit, ad portum sine perīculō adveniēmus.
5 sī dīligenter studueris, multa discēs.
6 cum domum redierō, omnia tibi nārrābō.

Exercise 27.5

Translate the following verbs forms

1	redīte	6	audiunt	11	posse
2	redībō	7	audient	12	possunt
3	redībāmus	8	audīvimus	13	potuit
4	redierint	9	audīverimus	14	poterāmus
5	rediērunt	10	audientēs	15	poterimus

Exercise 27.6

Translate into Latin

1 When we arrive at Rome, I will send you a letter without delay.
2 When Quintus has sailed to Greece, I shall return to Venusia.
3 If I leave Rome at once, I shall reach Venusia within ten days.
4 When I see you, you will hear everything.
5 If Antonius rouses the people, there will be civil war.

Chapter 28

Relative clauses

You have already met the relative pronoun **quī**, **quae**, **quod** = 'who', 'which' in the nominative case; you must now learn its full declension:

		singular			*plural*	
	m.	*f.*	*n.*	*m.*	*f.*	*n.*
nom.	quī	quae	quod	quī	quae	quae
gen.	cuius	cuius	cuius	quōrum	quārum	quōrum
dat.	cui	cui	cui	quibus	quibus	quibus
acc.	quem	quam	quod	quōs	quās	quae
abl.	quō	quā	quō	quibus	quibus	quibus

The relative pronoun is one of the few English words which still decline, e.g.:

		compare:	
nom.	who	he	she
gen.	whose	his	hers
acc.	whom	him	her

The relative pronoun agrees with its *antecedent* (the word it refers to) in gender and number (singular or plural), but its case depends upon its function (e.g. subject, object, indirect object) in its own clause, e.g.

1 **Scintilla (quae epistolam nōndum accēperat) trīstis erat.**
   Scintilla, who had not yet received a letter, was sad.

quae is feminine singular because it refers to **Scintilla**; it is in the nominative case because it is the subject of **accēperat**.

2 **amīcī (quōs in viā vīdimus) nōs salūtāvērunt.**
   The friends whom we saw in the road greeted us.

quōs is masculine plural because it refers to **amīcī**; it is in the accusative case because it is the object of **vīdimus**.

3 **Scintilla colōnōs (quī in agrīs labōrābant) salūtāvit.**
   Scintilla greeted the farmers who were working in the fields.

quī is masculine plural because it refers to **amīcōs**; it is in the nominative case because it is the subject of **labōrābant**.

Exercise 28.1

Translate

1 Flaccus, quī fīlium valēre iusserat, Rōmam rediit.
2 epistolam scrīpsit quam uxōrī statim mīsit.
3 Flaccus omnia quae Rōmae acciderant Scintillae nārrāvit.
4 Horātia tabellāriō (*postman*) occurrit, quī epistolam eī dedit.
5 Scintilla, cui Horātia epistolam trādidit, eam celeriter perlēgit.
6 māter Horātiae nārrāvit ea quae scrīpserat Flaccus.
7 Horātia amīcīs quibuscum lūdēbat tōtam rem exposuit.
8 amīcī, quōrum parentēs rem cognōscere cupiēbant, omnia eīs dīxērunt quae audīverant.
9 sīc brevī tempore omnēs Venusīnī omnia cognōverant quae scrīpserat Flaccus.

Exercise 28.2

Put the relative pronoun (in parentheses) into the correct form and translate the whole sentence

1 Quīntus, (*who*) in lītore stābat, nāvem spectābat.
2 pater, (*whose*) oculī lacrimīs plēnī erant, fīlium valēre iussit.
3 iter (*which*) Quīntus inībat longissimum erat.
4 nautae, (*whom*) Quīntus spectābat, nāvem solvere parābant.
5 nautae, (*to whom*) magister imperia dederat, nāvem solvērunt.
6 nāvis in (*which*) ad Graeciam nāvigābat nōn magna erat.
7 multī viātōrum (*with whom*) Quīntus colloquium faciēbat valdē ānxiī erant.
8 Quīntus tempestātem, (*which*) cēterōs terrēbat, nōn timuit.

Exercise 28.3

Put the following verb forms into (a) the future (b) the perfect (c) the future perfect

1 mittit   2 pōnunt   3 iubēmus   4 dat   5 reddit

Exercise 28.4

Translate into Latin

1 The captain, to whom Flaccus had given the money, called Quintus into the ship.
2 The ship, which the sailors had cast off, proceeded slowly out of the harbor.
3 Quintus approached two passengers who were standing in the stern (**puppis, puppis**).
4 One (**alter**) passenger with whom Quintus was talking (**colloquium facere**) was travelling to Puteoli.
5 The other (**alter**), whose parents lived in Greece, was returning home.

Chapter 29

Alter, uter and uterque

Because so many things come in pairs (eyes, hands, arms, legs, etc.), Latin has a special set of pronouns used with pairs.

Learn the following, which all have genitive singular -**īus** and dative singular -**ī**, all genders:

> **alter, altera, alterum** one or the other of two, e.g.
>
> **puer alterā manū librum ferēbat, alterā stilum.**
> In one hand the boy was carrying a book, in the other a pen.

duo hominēs forum iniērunt; alter iuvenis erat, alter senex.
Two men entered the forum; one was young, the other old.

uter, utra, utrum? which of two? e.g.
utrā manū librum ferēbat? In which hand was he carrying the book?

The neuter, **utrum**, is used in double questions followed by **an** = 'or', e.g.

utrum in urbe manēbis an domum redībis?
Will you stay in the city or return home? (literally: Which of two things, will you ...)

utrum ad Tirōnem epistolam scrībis an ad patrem?
Are you writing your letter to Tiro or to your father?

uterque, utraque, utrumque each of two, e.g.
librōs utrāque manū ferēbat. He was carrying books in each hand.

et Scintilla et Horātia Flaccum maximē dēsīderābant (*missed*); **ubi ille domum rediit, utraque laetissima erat.**
Both Scintilla and Horatia missed Flaccus very much; when he returned, each was very happy.

Exercise 29.1

Decline in the singular, all cases: **alter amīcus** *and* **utra manus**

Exercise 29.2

Translate

1 Quīntus duōbus cum viātōribus colloquium faciēbat.
2 uterque Rōmā vēnerat et ad Graeciam nāvigābat.
3 Quīntus alterī dīxit: 'utrum diū in Graeciā manēbis an brevī tempore Rōmam redībis?'
4 ille respondit: 'nōn diū in Graeciā manēbō. mercātor (*merchant*) sum. ubi prīmum negōtium cōnfēcī, Rōmam redībō.'
5 alter 'ego' inquit 'cupiō in Acadēmīā studēre. trēs annōs Athēnīs manēbō.'
6 Quīntus 'mihi quoque prōpositum (*intention*) est' inquit 'in Acadēmīā studēre. cuius scholās (*lectures*) audīre cupis?'
7 ille 'Theomnēstum' inquit 'in prīmīs (*especially*) audīre cupiō, quī, ut (*as*) dīcunt, optimus est doctōrum.'
8 Quīntus 'sine dubiō' inquit 'in Acadēmīā tē vidēbō. ego enim eiusdem doctōris scholīs aderō.'

Exercise 29.3

Put the words in parentheses into the correct case and translate the whole sentence

1 ante (diēs) surrēxit Quīntus et sine (mora) ad Acadēmīam prōcēdēbat.
2 trāns (agora) festīnāvit, cupiēns quam celerrimē advenīre.
3 ubi ad (Acadēmīa) advēnit, iuvenī quī prō (portae) stābat dīxit: 'sī vīs, mē ad Theomnēstum dūc.'
4 ille respondit: 'inveniēs eum prope (theātrum). venī mēcum.'
5 iuvenis eum dūxit ex (ātrium) ad tablīnum Theomnēstī, quī eum benignē accēpit.
6 post (merīdiēs) Quīntus manum iuvenum vīdit inter (quī) erat Marcus Cicerō.
7 ille Quīntum laetus salūtāvit eumque rogāvit dē (omnia) quae Rōmae fīēbant.
8 Quīntus eī omnia nārrāvit causamque exposuit propter (quae) pater eum Athēnās mīserat.

Exercise 29.4

Translate into Latin

1 Quintus was sitting in a pub (**taberna**) with Marcus drinking wine.
2 Two young men came up and greeted Marcus.
3 One, who was carrying a book in each hand, said, 'Will you come with me to the Lyceum or stay here drinking wine?'

4 The other said, 'Surely you don't want to listen to Cratippus, Marcus? Stay here with me.'

5 Quintus said, 'You must listen to Cratippus' lecture today. Don't you listen to him gladly (**libenter**)? Are you not his best pupil? That was what you wrote to Tiro. (= You wrote these things to Tiro.)'

Chapter 30

Active and passive

All the verb forms you have met so far have been in the active voice. In the *active* voice, the subject *acts*, e.g.

> Quintus *calls* Marcus.   Scintilla *leads* Horatia.

In the *passive* voice, the subject *is acted upon*, e.g.

> Marcus *is called* by Quintus.   Horatia *is led* by Scintilla.

In these sentences Marcus/Horatia are not acting but are the recipients of the action; he is being called, she is being led.

Exercise 30.1

Rewrite the following English sentences in passive form, e.g.

> Brutus killed Caesar = Caesar was killed by Brutus.

1 The captain gave the signal.

2 The sailors cast off the ship.

3 ⸳The sailors rowed the ship out of the harbour.

4 The storm frightened all the passengers.

5 But the captain saved the ship.

The perfect passive participle

You have already met a number of perfect passive participles, e.g.

apertus, -a, -um:	having been opened, open (from **aperiō**)
parātus, -a, -um:	having been prepared, prepared (from **parō**)
commōtus, -a, -um:	having been moved, moved (from **commoveō**)
territus, -a, -um:	having been terrified, terrified (from **terreō**)
dēsertus, -a, -um:	having been deserted, deserted (from **dēserō**).

The perfect passive participle is a verbal adjective, declined like **bonus, -a, -um**. It is formed from the supine of the verb. The *supine* is the fourth of the principal parts of verbs, which appears in all vocabularies from chapter 30 on; its uses will not be explained until Part III. It is most commonly formed by adding the suffix **-tum** (sometimes **-sum**) to the present verb stem. The perfect passive participle itself is formed by changing the final **-m** of the supine to **-s**, so:

supine	*perfect passive participle*	
parāt-um	**parāt-us, -a, -um**	having been prepared, prepared
monit-um	**monit-us, -a, -um**	having been warned, warned
rēct-um	**rēct-us, -a, -um**	having been ruled, ruled
capt-um	**capt-us, -a, -um**	having been taken, taken
audīt-um	**audīt-us, -a, -um**	having been heard, heard

Examples of verbs with supines in **-sum**:

iubeō, iubēre, iussī, iussum	iussus, -a, -um
videō, vidēre, vīdī, vīsum	vīsus, -a, -um
mittō, mittere, mīsī, missum	missus, -a, -um

In the following examples notice that the participles agree with the noun to which they refer in number, gender and case.

1 <u>Aenēas</u>, ā Mercuriō <u>monitus</u>, nāvēs parāvit.
   Aeneas, warned by Mercury, prepared the ships.
2 omnēs <u>cēnam</u> ā Scintillā <u>parātam</u> ēdērunt.
   They all ate the dinner prepared by Scintilla.
3 centuriō <u>hostēs</u> in proeliō <u>captōs</u> ad imperātōrem dūxit.
   The centurion led the soldiers (who had been) captured in battle to the general.
4 cōnsul <u>mīlitibus</u> <u>convocātīs</u> haec dīxit.
   The consul called together the soldiers and said this (these things).
   (Literally: The consul said this to the soldiers having been called together.)
5 Marcus <u>Quīntum</u> in viā <u>vīsum</u> in tabernam dūxit.
   Marcus saw Quintus in the street and led him to a pub. *or* When Marcus saw Quintus in the street, he led him to a pub. (literally: Marcus led Quintus having been seen in the street to a pub.)

NB 1 In the last three examples Latin and English idiom differ; English often uses a clause where Latin uses a participle. You must grasp the sense of the Latin and express it in natural English.

2 ā/ab = 'by' is always used with people (*agents*) but not with things (*instruments*), e.g.
   mīles ab hostibus vulnerātus the soldier wounded by the enemy
but:
   mīles hastā vulnerātus the soldier wounded by a spear

Exercise 30.2

What do the following words mean (and say what verb each comes from)?

   vocātus, territus, custōdītus, excitātus, scrīptus, doctus, factus, clausus, dēfēnsus, versus

Exercise 30.3

Translate

1 Caesar ā coniūrātīs occīsus prope statuam Pompēiī iacēbat.
2 coniūrātī ab Antōniō oppugnātī ex urbe fūgērunt.
3 Flaccus, cīvium tumultibus territus, cōnstituit Venusiam redīre.
4 Scintilla epistolam ā Quīntō scrīptam laeta accēpit.
5 Horātia Decimō spōnsāta (*betrothed*) ad nūptiās sē parāvit.
6 plūrimī amīcī ad nūptiās vocātī cēnam magnificam ā Scintillā parātam sūmpsērunt.
7 Decimus Horātiae, dominae familiae iam factae, aquam et ignem dedit.
8 Scintilla Flaccusque tōtā rē dēlectātī domum rediērunt.

Exercise 30.4

Translate the following sentences into natural English, e.g.

   Scintilla Horātiam salūtātam in casam dūxit.
   either Scintilla greeted Horatia and led her into the house.
   or When Scintilla had greeted Horatia, she led her into the house.

1 coniūrātī Caesarem occīsum in terrā iacentem relīquērunt.
2 Antōnius cīvēs in forum convocātōs ad furōrem excitāvit.
3 Flaccus Quīntum ad portum ductum valēre iussit.
4 Scintilla Horātiam māne excitātam ad nūptiās sē parāre iussit.
5 Decimus Horātiam ad novam domum ductam super līmen sustulit.

Exercise 30.5

Put the verbs in parentheses into the correct form of the perfect passive participle and translate the whole sentence

1 iuvenēs ad theātrum (convocāre) Cratippum exspectābant.
2 mox advēnit et ā discipulīs (salūtāre) nihil respondit.
3 iuvenēs vultū sevērō diū (īnspicere) sīc monuit.
4 'paucīs ante diēbus vōs iussī librum legere ā Platōne (scrībere).
5 vix quisquam vestrum (*of you*) hunc librum lēgit. omnēs, ā Marcō Cicerōne in tabernās (dūcere), tempus teritis (*you waste*) vīnum bibentēs.
6 itaque hodiē scholam vōbīs nōn habēbō. in urbem festīnāte et illum librum (emere) legite.'
7 iuvenēs, hīs verbīs (commovēre), omnia fēcērunt sīcut Theomnēstus iusserat.

Exercise 30.6

Translate into Latin

1 The girls, warned by their mother, stayed at home.
2 Flaccus, terrified by the riots, decided to return home.
3 The sailors, ordered by the captain, cast off the ship.
4 Scintilla quickly read the letter written by Quintus.
5 The young men bought the books praised by Cratippus.

Exercise 30.7

In the following sentences turn the first verb into a perfect passive participle and then translate into Latin, e.g.

The young men were called to the theatre and listened to the lecture = The young men, having been called..., listened... **iuvenēs ad theātrum vocātī scholam audīvērunt.**

1 Horatia was woken by her mother and prepared for the wedding.
2 Many friends were called to the wedding and joyful(ly) came to the house.
3 Decimus was led to the house by his friends and waited for Horatia.
4 All the guests (**hospitēs**) were called together by Flaccus and watched Horatia and Decimus joining (**cōnserere**) hands.
5 After dinner Decimus led Horatia through the streets and carried her into her new home (= Decimus carried Horatia having been led ...).

Exercise 30.8

Translate the following verb forms

1	dūcere	6	faciēmus	11	invenit
2	dūcēns	7	fēcerimus	12	invēnit
3	dūc	8	faciēns	13	inveniēns
4	ductus	9	facite	14	inventus
5	dūcet	10	factus	15	invenient

Chapter 31

Perfect, future perfect and pluperfect passive

The *perfect passive* consists of the perfect passive participle plus the present of **sum**:

parātus sum	I was prepared, I have been prepared
parātus es	you were prepared, you have been prepared
parātus/a est	he/she was prepared, he/she has been prepared
parātī sumus	we were prepared, we have been prepared
parātī estis	you were prepared, you have been prepared
parātī sunt	they were prepared, they have been prepared

Notice that the participle, being an adjective, agrees with the subject, e.g.

puer parāt-us est; puell-a parāt-a est
puer-ī parāt-ī sunt; puell-ae parāt-ae sunt

So also:

monitus sum	I was warned, I have been warned
rēctus sum	I was ruled, I have been ruled
audītus sum	I was heard, I have been heard

The *future perfect passive* consists of the perfect passive participle plus the future of **sum**:

parātus erō	I shall have been prepared
monitus erō	I shall have been warned
rēctus erō	I shall have been ruled
audītus erō	I shall have been heard

The *pluperfect passive* consists of the perfect passive participle plus the imperfect of **sum**:

parātus eram	I had been prepared
monitus eram	I had been warned
rēctus eram	I had been ruled
audītus eram	I had been heard

(For the full paradigms, see the Reference grammar, p. 158.)

The meanings of the perfect passive

You will remember that the *perfect active* has two different meanings, e.g.

Flaccus Quīntum Rōmam dūxit.
either Flaccus led Quintus to Rome.
or (in a present context) Flaccus has led Quintus to Rome.

So, in the *passive*:

Quīntus Rōmam ā Flaccō ductus est.
either Quintus was led to Rome by Flaccus.
or (in a present context) Quintus has been led to Rome by Flaccus.

e.g. **Quīntus Rōmam ductus est; in lūdō Orbiliī studēbat.**
Quintus was led to Rome; he studied in the school of Orbilius.

Quīntus Rōmam ductus est; in lūdō Orbiliī studet.
Quintus has been led to Rome; he is studying in the school of Orbilius.

Exercise 31.1

Translate the following verb forms

1	vincet	6	captī erāmus	11	mīsī
2	victus sum	7	capit	12	missae sumus
3	victī erimus	8	cēpit	13	mittēns
4	vīcistī	9	capta est	14	missus eram
5	victī erant	10	capite	15	missa erit

Exercise 31.2

Translate

1 Marcus Athēnās ā patre missus erat.
2 Quīntus ā Marcō vocātus est.
3 iuvenēs valdē commōtī sunt.
4 domum redīre iussae sumus.

5 epistola ā Quīntō scrīpta erat.
6 epistola iam ā Scintillā accepta erit.
7 nōnne ā canibus territae estis?
8 canēs ā colōnō retentī sunt.

Exercise 31.3

Rewrite the following sentences in the passive voice and translate, e.g.

iuvenēs Brūtum vīdērunt.
Brūtus ā iuvenibus vīsus est. Brutus was seen by the young men.

1 Horātia Argum servāvit.
2 Horātiam pater laudāvit.
3 iuvenēs Cratippum audīverant.

4 Brūtus lībertātem dēfendit.
5 pater mē monuerat.
6 amīcī vōs curāverint.

Exercise 31.4

Translate

1 Cicerō rūmōribus, quōs dē Marcō accēperat, maximē vexātus est.
2 epistola ā Tīrōne ad Marcum scrīpta erat.
3 hāc epistolā Marcus valdē commōtus est; nam pater Athēnās veniēbat.
4 sed alterā epistolā cūrā līberātus est; pater enim Rōmae rēbus pūblicīs retentus erat.
5 iuvenēs ad theātrum convocātī erant.
6 omnēs Theomnēstum exspectābant, cum Brūtus in theātrum ductus est.
7 Horātia ā Scintillā domum vocāta erat.
8 Horātia, ubi advēnit, 'cūr ā tē vocāta sum?' inquit.
9 Scintilla 'Argus, ā lupō oppugnātus,' inquit, 'graviter vulnerātus est.'
10 Horātia hīs verbīs commōta est. ad canem festīnāvit eumque cūrāvit.

Exercise 31.5

Translate into Latin

1 Argus was saved by Horatia.
2 The dog had been left in the house by Scintilla.
3 When Horatia returned from the fountain, she saw the house on fire (= burning).
4 She was terrified, but she dragged Argus into the garden.
5 Flaccus was called by Scintilla; but when he arrived, the fire had been overcome.
6 Horatia was praised by her father, because she had saved Argus.

Chapter 32

Present, future and imperfect passive

A new set of person endings must be learnt for the present, future and imperfect passive; these are set out below in parallel with the person endings of the active:

	active	passive	e.g.	active I prepare, I am preparing	passive I am prepared, I am being prepared
I	-ō/m	-r		par-ō	par-or
you	-s	-ris		parā-s	parā-ris
he/she	-t	-tur		para-t	parā-tur
we	-mus	-mur		parā-mus	parā-mur
you	-tis	-minī		parā-tis	parā-minī
they	-nt	-ntur·		para-nt	para-ntur

Write out the present passive of **mone-ō** and **audi-ō** (check the forms in the Reference grammar, p. 158).

The present passive of 3rd conjugation verbs e.g.	The present passive of 3rd conjugation -iō verbs e.g.
reg-or	capi-or
reg-eris	cap-eris
reg-itur	cap-itur
reg-imur	cap-imur
reg-iminī	cap-iminī
reg-untur	capi-untur

Future passive:

parā-bor *I shall be prepared*	monē-bor *I shall be warned*	reg-ar *I shall be ruled*
parā-beris	monē-beris	reg-ēris
parā-bitur	monē-bitur	reg-ētur
parā-bimur	monē-bimur	reg-ēmur
parā-biminī	monē-biminī	reg-ēminī
parā-buntur	monē-buntur	reg-entur
capi-ar *I shall be taken*	audi-ar *I shall be heard*	
capi-ēris	audi-ēris	
capi-ētur	audi-ētur	
capi-ēmur	audi-ēmur	
capi-ēminī	audi-ēminī	
capi-entur	audi-entur	

Imperfect passive:

parā-bar *I was being prepared*	monē-bar *I was being warned*	regē-bar *I was being ruled*
parā-bāris	monē-bāris	regē-bāris
parā-bātur	monē-bātur	regē-bātur
parā-bāmur	monē-bāmur	regē-bāmur
parā-bāminī	monē-bāminī	regē-bāminī
parā-bantur	monē-bantur	rege-bantur
capi-ēbar *I was being taken*	audi-ēbar *I was being heard*	
capi-ēbāris	audi-ēbāris	
capi-ēbātur	audi-ēbātur	
capi-ēbāmur	audi-ēbāmur	
capi-ēbāminī	audi-ēbāminī	
capi-ēbantur	audi-ēbantur	

Exercise 32.1

Translate

amantur, regitur, audīminī, monēris, dūcēbāris, vidēbimur, oppugnābantur, trāditur, trādētur, mittēris, mitteris

Exercise 32.2

Translate the following verb forms

1	vocābimur	8	terrēbantur	15	pōnor
2	vocātī estis	9	terrētur	16	pōnēris
3	vocābātur	10	territī sunt	17	pōneris
4	vocātus eram	11	terrēbant	18	posuērunt
5	vocābant	12	territa erat	19	positae erant
6	vocāris	13	terrēmur	20	posueram
7	vocāvī	14	terruit	21	positī sunt

Exercise 32.3

Translate

1 cotīdiē nūntiī peiorēs Venusiam Rōmā afferēbantur.
2 Flaccus hīs rūmōribus magnopere commovēbātur.
3 cum amīcīs in tabernā sedēbat, quibus nūntius novus nūper allātus erat.
4 Flaccus 'quid sentītis?' inquit. 'rēspūblica in bellum cīvīle iterum trahitur. nec iūs nec lēgēs valēbunt.'
5 Ganymēdēs 'nōlī tē vexāre,' inquit; 'Rōmā longē absumus; nōs bellō cīvīlī nōn vexābimur.'
6 Flaccus 'nōlī nūgās (*nonsense*) nārrāre,' inquit; 'tōta Italia ēvertētur, immō (*or rather*) tōtus orbis terrārum.
7 fīlius meus Athēnīs studet; in bellum ā Brūtō trahētur.'
8 amīcī eum iussērunt meliōra dīcere; 'nōlī dēspērāre, Flacce,' inquiunt; 'pāx sine dubiō servābitur; ducēs in concordiam (*agreement, harmony*) addūcentur.'
9 Flaccus tamen eīs nōn crēdēbat. hīs rūmōribus semper vexābātur, propter quōs et prō rēpūblicā et prō fīliō suō timēbat.

Exercise 32.4

Change the following Latin sentences into passive form and then translate them; e.g.

Decimus Horātiam domum dūcēbat = Horātia ā Decimō domum dūcēbātur.
Horatia was being led home by Decimus.

1 Brūtus multōs iuvenēs Athēnīs in Macedoniam dūxit.
2 Antōnius patrem Marcī occīderat.
3 ego patris meī mortem vindicābō (**vindicō** = I avenge).
4 Brūtus sōlus lībertātem dēfendit.
5 Brūtī mīlitēs exercitum Antōniī superābunt.
6 omnēs cīvēs et Brūtum et mīlitēs eius laudābunt.

Exercise 32.5

Translate into Latin

1 Marcus was being led to a tavern by a friend.
2 Suddenly someone called him; 'By whom was I called?' he said.
3 His friend replied: 'Look! You are being called by Brutus.'
4 Marcus looked back and saw Brutus approaching.
5 Brutus greeted him and said, 'Marcus, are you willing to come with me to Macedonia?
6 If you fight with me for freedom, you will be praised by all.'
7 Marcus, greatly moved by these words, said, 'I will fight with you; for freedom is being defended by you alone.'
8 Soon he had packed (**compōnō**) his things and was led by Brutus to Macedonia.

Appendix · Cena Trimalchionis

The following passage is adapted from the *Satyricon* of Petronius, who died in AD 66. The *Satyricon* is an immensely long novel which centers around the adventures of two disreputable students, Encolpius and Ascyltos, who get into various scrapes. When our extracts begin, they are studying rhetoric in the town of Puteoli and have been befriended by their professor, Agamemnon. They are sitting in their lodgings, expecting trouble from their latest escapade, when Agamemnon's slave bursts in and tells them that his master has procured them an invitation to dinner with Trimalchio.

Trimalchio is a vulgar, boastful and fabulously rich freedman. He has asked Agamemnon to bring along a couple of his students to raise the tone of his party; the other guests are uneducated freedmen. As usual at a Roman dinner party, there were nine dining in all, including the host. They reclined on three couches placed in a square around the table, with one end open for serving the food.

The narrator of the story is Encolpius.

(Words which occur in the General vocabulary are not glossed; you may have to look some up there.)

Itaque domī sedēbāmus cum intrāvit servus Agamemnonis et 'quid?' inquit; 'nōnne scītis? hodiē vōs ad cēnam invītāvit Trimalchiō, lautissimus homō. venīte igitur; nōlīte cessāre.' celeriter igitur vestīmenta induimus et ad balnea prōcessimus. in
5 balneīs senem calvum vīdimus quī inter puerōs capillātōs pilā lūdēbat. accurrit aliquis ad nōs et 'ille est' inquit 'Trimalchiō, quī vōs ad cēnam invītāvit.' vix haec dīxerat cum Trimalchiō digitōs concrepuit; aquam poposcit et digitōs lāvit. deinde servī eum in lectīcam imposuērunt domumque auferēbant.

10   ad iānuam Trimalchiōnis aedium cum Agamemnone pervēnimus. ātrium magnificum erat, sed ego, dum omnia spectō, paene cecidī et crūra mea frēgī. in mūrō enim pictus est canis ingēns, superque scrīptum CAVE CANEM. comitēs mē rīsērunt; ego autem spīritum collēgī et tōtum mūrum īnspicere incēpī. erat enim
15 vēnālicium cum titulīs pictum; deinde ipse Trimalchiō Rōmam intrābat. deinde omnia quae fēcerat Trimalchiō pictor cum īnscrīptiōne dīligenter reddiderat. prīmum Trimalchiō ratiōnēs facere discēbat, deinde dispēnsātor factus est, dēnique Mercurius eum tollēbat et in tribūnal altum rapiēbat; ibi erat Fortūna, quae
20 cornū abundantī dīvitiās effundēbat.

nōs in trīclīnium iam pervēnerāmus et mox omnēs discubuerant praeter ipsum Trimalchiōnem. servī gustātiōnem

lautissimus very grand

calvum bald; **capillātōs** long-haired
pilā with a ball
digitōs concrepuit snapped his fingers
lectīcam a litter

crūra legs
pictus est was painted
spīritum my breath
vēnālicium slave sale

ratiōnēs facere to keep accounts
dispēnsātor factus est was appointed a steward
tribūnal (n.) a platform
cornū abundantī from her horn of plenty
effundēbat was pouring out
trīclīnium dining-room
discubuerant had taken our places (at table); **praeter** except
gustātiōnem hors d'oeuvre, snacks

valdē lautam intulērunt. nam asellum argenteum cum bisacciō
nōbīs prōposuērunt, quī habēbat olīvās in alterā parte albās, in
25   alterā nigrās.

hāc gustātiōne gaudēbāmus cum ipse Trimalchiō intrāvit ad
symphōniam. ubi lectō accubuit, 'amīcī,' inquit, 'nōndum voluī in
trīclīnium venīre; tesserīs enim lūdēbam. sed omnem voluptātem
mihi negāvī. lūdum tamen sine mē cōnficere.' intrāvit puer
30   tabulam portāns et crystallinās tesserās.

iam Trimalchiō lūdum cōnfēcerat, cum puerī amphorās
attulērunt quārum in cervīcibus pittacia fīxa sunt cum hāc
īnscrīptiōne: 'Falernum Opīmiānum annōrum centum'. dum nōs
īnscrīptiōnem legimus, Trimalchiō 'ergō' inquit 'diūtius vīnum
35   vīvit quam homō. līberē igitur bibite. vērum Opīmiānum vōbīs
dō. herī vīnum nōn tam bonum posuī et multō honestiōrēs
mēcum cēnābant.'

advēnērunt subitō servī quī torālia prōposuērunt; in eīs rētia
picta erant vēnātōrēsque et tōtus vēnātiōnis apparātus. dum haec
40   spectāmus admīrātiōne plēnī, clāmōrem ingentem audīmus et,
ecce, canēs Lacōnicī circum mēnsam currere incēpērunt. deinde
puer repositōrium intulit, in quō erat aper maximus. accessit
barbātus ingēns, vēnātōris vestīmenta gerēns, quī ventrem aprī
vehementer percussit. ubi hoc fēcit, avēs ē ventre aprī
45   ēvolāvērunt. parātī erant servī quī avēs circum trīclīnium
volantēs celeriter cēpērunt.

ubi servī hoc ferculum abstulērunt, surrēxit Trimalchiō et ē
trīclīniō discessit. nōs colloquium facere incēpimus. itaque Dāma
prīmus pōtiōnem rogāvit et 'diēs' inquit 'nihil est. dum vertis tē,
50   nox fit. itaque nihil est melius quam dē cubiculō rēctā in
trīclīnium īre. et ācre frīgus habuimus. vix mē balneum calfēcit.
calida tamen pōtiō vestiārius est. plūrimum bibī et ēbrius sum.
vīnum in caput meum abiit.'

Seleucus, ubi haec audīvit, 'ego' inquit 'nōn cotīdiē mē lavō;
55   balneum enim corpus dīlacerat. neque hodiē mē lavāre potuī. īvī
enim ad fūnus. homō bellus, tam bonus Chrȳsanthus, diem suum
obiit. modo, modo mē salūtāvit. medicī eum perdidērunt, immō
malum fātum; medicus enim nihil aliud est quam animī
cōnsōlātiō. optimum tamen fūnus erat, etiam sī uxor nōn multum
60   eum plōrāvit.'

molestus fuit, et Philerōs clāmāvit: 'nōlī molestus esse.
vīvōrum meminerīmus. ille habet quod sibi dēbēbātur. honestē
vīxit, honestē obiit. ab asse crēvit et parātus fuit quadrantem

---

asellum argenteum a silver donkey
bisacciō double panniers

ad symphōniam to (the sound of) a band
tesserīs with dice
voluptātem pleasure
negāvī I denied
tabulam a (playing) board
amphorās wine jars
quārum in cervīcibus on the necks of which; **pittacia** labels
Falernum Opīmiānum Falernian wine made in the consulship of Opimius (121 BC)
multō honestiōrēs much more important people
torālia (n. pl.) tapestries
rētia (n. pl.) hunting nets
vēnātōrēs huntsmen
canēs Lacōnicī Spartan hounds
repositōrium a dish; **aper** a boar
barbātus ingēns a huge bearded man
ventrem the belly; **percussit** struck

ferculum course

pōtiōnem a drink
dē cubiculō from the bedroom
rēctā straight; **ācre frīgus** (acc. n.) a sharp cold (spell)
calfēcit has warmed; **calida** hot
vestiārius est is (as good as) an overcoat
dīlacerat tears apart
homō bellus a nice man
obiit has met (i.e. has died)
modo, modo just lately
medicī the doctors
immō or rather; **plōrāvit** mourned

molestus tiresome, boring
vīvōrum meminerīmus let's remember the living
dēbēbātur was owing; **ab asse** from a penny; **quadrantem** a farthing

dē stercore dentibus tollere. itaque crēvit tamquam favus. dī
65 immortālēs, relīquit solida centum.'

Ganymēdēs, ubi haec audīvit, 'merās nūgās' inquit
'nārrātis. nēmō intereā cūrat quam cārum sit frūmentum.
hodiē nōn buccam pānis invenīre potuī. iam tōtum annum
ēsurītiō fuit. heu, heu cotīdiē peius. quid enim futūrum est, sī
70 nec deī neque hominēs hanc colōniam adiuvant? omnia haec,
ut ego crēdō, deī faciunt. nēmō enim Iovem pilī facit, sed
omnēs opertīs oculīs bona sua computant.'

Echiōn tamen 'ōrō tē;' inquit 'meliōra dīcite. ecce, mox
habitūrī sumus mūnus optimum. Titus noster magnum
75 animum habet. ferrum optimum datūrus est, sine fugā,
carnārium in mediō.' haec ubi dīxit, ad Agamemnona sē vertit,
et 'tū, Agamemnon, tibi dīcis, ut crēdō, "cūr ille molestus
nūgās nārrat?" quod tū, quī potes dīcere, nihil dīcis. tū prae
litterīs fatuus es. omnēs id scīmus. sed tibi discipulus crēscit
80 fīliolus meus. iam quattuor partēs dīcit. sī vīxerit, habēbis
bonum discipulum.'

tālia dīcēbāmus cum Trimalchiō rediit et 'ignōscite mihi'
inquit, 'amīcī. multōs iam diēs venter meus nōn respondet, nec
medicī mē iuvāre possunt. prōfuit tamen mihi mālicorium et,
85 ut spērō, aliquid recreātus sum.'

iam discubuerat Trimalchiō cum servus trēs albōs porcōs
in trīclīnium dūxit. Trimalchiō, porcōs īnspiciēns, 'quem ex
eīs' inquit 'vultis edere?' tum cocum vocāvit eumque iussit
maximum in cēnam occīdere.

90 deinde Trimalchiō vultū benignō ad nōs respexit et 'sī
vīnum' inquit 'vōbīs nōn placet, mūtābō. deōrum beneficiō
nihil emō. hoc vīnum ā praediō venit quod ego adhūc nōn
vīdī. est prope Tarentum, ut mihi dīcunt. nunc Siciliam volō
coniungere agrīs meīs; sīc, cum in Africam voluerō īre, per
95 meōs fīnēs nāvigābō. sed tū, Agamemnōn, dīc mihi; quam
contrōversiam hodiē ēgistī? litterās enim nōn contemnō. duās
bibliothēcās habeō, ūnam Graecam, alteram Latīnam.'

tālia efflābat cum duō servī repositōrium cum porcō
ingentī in mēnsā posuērunt. nōs admīrātiōne plēnī erāmus;
100 nam cocus nē gallum quidem tam celeriter coquere potuit.
deinde Trimalchiō porcum īnspiciēns 'quid? quid?' inquit 'hic
porcus nōn est exinterātus? nōn mehercule est. vocā, vocā
cocum.' intrāvit cocus et trīstis prope mēnsam cōnstitit.
'oblītus sum' inquit 'porcum exinterāre.' Trimalchiō exclāmat
105 'quid? oblītus? dēspoliā eum.'

---

dē stercore from the dung
tamquam favus like a honeycomb
solida centum a solid 100,000 (i.e. a
  fortune); **merās nūgās** pure rubbish
quam cārum sit frūmentum how dear
  grain is; **buccam pānis** a mouthful of
  bread; **ēsurītiō** a famine
futūrum going to happen
pilī facit cares a straw (a jot) for
opertīs oculīs with their eyes closed
computant reckon up

habitūrī going to have; **mūnus** (n.)
  gladiatorial show; **Titus** the magistrate
  who will give the show
ferrum optimum datūrus going to give
  (the gladiators) really good steel
carnārium a butcher's shambles
prae litterīs fatuus mad with literature
quattuor partēs his four times table

ignōscite (+ dat.) forgive!
venter meus nōn respondet my bowels
  have not performed
prōfuit mihi has done me good
mālicorium pomegranate (a laxative)
aliquid recreātus a bit better
albōs porcōs white pigs
cocum the cook

mūtābō I will change (it)
beneficiō by the kindness
praediō an estate
agrīs meīs to my fields
fīnēs territory, property
quam contrōversiam? what debate?
contemnō I despise
bibliothēcās libraries
efflābat was puffing out
repositōrium dish
nē gallum quidem not even a chicken

exinterātus gutted
mehercule by Hercules!
oblītus sum I forgot
dēspoliā strip!

sine morā cocus dēspoliātus inter duōs tortōrēs cōnstitit. nōs
omnēs ōrāre prō eō incēpimus et dīcere: 'tē rogāmus, eī ignōsce.
sī iterum hoc fēcerit, nēmō nostrum ōrābit prō illō.' Trimalchiō
vultum in rīsum relaxāvit et 'quod tam malae memoriae es,'
110 inquit 'palam nōbīs porcum exinterā.' cocus tunicam recēpit
porcīque ventrem timidā manū secuit. sine morā ex plāgīs
crēscentibus tomācula cum botulīs effūsa sunt.

plausum post hoc servī dedērunt et 'Gāiō fēlīciter'
conclāmāvērunt. et cocus pōtiōne honōrātus est et argenteā
115 corōnā.

deinde Trimalchiō ad Nīcerōtem respexit et 'solēbas' inquit
'suāvior esse in convīctū. cūr nunc tacēs nec quicquam dīcis?
ōrō tē, nārrā nōbīs id quod tibi iuvenī accidit.' Nīcerōs
dēlectātus affābilitāte amīcī, 'gaudeō' inquit 'quod tē tam
120 hilarem videō. itaque faciam id quod rogās.

'ubi adhūc servus eram, habitābam in vīcō angustō; nunc
Gavillae domus est. ibi amāre incēpī uxōrem Terentiī; Melissam
cognōverātis, pulcherrimum baciballum. sed nōn mehercule
corporāliter eam amābam sed magis quod bonō ingeniō fuit. sī
125 quid ab illā petiī, numquam mihi negāvit; sī fēcit assem, ego
sēmissem habuī. huius marītus in vīllā diem obiit. itaque
temptābam omnibus modīs ad eam pervenīre.

forte dominus meus Capuam exierat; nam negōtium
quoddam expedīre voluit. ego occāsiōnem habuī. hospitī nostrō
130 persuāsī mēcum venīre. ille mīles erat, fortis tamquam Orcus.
iter iniimus circā gallicinia; lūna lūcēbat tamquam merīdiē.
vēnimus inter monumenta. comes meus ad stēlās abiit. sedeō
ego stēlāsque numerō. deinde, ubi respexī ad comitem, ille exuit
sē et omnia vestīmenta secundum viam posuit. valdē territus
135 eram; stābam tamquam mortuus. sed ille circummīnxit
vestīmenta sua et subitō lupus factus est.

mihi crēdite; ululāvit et in silvās fūgit. ego accessī
vestīmentaque eius tollere temptābam; sed illa lapidea facta
sunt. paene timōre periī. gladium tamen strīnxī et in tōtā viā
140 umbrās cecīdī, dōnec ad vīllam amīcae meae pervēnī. tamquam
larva intrāvī; oculī mortuī erant. Melissa mea mē rogāvit: 'cūr
tam sērō ambulās? cūr nōn anteā advēnistī? nōs adiuvāre
potuistī. lupus enim vīllam intrāvit et omnia pecora oppugnāvit;
tamquam lanius sanguinem illīs mīsit. nōn tamen nōs dērīsit,
145 etiam sī effūgit. servus enim noster lanceā collum eius trāiēcit.'

haec ubi audīvī, operīre oculōs nōn potuī sed domum fūgī. et
ubi vēnī in eum locum, in quō lapidea vestīmenta facta erant,
nihil invēnī nisi sanguinem. ubi domum vēnī, iacēbat mīles

tortōrēs torturers

palam nōbīs in our presence
secuit cut; **ex plāgīs crēscentibus**
   from the growing slits
tomācula (n. pl.) black puddings
botulīs sausages
effūsa sunt (were) poured out
plausum applause
Gāiō fēlīciter good luck to Gaius!
argenteā corōnā with a silver crown
solēbas…esse you used to be
suāvior in convīctū better company at
   a party

vīcō angustō a narrow street

baciballum peach
corporāliter physically
sī quid if…anything
negāvit she denied, refused
sēmissem a halfpenny
omnibus modīs by all means
forte by chance
expedīre to deal with; **occāsiōnem** an
   opportunity; **hospitī** our guest
fortis tamquam Orcus as brave as hell
circā gallicinia around cockcrow
inter monumenta among the
   monuments, i.e. the graveyard
stēlās gravestones
secundum (+ acc.) beside
circummīnxit piddled around
ululāvit he howled
lapidea made of stone
strīnxī I drew
cecīdī I struck at; **dōnec** until
tamquam larva like a ghost

pecora (n. pl.) the flocks
tamquam lanius like a butcher
nōn … nōs dērīsit he didn't have the
   laugh on us
lanceā with a spear
operīre to close

meus in lectō tamquam bōs, et collum eius medicus cūrābat.
150 tum rem intellēxī: versipellis erat; nec posteā cum eō pānem
gustāre potuī. crēdite mihi, vēra sunt ea quae dīcō.'

omnēs admīrātiōne attonitī erāmus et Trimalchiō 'tibi crēdō'
inquit; 'pilī mihi inhorruērunt, quod Nīcerōs nōn nūgās nārrat,
sed certus neque umquam mendācia dīcit.'

155 inter haec aliquis trīclīniī iānuam pulsāvit intrāvitque
cōmissātor cum ingentī turbā. ego māiestāte eius territus sum et
temptāvī surgere. sed Agamemnōn mē rīsit et 'continē tē' inquit;
'hic est Habinnas, amīcus Trimalchiōnis.' ille ēbrius erat
manūsque uxōris umerīs imposuerat. sē posuit ad mēnsam
160 continuōque vīnum et calidam aquam poposcit. dēlectātus hāc
hilaritāte ipse Trimalchiō maiōrem poposcit phialam et
Habinnam rogāvit 'quōmodo acceptus es?' ille 'omnia habuimus'
inquit 'praeter tē. sed dīc mihi, Gāī, cur Fortūnāta nōn recumbit?
nisi illa recumbit, ego abeō.'

165 surgēbat Habinnās, sed tōta familia Fortūnātam quater
vocāvit. illa trīclīnium iniit et sūdāriō manūs tergēns accubuit in
illō lectō in quō Scintilla, Habinnae uxor, discumbēbat. omnēs
iam ēbriī erant, cum Trimalchiō servum iussit exemplar
testāmentī suī afferre et tōtum ā prīmō ad ultimum recitāvit.
170 deinde respiciēns ad Habinnam 'quid dīcis, cārissimē?' inquit;
'aedificābis monumentum meum quemadmodum tē iussī?
secundum pedēs statuae meae catellam pōnē et corōnās et
unguentum; sīc tuō beneficiō post mortem vīvam. valdē enim
stultum est, sī vīvī domōs pulchrās aedificāmus, nōn tamen
175 cūrāmus eās ubi diūtius dēbēmus habitāre. ad dextram meam
pōne statuam Fortūnātae columbam tenentis. et hanc
īnscrīptiōnem scrībe in monumentō:
C. POMPEIUS TRIMALCHIO HIC REQUIESCIT. PIUS, FORTIS,
FIDELIS, EX PARVO CREVIT, SESTERTIUM RELIQUIT
180 TRECENTIES, NEC UMQUAM PHILOSOPHUM AUDIVIT. VALE.'

deinde Trimalchiō, iam valdē ēbrius, cornicinēs in trīclīnium
addūcī iussit. extendit sē super lectum et 'fingite' inquit 'mē
mortuum esse. dīcite aliquid bellī dē mē.' cōnsonuērunt
cornicinēs tōtamque excitāvērunt vīcīniam. itaque vigilēs, quī
185 vīcīniam custōdiēbant, dīxērunt 'ardet Trimalchiōnis domus.'
iānuam subitō frēgērunt et cum aquā secūribusque tumultum
facere incēpērunt. nōs hanc occāsiōnem nōn āmīsimus; celeriter
fūgimus tamquam ex vērō incendiō.

---

tamquam bōs like an ox
versipellis a werewolf
pānem gustāre to taste bread

pilī mihi my hair
inhorruērunt stood on end
mendācia lies

cōmissātor reveller
continē tē restrain yourself

umerīs on the shoulders

phialam cup

praeter tē except you
Fortūnāta Trimalchio's wife
recumbit reclines (at table)
quater four times
sūdāriō on a dish cloth
tergēns wiping
exemplar testāmentī suī a copy of
    his will

quemadmodum as
secundum pedēs beside the feet
catellam my puppy
unguentum scent bottle

columbam dove

pius pious
fīdēlis loyal
sēstertium trecentiēs 30,000,000
    sestertii; **valē** goodbye (addressed to
    the reader of the inscription)
cornicinēs trumpeters; **addūcī** to be
    brought; **extendit sē** he stretched
    himself out; **fingite** pretend
mē mortuum esse that I am dead
aliquid bellī something nice
cōnsonuērunt blared out
vīcīniam neighbourhood
vigilēs watchmen, fire brigade
secūribus axes
occāsiōnem opportunity
āmīsimus we lost; **tamquam** as if

Reference grammar

NOUNS

	1st declension	2nd declension			
	stems in **-a**	stems in **-o**			
	feminine	*masculine*			*neuter*
singular					
nom.	puell-a	colōn-us	puer	ager	bell-um
gen.	puell-ae	colōn-ī	puer-ī	agr-ī	bell-ī
dat.	puell-ae	colōn-ō	puer-ō	agr-ō	bell-ō
acc.	puell-am	colōn-um	puer-um	agr-um	bell-um
abl.	puell-ā	colōn-ō	puer-ō	agr-ō	bell-ō
voc.	puell-a	colōn-e	puer	ager	bell-um
plural					
nom.	puell-ae	colōn-ī	puer-ī	agr-ī	bell-a
gen.	puell-ārum	colōn-ōrum	puer-ōrum	agr-ōrum	bell-ōrum
dat.	puell-īs	colōn-īs	puer-īs	agr-īs	bell-īs
acc.	puell-ās	colōn-ōs	puer-ōs	agr-ōs	bell-a
abl.	puell-īs	colōn-īs	puer-īs	agr-īs	bell-īs
voc.	puell-ae	colōn-ī	puer-ī	agr-ī	bell-a

Notes

1 All nouns of the 1st declension are feminine except for a very few which are masculine by meaning, e.g. **nauta** a sailor.

2 The vocative is the same as the nominative except for the vocative singular of 2nd declension nouns with nominative **-us**, e.g. **colōn-e**.

The vocative of 2nd declension nouns with nominative **-ius** ends **-ī**, not **-e**, e.g. **fīlī**.

3 The following 2nd declension nouns have minor irregularities: **deus** has nominative plural **deī** or **dī**, genitive plural **deōrum** or **deum**, ablative plural **deīs** or **dīs**; **vir**, **virī** has genitive plural **virōrum** or **virum**.

	3rd declension			
	stems in consonants		stems in **-i**	
	masc. & fem.	*neuter*	*masc. & fem.*	*neuter*
singular				
nom.	rēx	lītus	nāvis	mare
gen.	rēg-is	lītor-is	nāv-is	mar-is
dat.	rēg-ī	lītor-ī	nāv-ī	mar-ī
acc.	rēg-em	lītus	nāv-em	mare
abl.	rēg-e	lītor-e	nāv-e	mar-ī
plural				
nom.	rēg-ēs	lītor-a	nāv-ēs	mar-ia
gen.	rēg-um	lītor-um	nāv-ium	mar-ium
dat.	rēg-ibus	lītor-ibus	nāv-ibus	mar-ibus
acc.	rēg-ēs	lītor-a	nāv-ēs	mar-ia
abl.	rēg-ibus	lītor-ibus	nāv-ibus	mar-ibus

Notes

1 The vocative case is the same as the nominative in all 3rd declension nouns and adjectives.

2 Masculine and feminine nouns with stems in **-i** nearly all decline like those with stems in consonants except in the genitive plural, where the **-i** is retained, e.g. **nāvium**; neuter nouns with stems in **-i** keep the **-i** in ablative singular, and the nominative, accusative and genitive plural (see **mare** above).

Nouns ending in two consonants (the second **-s**), e.g. **mōns**, **urbs** (originally spelt **monis**, **urbis**) have genitive plural **-ium**.

3 **iuvenis**, **senex** and **canis** have genitive plural **-um**.

4 A few 3rd declension nouns can, by sense, be either masculine or feminine in gender, e.g. **comes**, **comitis** a companion; these are marked *c.* (= common) in vocabulary lists.

	4th declension		5th declension
	stems in **-u**		stems in **-e**
	masc.	*neuter*	*feminine*
singular			
nom.	grad-us	corn-ū	r-ēs
gen.	grad-ūs	corn-ūs	r-eī
dat.	grad-uī	corn-uī	r-eī
acc.	grad-um	corn-ū	r-em
abl.	grad-ū	corn-ū	r-ē
plural			
nom.	grad-ūs	corn-ua	r-ēs
gen.	grad-uum	corn-uum	r-ērum
dat.	grad-ibus	corn-ibus	r-ēbus
acc.	grad-ūs	corn-ua	r-ēs
abl.	grad-ibus	corn-ibus	r-ēbus

Notes

1 Most 4th declension nouns are masculine; **manus** is the only common noun which is feminine. There are a very few neuter nouns; the only common one is **cornū**.

2 All 5th declension nouns are feminine except for **diēs**, which is masculine.

ADJECTIVES

Masculine & neuter 2nd declension; feminine 1st declension

singular	*m.*	*f.*	*n.*
nom.	bon-us	bon-a	bon-um
gen.	bon-ī	bon-ae	bon-ī
dat.	bon-ō	bon-ae	bon-ō
acc.	bon-um	bon-am	bon-um
abl.	bon-ō	bon-ā	bon-ō
voc.	bon-e	bon-a	bon-um
plural			
nom.	bon-ī	bon-ae	bon-a
gen.	bon-ōrum	bon-ārum	bon-ōrum
dat.	bon-īs	bon-īs	bon-īs
acc.	bon-ōs	bon-ās	bon-a
abl.	bon-īs	bon-īs	bon-īs
voc.	bon-ī	bon-ae	bon-a

So also:
miser, miser-a, miser-um, etc.,
pulcher, pulchr-a, pulchr-um, etc.

For **miser** and **pulcher** types of adjective the vocative is the same as the nominative.

3rd declension

	consonant stems		stems in **-i**	
singular	*m. & f.*	*n.*	*m. & f.*	*n.*
nom.	pauper	pauper	omnis	omn-e
gen.	pauper-is	pauper-is	omn-is	omn-is
dat.	pauper-ī	pauper-ī	omn-ī	omn-ī
acc.	pauper-em	pauper	omn-em	omn-e
abl.	pauper-e	pauper-e	omn-ī	omn-ī

Notes

1 The vocative is the same as the nominative.

2 Most 3rd declension adjectives have stems in **-i**; these keep the **-i** in ablative singular, genitive plural, and in neuter nominative and accusative plural.

3 Other types of 3rd declension adjectives with stems in **-i** are:

plural	consonant stems		stems in -i	
	m. & f.	*n.*	*m. & f.*	*n.*
nom.	pauper-ēs	pauper-a	omn-ēs	omn-ia
gen.	pauper-um	pauper-um	omn-ium	omn-ium
dat.	pauper-ibus	pauper-ibus	omn-ibus	omn-ibus
acc.	pauper-ēs	pauper-a	omn-ēs	omn-ia
abl.	pauper-ibus	pauper-ibus	omn-ibus	omn-ibus

	m. & f.	*n.*
nom.	ingēns	ingēns
gen.	ingentis	ingentis
nom.	fēlīx	fēlīx
gen.	fēlīcis	fēlīcis

4 3rd declension adjectives with stems in consonants are few, e.g. **dīves, dīvit-is**; **pauper, pauper-is**; **vetus, veter-is**; and the comparative adjective, e.g. **fortior** (*n.* **fortius**), genitive **fortiōr-is**.

	alter (one or the other of two)			**uter** (which of two?)		
	m.	*f.*	*n.*	*m.*	*f.*	*n.*
nom.	alter	altera	alterum	uter	utra	utrum
gen.	alterīus	alterīus	alterīus	utrīus	utrīus	utrīus
dat.	alterī	alterī	alterī	utrī	utrī	utrī
acc.	alterum	alteram	alterum	utrum	utram	utrum
abl.	alterō	alterā	alterō	utrō	utrā	utrō

Plural like that of **bon-ī, bon-ae, bon-a**.

Similarly: **uterque, utraque, utrumque** (each of two).

The following adjectives have the same characteristic, i.e. gen. sing. **-īus**, dat. sing. **-ī**:

alius, alia, aliud	other	*gen. sing.* **alīus**	*dat. sing.*	**aliī**
nūllus, nūlla, nūllum	no	**nūllīus**		**nūllī**
ūllus, ūlla, ūllum	any	**ūllīus**		**ūllī**
sōlus, sōla, sōlum	only	**sōlīus**		**sōlī**
tōtus, tōta, tōtum	whole	**tōtīus**		**tōtī**
ūnus, ūna, ūnum	one	**ūnīus**		**ūnī**

For the comparison of adjectives, see the grammar sections of chapters 24 and 25.

ADVERBS

1 From **bonus** type adjectives, adverbs are usually formed by adding **-ē** to the stem, e.g. **mal-us** bad: **mal-e** badly; **miser** miserable: **miser-ē** miserably. A few add **-ō**, e.g. **subit-us** sudden: **subit-ō** suddenly.
Irregular: **bon-us** good, **ben-e** well; **mult-us** much, **mult-um** much; **prīmus** first, **prīmum** first(ly).

2 From 3rd declension adjectives, adverbs are usually formed by adding **-ter** to the stem, e.g. **fēlīx** fortunate: **fēlīci-ter** fortunately; **celer** quick: **celeri-ter** quickly. A few 3rd declension adjectives use the accusative neuter singular as an adverb, e.g. **facilis** easy, **facile** easily; so also comparative adverbs, e.g. **fortior** braver, **fortius** more bravely.

3 There are many adverbs which have no corresponding adjectival form, e.g. **diū, quandō? iam, semper**.

4 For the comparison of adverbs, see the grammar section of chapter 25.

NUMERALS

	cardinals			ordinals	
1	ūnus	I	1st	prīmus, -a, -um
2	duo	II	2nd	secundus, -a, -um/alter, -a, -um
3	trēs	III	3rd	tertius, -a, -um
4	quattuor	IV	4th	quārtus, -a, -um
5	quīnque	V	5th	quīntus, -a, -um
6	sex	VI	6th	sextus, -a, -um
7	septem	VII	7th	septimus, -a, -um
8	octō	VIII	8th	octāvus, -a, -um
9	novem	IX	9th	nōnus, -a, -um
10	decem	X	10th	decimus, -a, -um
11	ūndecim	XI		
12	duodecim	XII		
13	tredecim	XIII		
14	quattuordecim	XIV		
15	quīndecim	XV		
16	sēdecim	XVI		
17	septendecim	XVII		
18	duodēvīgintī	XVIII		
19	ūndēvīgintī	XIX		
20	vīgintī	XX	20th	vīcēsimus, -a, -um
30	trīgintā	XXX		
40	quadrāgintā	XL		
50	quīnquāgintā	L		
100	centum	C	100th	centēsimus, -a, -um
200	ducentī, -ae, -a	CC		
300	trecentī, -ae, -a	CCC		
400	quadringentī, -ae, -a	CCCC		
1,000	mīlle	M	1,000th	mīllēsimus, -a, -um
2,000	duo mīlia			

Note

The numbers 4–100 do not decline; 200–900 decline like **bonī, -ae, -a.**

mīlle does not decline; **mīlia** is a 3rd declension noun, so:

mīlle passūs = 1,000 paces (a mile)
duo mīlia passuum = 2,000 (of) paces (2 miles)

Declension of **ūnus, duo, trēs**

	m.	*f.*	*n.*	*m.*	*f.*	*n.*	*m.*	*f.*	*n.*
nom.	ūnus	ūna	ūnum	duo	duae	duo	trēs	trēs	tria
gen.	ūnīus	ūnīus	ūnīus	duōrum	duārum	duōrum	trium	trium	trium
dat.	ūnī	ūnī	ūnī	duōbus	duābus	duōbus	tribus	tribus	tribus
acc.	ūnum	ūnam	ūnum	duōs	duās	duo	trēs	trēs	tria
abl.	ūnō	ūnā	ūnō	duōbus	duābus	duōbus	tribus	tribus	tribus

PRONOUNS

singular

					Possessive adjectives:
nom.	ego (I)	tū (you)			
gen.	meī	tuī	suī		meus, -a, -um (my)
dat.	mihi	tibi	sibi		tuus, -a, -um (your)
acc.	mē	tē	sē (himself, herself)		suus, -a, -um (his own)
abl.	mē	tē	sē		

plural

nom.	nōs (we)	vōs (you)		noster, nostra, nostrum (our)		
gen.	nostrum, nostrī	vestrum, vestrī	suī	vester, vestra, vestrum (your)		
dat.	nōbīs	vōbīs	sibi	suus, -a, -um (their own)		
acc.	nōs	vōs	sē (themselves)	All decline like **bonus, -a, -um,**		
abl.	nōbīs	vōbīs	sē	but the vocative of **meus** is **mī**		

singular

	m.	*f.*	*n.*	*m.*	*f.*	*n.*	*m.*	*f.*	*n.*
nom.	hic	haec	hoc (this)	ille	illa	illud (that)	is	ea	id (he, she, it;
gen.	huius	huius	huius	illīus	illīus	illīus	eius	eius	eius
dat.	huic	huic	huic	illī	illī	illī	eī	eī	eī
acc.	hunc	hanc	hoc	illum	illam	illud	eum	eam	id that)
abl.	hōc	hāc	hōc	illō	illā	illō	eō	eā	eō

plural

	m.	*f.*	*n.*	*m.*	*f.*	*n.*	*m.*	*f.*	*n.*
nom.	hī	hae	haec	illī	illae	illa	eī	eae	ea
gen.	hōrum	hārum	hōrum	illōrum	illārum	illōrum	eōrum	eārum	eōrum
dat.	hīs	hīs	hīs	illīs	illīs	illīs	eīs	eīs	eīs
acc.	hōs	hās	haec	illōs	illās	illa	eōs	eās	ea
abl.	hīs	hīs	hīs	illīs	illīs	illīs	eīs	eīs	eīs

singular   relative pronoun

	m.	*f.*	*n.*	*m.*	*f.*	*n.*	*m.*	*f.*	*n.*
nom.	ipse	ipsa	ipsum (self)	īdem	eadem	idem (the same)	quī	quae	quod (who, which)
gen.	ipsīus	ipsīus	ipsīus	eiusdem	eiusdem	eiusdem	cuius	cuius	cuius
dat.	ipsī	ipsī	ipsī	eīdem	eīdem	eīdem	cui	cui	cui
acc.	ipsum	ipsam	ipsum	eundem	eandem	idem	quem	quam	quod
abl.	ipsō	ipsā	ipsō	eōdem	eādem	eōdem	quō	quā	quō

plural

	m.	*f.*	*n.*	*m.*	*f.*	*n.*	*m.*	*f.*	*n.*
nom.	ipsī	ipsae	ipsa	eīdem	eaedem	eadem	quī	quae	quae
gen.	ipsōrum	ipsārum	ipsōrum	eōrundem	eārundem	eōrundem	quōrum	quārum	quōrum
dat.	ipsīs	ipsīs	ipsīs	eīsdem	eīsdem	eīsdem	quibus	quibus	quibus
acc.	ipsōs	ipsās	ipsa	eōsdem	eāsdem	eadem	quōs	quās	quae
abl.	ipsīs	ipsīs	ipsīs	eīsdem	eīsdem	eīsdem	quibus	quibus	quibus

quīdam (a certain, a) declines like the relative pronoun with the suffix **-dam**:

nom.	quīdam	quaedam	quoddam
acc.	quendam	quandam	quoddam etc.

The interrogative pronoun **quis?** (who? what?):

nom.	quis?	quis?	quid?
acc.	quem?	quam?	quid? (the rest exactly like the relative pronoun)

The interrogative adjective **quī?** (which? what?):

nom.	quī?	quae?	quod? (exactly like the relative pronoun)

The indefinite pronoun **aliquis** (someone, something) declines like **quis?** with the prefix **ali-**:

nom.	aliquis	aliquis	aliquid etc.

quisquam, quicquam (anyone, anything, after a negative) declines like **quis** with the suffix **-quam**:

nom.	quisquam	quisquam	quicquam

VERBS

Active

	1st conjugation	*2nd conjugation*	*3rd conjugation*	*3rd conjugation* -**iō**	*4th conjugation*
	stems in -**a**	stems in -**e**	stems in consonants		stems in -**i**
present					
singular	1 par-ō	mone-ō	reg-ō	capi-ō	audi-ō
	2 parā-s	monē-s	reg-is	capi-s	audī-s
	3 para-t	mone-t	reg-it	capi-t	audi-t
plural	1 parā-mus	monē-mus	reg-imus	capi-mus	audī-mus
	2 parā-tis	monē-tis	reg-itis	capi-tis	audī-tis
	3 para-nt	mone-nt	reg-unt	capi-unt	audi-unt
future					
singular	1 parā-bō	monē-bō	reg-am	capi-am	audi-am
	2 parā-bis	monē-bis	reg-ēs	capi-ēs	audi-ēs
	3 parā-bit	monē-bit	reg-et	capi-et	audi-et
plural	1 parā-bimus	monē-bimus	reg-ēmus	capi-ēmus	audi-ēmus
	2 parā-bitis	monē-bitis	reg-ētis	capi-ētis	audi-ētis
	3 parā-bunt	monē-bunt	reg-ent	capi-ent	audi-ent
imperfect					
singular	1 parā-bam	monē-bam	regē-bam	capiē-bam	audiē-bam
	2 parā-bās	monē-bās	regē-bās	capiē-bās	audiē-bās
	3 parā-bat	monē-bat	regē-bat	capiē-bat	audiē-bat
plural	1 parā-bamus	monē-bāmus	regē-bāmus	capiē-bāmus	audiē-bāmus
	2 parā-bātis	monē-bātis	regē-bātis	capiē-bātis	audiē-bātis
	3 parā-bant	monē-bant	regē-bant	capiē-bant	audiē-bant
perfect					
singular	1 parāv-ī	monu-ī	rēx-ī	cēp-ī	audīv-ī
	2 parāv-istī	monu-istī	rēx-istī	cēp-istī	audīv-istī
	3 parāv-it	monu-it	rēx-it	cēp-it	audīv-it
plural	1 parāv-imus	monu-imus	rēx-imus	cēp-imus	audīv-imus
	2 parāv-istis	monu-istis	rēx-istis	cēp-istis	audīv-istis
	3 parāv-ērunt	monu-ērunt	rēx-ērunt	cēp-ērunt	audīv-ērunt
future perfect					
singular	1 parāv-erō	monu-erō	rēx-erō	cēp-erō	audīv-erō
	2 parāv-eris	monu-eris	rēx-eris	cēp-eris	audīv-eris
	3 parāv-erit	monu-erit	rēx-erit	cēp-erit	audīv-erit
plural	1 parāv-erimus	monu-erimus	rēx-erimus	cēp-erimus	audīv-erimus
	2 parāv-eritis	monu-eritis	rēx-eritis	cēp-eritis	audīv-eritis
	3 parāv-erint	monu-erint	rēx-erint	cēp-erint	audīv-erint
pluperfect					
singular	1 parāv-eram	monu-eram	rēx-eram	cēp-eram	audīv-eram
	2 parāv-erās	monu-erās	rēx-erās	cēp-erās	audīv-erās
	3 parāv-erat	monu-erat	rēx-erat	cēp-erat	audīv-erat
plural	1 parāv-erāmus	monu-erāmus	rēx-erāmus	cēp-erāmus	audīv-erāmus
	2 parāv-erātis	monu-erātis	rēx-erātis	cēp-erātis	audīv-erātis
	3 parāv-erant	monu-erant	rēx-erant	cēp-erant	audīv-erant
Infinitive	parā-re	monē-re	reg-ere	cap-ere	audī-re

Imperative

singular	parā	monē	reg-e	cap-e	audī
plural	parā-te	monē-te	reg-ite	cap-ite	audī-te

Passive

	1st conjugation	2nd conjugation	3rd conjugation	3rd conjugation -**iō**	4th conjugation
	stems in **-a**	stems in **-e**	stems in consonants		stems in **-i**

present

		1st conjugation	2nd conjugation	3rd conjugation	3rd conjugation -iō	4th conjugation
singular	1	par-or	mone-or	reg-or	capi-or	audi-or
	2	parā-ris	monē-ris	reg-eris	cap-eris	audī-ris
	3	parā-tur	monē-tur	reg-itur	cap-itur	audī-tur
plural	1	parā-mur	monē-mur	reg-imur	cap-imur	audī-mur
	2	parā-minī	monē-minī	reg-iminī	cap-iminī	audī-minī
	3	para-ntur	mone-ntur	reg-untur	capi-untur	audi-untur

future

		1st conjugation	2nd conjugation	3rd conjugation	3rd conjugation -iō	4th conjugation
singular	1	parā-bor	monē-bor	reg-ar	capi-ar	audi-ar
	2	parā-beris	monē-beris	reg-ēris	capi-ēris	audi-ēris
	3	parā-bitur	monē-bitur	reg-ētur	capi-ētur	audi-ētur
plural	1	parā-bimur	monē-bimur	reg-ēmur	capi-ēmur	audi-ēmur
	2	parā-biminī	monē-biminī	reg-ēminī	capi-ēminī	audi-ēminī
	3	parā-buntur	monē-buntur	reg-entur	capi-entur	audi-entur

imperfect

		1st conjugation	2nd conjugation	3rd conjugation	3rd conjugation -iō	4th conjugation
singular	1	parā-bar	monē-bar	reg-ēbar	capi-ēbar	audi-ēbar
	2	parā-bāris	monē-bāris	reg-ēbāris	capi-ēbāris	audi-ēbāris
	3	parā-bātur	monē-bātur	reg-ēbātur	capi-ēbātur	audi-ēbātur
plural	1	parā-bāmur	monē-bāmur	reg-ēbāmur	capi-ēbāmur	audi-ēbāmur
	2	parā-bāminī	monē-bāminī	reg-ēbāminī	capi-ēbāminī	audi-ēbāminī
	3	parā-bantur	monē-bantur	reg-ēbantur	capi-ēbantur	audi-ēbantur

perfect

		1st conjugation	2nd conjugation	3rd conjugation	3rd conjugation -iō	4th conjugation
singular	1	parātus sum	monitus sum	rēctus sum	captus sum	audītus sum
	2	parātus es	etc.	etc.	etc.	etc.
	3	parātus est				
plural	1	parātī sumus				
	2	parātī estis				
	3	parātī sunt				

future perfect

		1st conjugation	2nd conjugation	3rd conjugation	3rd conjugation -iō	4th conjugation
singular	1	parātus erō	monitus erō	rēctus erō	captus erō	audītus erō
	2	parātus eris	etc.	etc.	etc.	etc.
	3	parātus erit				
plural	1	parātī erimus				
	2	parātī eritis				
	3	parātī erunt				

pluperfect

		1st conjugation	2nd conjugation	3rd conjugation	3rd conjugation -iō	4th conjugation
singular	1	parātus eram	monitus eram	rēctus eram	captus eram	audītus eram
	2	parātus erās	etc.	etc.	etc.	etc.
	3	parātus erat				
plural	1	parātī erāmus				
	2	parātī erātis				
	3	parātī erant				

Participles

present active

	parāns, parantis *preparing*	monēns, monentis *warning*	regēns, regentis *ruling*	audiēns, audientis *hearing*	capiēns, capientis *taking*

perfect passive

	parātus, -a, -um *having been prepared*	monitus, -a, -um *having been warned*	rēctus, -a, -um *having been ruled*	audītus, -a, -um *having been heard*	captus, -a, -um *having been taken*

Irregular verbs

	sum: infinitive **esse** I am	**possum**: infinitive **posse** (**pot + sum**) I am able	**eō**: infinitive **īre** (stem **i-**) I go
present			
singular	1 sum	possum	eō
	2 es	potes	īs
	3 est	potest	it
plural	1 sumus	possumus	īmus
	2 estis	potestis	ītis
	3 sunt	possunt	eunt
future			
singular	1 erō	pot-erō	ī-bō
	2 eris	pot-eris	ī-bis
	3 erit	pot-erit	ī-bit
plural	1 erimus	pot-erimus	ī-bimus
	2 eritis	pot-eritis	ī-bitis
	3 erunt	pot-erunt	ī-bunt
imperfect			
singular	1 eram	pot-eram	ī-bam
	2 erās	pot-erās	ī-bās
	3 erat	pot-erat	ī-bat
plural	1 erāmus	pot-erāmus	ī-bāmus
	2 erātis	pot-erātis	ī-bātis
	3 erant	pot-erant	ī-bant
perfect stem	**fu-**	**potu-**	**i-**
singular	1 fu-ī	potu-ī	i-ī
	2 fu-istī	potu-istī	īstī
	3 fu-it	potu-it	i-it
plural	1 fu-imus	potu-imus	i-imus
	2 fu-istis	potu-istis	īstis
	3 fu-ērunt	potu-ērunt	i-ērunt
future perfect	fu-erō etc.	potu-erō etc.	i-erō etc.
pluperfect	fu-eram etc.	potu-eram etc.	i-eram etc.
imperatives *singular*	es, estō		ī
plural	este		īte
present participle	–	–	iēns, euntis

volō, velle, voluī	I wish, I am willing			
nōlō, nōlle, nōluī	I am unwilling, I refuse			
mālō, mālle, māluī	I prefer			
ferō, ferre, tulī, lātum	I carry, bear			

present				*active*	*passive*
singular	1 volō	nōlō	mālō	ferō	feror
	2 vīs	nōn vīs	māvīs	fers	ferris
	3 vult	nōn vult	māvult	fert	fertur
plural	1 volumus	nōlumus	mālumus	ferimus	ferimur
	2 vultis	nōn vultis	māvultis	fertis	feriminī
	3 volunt	nōlunt	mālunt	ferunt	feruntur
future					
singular	1 volam	nōlam	mālam	feram	ferar
	2 volēs	nōlēs	mālēs	ferēs	ferēris
	3 volet etc.	nōlet etc.	mālet etc.	feret etc.	ferētur etc.
imperfect	volēbam etc.	nōlēbam etc.	mālēbam etc.	ferēbam etc.	ferēbar etc.
perfect	voluī etc.	nōluī etc.	māluī etc.	tulī etc.	lātus sum etc.
future perfect	voluerō etc.	nōluerō etc.	māluerō etc.	tulerō etc.	lātus erō etc.
pluperfect	volueram etc.	nōlueram etc.	mālueram etc.	tuleram etc.	lātus eram etc.
imperatives	–	nōlī	–	fer	ferre
	–	nōlīte	–	ferte	feriminī
infinitive	velle	nōlle	mālle	ferre	ferrī
participle	volēns	nōlēns	–	ferēns	lātus, -a, -um
	volentis	nōlentis	–	ferentis	

Principal parts of verbs

Regular verbs of 1st, 2nd and 4th conjugations

	present	*infinitive*	*perfect*	*supine*
1st	parō	parāre	parāvī	parātum
2nd	moneō	monēre	monuī	monitum
4th	audiō	audīre	audīvī	audītum

The following are irregular:

1st conjugation

dō, dare, dedī, datum	I give
stō, stāre, stetī, statum	I stand
iuvō, iuvāre, iūvī, iūtum	I help
lavō, lavāre, lāvī, lautum	I wash

2nd conjugation

ardeō, ardēre, arsī, arsum	I burn, am on fire
augeō, augēre, auxī, auctum	I increase
doceō, docēre, docuī, doctum	I teach
faveō, favēre, fāvī, fautum + dat.	I favor
fleō, flēre, flēvī, flētum	I weep
iubeō, iubēre, iussī, iussum	I order
maneō, manēre, mānsī, mānsum	I stay, remain
moveō, movēre, mōvī, mōtum	I move
persuādeō, persuādēre, persuāsī, persuāsum + dat.	I persuade
respondeō, respondēre, respondī, respōnsum	I answer
rīdeō, rīdēre, rīsī, rīsum	I laugh
sedeō, sedēre, sēdī, sessum	I sit
teneō, tenēre, tenuī, tentum	I hold
videō, vidēre, vīdī, vīsum	I see

4th conjugation

aperiō, aperīre, aperuī, apertum	I open
veniō, venīre, vēnī, ventum	I come

3rd conjugation verbs, arranged by type

1a Perfect **-sī**, supine **-tum** (see chapter 17)

dīcō, dīcere, dīxī, dictum	I say, tell
dūcō, ducere, dūxī, ductum	I lead
gerō, gerere, gessī, gestum	I carry, wear
regō, regere, rēxī, rēctum	I rule
scrībō, scrībere, scrīpsī, scrīptum	I write
surgō*, surgere, surrēxī, surrēctum	I rise, get up (surrigo)
trahō*, trahere, trāxī, tractum	I drag (tragho)
vehō*, vehere, vēxī, vectum	I carry (vegho)
vīvō*, vīvere, vīxī, vīctum	I live (vigvo)

1b Perfect **-sī**, supine **-sum** (see chapter 17)

cēdō, cēdere, cessī, cessum	I yield ('go' in compounds)
claudō, claudere, clausī, clausum	I shut
ēvādō, ēvādere, ēvāsī, ēvāsum	I escape
lūdō, lūdere, lūsī, lūsum	I play
mittō, mittere, mīsī, missum	I send

Notes

1 verbs marked *: the forms in brackets are the original form of the verb.

2 regō, surgō, mittō lengthen the vowel of the stem in the perfect.

3 Compound verbs usually form the perfect in the same way as the simple verb, e.g.

prōcēdō, prōcēdere, prōcessī, prōcessum

remittō, remittere, remīsī, remissum

2a Perfect stem the same as the present, supine **-tum** (see chapter 18)

cōnstituō, cōnstituere, cōnstituī, cōnstitūtum	I decide
contendō, contendere, contendī, contentum	I march, hasten
induō, induere, induī, indūtum	I put on
solvō, solvere, solvī, solūtum	I loosen

2b Perfect stem the same as the present, supine **-sum** (see chapter 18)

accendō, accendere, accendī, accēnsum	I light (a fire)
ascendō, ascendere, ascendī, ascēnsum	I climb
dēscendō, dēscendere, dēscendī, dēscēnsum	I climb down
dēfendō, dēfendere, dēfendī, dēfēnsum	I defend

2c Perfect stem the same as the present but no supine:

bibō, bibere, bibī	I drink
vīsō, vīsere, vīsī	I go to see

3 Verbs lengthening stem vowel in the perfect, supine **-tum** (see chapter 19)

agō, agere, ēgī, actum	I do, I drive
cōgō, cōgere, coēgī, coāctum	I drive together, I compel
emō, emere, ēmī, ēmptum	I buy
legō, legere, lēgī, lēctum	I read, I gather
frangō*, frangere, frēgī, frāctum	I break
relinquō*, relinquere, relīquī, relictum	I leave
rumpō*, rumpere, rūpī, ruptum	I burst open
vincō*, vincere, vīcī, victum	I conquer

NB *these verbs insert **n** (**m** before **p**) in the present, which is dropped in perfect and supine, e.g. **fra-n-gō**, original stem **fragō**, hence **frēgī, frāctum**.

4a Verbs with reduplicated perfect, supine **-tum** (see chapter 20)

addō, addere, addidī, additum	I add (so all compounds of **dō**)
canō, canere, cecinī, cantum	I sing

Note also 1st conjugation:

dō, dare, dedī, datum	I give
stō, stāre, stetī, statum	I stand
instō, instāre, institī, instatum	I press hard on

4b Verbs with reduplicated perfect, supine **-sum** (see chapter 20)

cadō, cadere, cecidī, casum	I fall
currō, currere, cucurrī, cursum	I run
pellō, pellere, pepulī, pulsum	I drive

Note that compounds of **cadō**, **currō** and **pellō** do not have reduplicated perfects, e.g.

expellō, expellere, expulī, expulsum	I drive out
incidō, incidere, incidī, incāsum	I fall down
occurrō, occurrere, occurrī, occursum	I run to meet, meet

5 Verbs forming perfect **-vī/-uī** (see chapter 21)

arcessō, arcessere, arcessīvī, arcessītum	I summon
colō, colere, coluī, cultum	I cultivate
petō, petere, petīvī, petītum	I seek
pōnō, pōnere, posuī, positum	I place
quaerō, quaerere, quaesīvī, quaesītum	I ask, seek
sinō, sinere, sīvī, situm	I allow
dēsinō, dēsinere, dēsiī, dēsitum	I cease

Note also 4th conjugation:

aperiō, aperīre, aperuī, apertum	I open

6 Inceptive verbs (see chapter 22)

cognōscō, cognōscere, cognōvī, cognitum	I get to know, learn
crēscō, crēscere, crēvī, crētum	I grow
nōscō, nōscere, nōvī, nōtum	I get to know
quiēscō, quiēscere, quiēvī, quiētum	I rest

7 3rd conjugation **-iō**

capiō, capere, cēpī, captum	I take
cupiō, cupere, cupīvī, cupītum	I desire
faciō, facere, fēcī, factum	I make, do
fugiō, fugere, fūgī, fugitum	I flee
iaciō, iacere, iēcī, iactum	I throw
rapiō, rapere, rapuī, raptum	I seize
(īn)spiciō, (īn)spicere, (īn)spexi, (īn)spectum	I look at

PREPOSITIONS

The following take the accusative:

ad	to, towards
ante	before
circum	around
contrā	against
extrā	outside
in	into, onto
inter	among
per	through
post	after, behind
prope	near
propter	on account of
super	above
trāns	across

The following take the ablative:

ā/ab	from
cum	with
dē	down from; about
ē/ex	out of
in	in, on
prō	in front of, on behalf of
sine	without
sub	under

CONJUNCTIONS

Coordinating

atque	and
aut	or
aut...aut	either...or
enim*	for
ergō	and so
et	and
et...et	both...and
igitur*	therefore, and so
itaque	and so
nam	for
nec/neque	and not, nor
nec/neque...nec/neque	neither...nor
-que	and
sed	but
tamen*	but, however

Subordinating

cum	when
dum	while
nisi	unless
quamquam	although
quod	because
sī	if
ubi	when
ut	as

*these come second word in their sentence

Vocabulary — Latin – English

The numbers after the words indicate the chapter vocabularies in which the words occur; those with no number have not been learned.
Principal parts of all verbs are given except for regular verbs of the 1st conjugation, which are listed with infinitive only.

ā/ab + abl. (7) from; by
abhinc ago
absum, abesse, āfuī + abl. (18) I am away from, I am absent
ac/atque and
accēdō, accēdere, accessī, accessum (4) I approach
accendō, accendere, accendī, accēnsum (27) I set fire to
accidit, accidere, accidit (26) it happens
accipiō, accipere, accēpī, acceptum (9) I receive
accurrō, accurrere, accurrī, accursum I run to
ad + acc. (3) towards, to
addō, addere, addidī, additum I add
addūcō, addūcere, addūxī, adductum I lead to; I influence
adhūc (18) still
adiuvō, adiuvāre, adiūvī, adiūtum (33) I help
administrō, administrāre (33) I manage, administer
admīrātiō, admīrātiōnis, f. (16) wonder
adoptō, adoptāre I adopt
adsum, adesse, adfuī (4) I am present
adveniō, advenīre, advēnī, adventum (5) I arrive
adventus, adventūs, m. (29) arrival
adversus, -a, -um (32) facing, contrary, against
aedēs, aedium, f. pl. (21) house
aedificium, -ī, n. (19) building
aedificō, aedificāre (11) I build
aeger, aegra, aegrum (23) sick, ill
aegrē with difficulty
aequus, -a, -um (30) equal, fair
afficiō, afficere, affēcī, affectum I affect
affīgō, affīgere, affīxī, affīxum I affix
age! come on!
ager, agrī, m. (3) field
agō, agere, ēgī, actum (19) I drive; I do, manage
agora, -ae, f. agora, city centre
aliquis, aliquid (21) someone, something
alius, alia, aliud (5) other, another
  aliī ... aliī some ... others
alter, altera, alterum (29) one or the other (of two); second
altus, -a, -um (19) high, deep
ambulō, ambulāre (1) I walk
amīcus, -ī, m. (4) friend
amīcus, -a, -um friendly
amō, amāre (12) I love
amor, amōris, m. (12) love
an? (29) or?

animus, -ī, m. (12) mind
  in animō habeō I have in mind, intend
annus, -ī, m. (18) year
ante + acc. (12) before
anteā (adv.) before
antīquus, -a, -um (30) old, ancient
ānxietās, ānxietātis, f. (23) anxiety
ānxius, -a, -um (3) anxious
aperiō, aperīre, aperuī, apertum (19) I open
apertus, -a, -um (19) open
appellō, appellāre (20) I call (by name)
aqua, -ae, f. (2) water
arbor, arboris, f. (13) tree
arcessō, arcessere, arcessīvī, arcessītum (30) I summon
ardeō, ardēre, arsī, arsum (26) I am on fire
argentum, -ī, n. (28) silver, money
arithmētica, -ae, f. arithmetic
arma, armōrum, n. pl. (11) arms, weapons
armātus, -a, -um (26) armed
ascendō, ascendere, ascendī, ascēnsum (3) I climb
asinus, -ī, m. ass
atque (32) and
ātrium, -ī, n. (21) hall
attendō, attendere, attendī, attentum I attend
attentē attentively
attonitus, -a, -um astonished
audiō, audīre, audīvī, audītum (3) I hear
audītor, audītōris, m. listener, audience
auferō, auferre, abstulī, ablātum I carry away
augeō, augēre, auxī, auctum (27) I increase
aula, -ae, f. courtyard
aura, -ae, f. (13) breeze, air
aut ... aut (12) either ... or
auxilium, -ī, n. (15) help
avis, avis, f. bird

balnea, -ōrum, n. pl. (23) baths
bellum, -ī, n. (11) war
bene (8) well
benignus, -a, -um (27) kind
bibō, bibere, bibī (9) I drink
bona, -ōrum, n. pl. (32) goods
bonus, -a, -um (5) good
brevis, breve (25) short

cadō, cadere, cecidī, cāsum (3) I fall
caelum, -ī, n. (10) sky, heaven
campus, -ī, m. (25) field, plain
candidātus, -ī, m. (17) candidate
candidus, -a, -um (17) white
canis, canis, c. (7) dog

canō, canere, cecinī, cantum (14) I sing
capiō, capere, cēpī, captum (7) I take
capsula, -ae, f. box, satchel
caput, capitis, n. (26) head
carmen, carminis, n. (14) song
cārus, -a, -um (7) dear
casa, -ae, f. (1) house, cottage
castra, castrōrum, n. pl. (11) camp
cāsus, -ūs, m. (22) mishap, misfortune
caupōna, -ae, f. inn
causa, -ae, f. (26) cause, reason
cautus, -a, -um (33) cautious
caveō, cavēre, cāvī, cautum (24) I beware
celebrō, celebrāre I celebrate
celer, celeris quick
celeritās, celeritātis, f. (23) speed
celeriter (6) quickly
cēlō, cēlāre I hide
cēna, -ae, f. (1) dinner
cēnō, cēnāre (1) I dine
centum a hundred
centuriō, centuriōnis, m. (14) centurion
certē certainly
certus, -a, -um (33) certain; resolved
   aliquem certiōrem faciō (32) I inform someone
cessō, cessāre I idle, linger
cēterī, cēterae, cētera (6) the others, the rest
chorus, -ī, m. (30) chorus
cibus, -ī, m. (3) food
circum + acc. (8) round
circumspectō, circumspectāre I look round
circumstō, -stāre, -stetī, -statum I stand round
circumveniō, -venīre, -vēnī, -ventum (15) I surround
circumvolō, circumvolāre I fly round
cīvīlis, cīvīle (27) of citizens, civil
cīvis, cīvis, c. (15) citizen
clam (32) secretly
clāmō, clāmāre (5) I shout
clāmor, clāmōris, m. (10) shout
clārus, -a, -um (21) clear, bright, famous
claudō, claudere, clausī, clausum (19) I shut
cliēns, clientis, m. (24) client, dependant
coepī, coepisse I began
cōgitō, cōgitāre I think, reflect
cognōscō, cognōscere, cognōvī, cognitum (11) I get to
   know, learn
cōgō, cōgere, coēgī, coactum (32) I compel
colligō, colligere, collēgī, collēctum (27) I gather, collect
collis, collis, m. (11) hill
colloquium, -ī, n. conversation, talk
collum, -ī, n. neck
colō, colere, coluī, cultum (13) I till; I worship
colōnus, -ī, m. (3) farmer
comes, comitis, c. (7) companion
cōmis, cōme friendly
comitia, -ōrum, n. pl. elections

commendō, commendāre I introduce, commend
committō, committere, commīsī, commissum (33) I
   entrust
commōtus, -a, -um (12) moved
commoveō, commovēre, commōvī, commōtum I move
   deeply
comparō, comparāre (32) I acquire, get
compōnō, compōnere, composuī, compositum I put
   together, compose
conclāmō, conclāmāre I shout aloud
concurrō, concurrere, concurrī, concursum I run
   together
condō, condere, condidī, conditum (29) I found
condūcō, condūcere, condūxī, conductum I hire
cōnfectus, -a, -um (19) finished
cōnficiō, cōnficere, cōnfēcī, cōnfectum (21) I finish
cōnfīdō, cōnfīdere, cōnfīsus + dat. (29) I trust
coniciō, conicere, coniēcī, coniectum (8) I hurl
coniungō, coniungere, coniūnxī, coniūnctum I join
   together
coniūrātus, -ī, m. conspirator
cōnscendō, cōnscendere, cōnscendī, cōnscēnsum (9) I
   board (a ship)
cōnsilium, -ī, n. (11) plan
cōnsistō, cōnsistere, cōnstitī, cōnstitum (32) I halt, stand
   still
cōnsōlātiō, cōnsōlātiōnis, f. consolation, comfort
cōnspectus, cōnspectūs, m. (24) sight, view
cōnspiciō, cōnspicere, cōnspexī, cōnspectum (18) I catch
   sight of
cōnstituō, cōnstituere, cōnstituī, cōnstitūtum (6) I decide
cōnsul, cōnsulis, m. (15) consul
cōnsūmō, cōnsūmere, cōnsūmpsī, cōnsūmptum I
   consume, eat
contendō, contendere, contendī, contentum (14) I walk,
   march
contentus, -a, -um (22) content
continuō (19) immediately
conveniō, convenīre, convēnī, conventum (9) I come
   together, meet
conventus, -ūs, m. meeting
convocō, convocāre (7) I call together
cōpiae, -ārum, f. pl. (32) forces
corōna, -ae, f. crown, garland
corpus, corporis, n. body
corripiō, corripere, corripuī, correptum (32) I seize, steal
cotīdiē (21) every day
crās (27) tomorrow
crēdō, crēdere, crēdidī, crēditum + dat. (17) I believe,
   trust
crēscō, crēscere, crēvī, crētum (28) I grow, increase
crūdēlis, crūdēle (24) cruel
cubō, cubāre, cubuī, cubitum I lie down
cum + abl. (5) with
cum (conjunction) (17) when
   cum prīmum (28) as soon as

cupiō, cupere, cupīvī, cupītum (6) I desire, want
cūr? (4) why
cūra, -ae, *f.* care
cūrō, cūrāre (4) I care for, look after
currō, currere, cucurrī, cursum (3) I run
currus, -ūs, *m.* (22) chariot
cursus, -ūs, *m.* (22) running; a course
custōdiō, custōdīre, custōdīvī, custōdītum (16) I guard
custōs, custōdis, *m.* (16) guard

dē + abl. (10) down from
dē + abl. (15) about
dea, -ae, *f.* (12) goddess
dēbeō, dēbēre, dēbuī, dēbitum (7) I ought, must
dēcidō, dēcidere, dēcidī I fall down
decimus, -a, -um tenth
dēdō, dēdere, dēdidī, dēditum (15) I give up, surrender
dēfendō, dēfendere, dēfendī, dēfēnsum (7) I defend
dēfēnsor, dēfēnsōris, *m.* defender, protector
deinde (17) then, next
dēlectō, dēlectāre (30) I please, delight
dēnārius, dēnāriī, *m.* a penny
dēnique (24) finally, lastly
dēpōnō, dēpōnere, dēposuī, dēpositum (13) I put down
dēscendō, dēscendere, dēscendī, dēscēnsum I descend, come down
dēserō, dēserere, dēseruī, dēsertum I desert
dēsertus, -a, -um deserted
dēsistō, dēsistere, dēstitī, destitum I cease from
dēspērō, dēspērāre (12) I despair
deus, -ī, *m.* (12) god
dēvōrō, dēvōrāre I swallow down, devour
dexter, dextra, dextrum (28) right
  dextrā (manū) (28) on the right (hand)
dī immortālēs! immortal gods!
dīcō, dīcere, dīxī, dictum (5) I say
dictātor, dictātōris, *m.* (15) dictator
dictō, dictāre I dictate
diēs, diēī, *m.* (18) day
difficilis, difficile (19) difficult
diffugiō, diffugere, diffūgī I flee away
dignus, -a, -um + abl. (16) worthy (of)
dīligenter (6) carefully, hard
dīligentia, -ae, *f.* (25) care, diligence
dīmittō, dīmittere, dīmīsī, dīmissum (6) I send away, dismiss
discēdō, discēdere, discessī, discessum (17) I go away, depart
discipulus, -ī, *m.* (20) pupil
discō, discere, didicī (18) I learn
disserō, disserere, disseruī, dissertum (31) I discuss
diū (4) for a long time
diūtius for a longer time, longer
dīves, dīvitis (30) rich
dīvidō, dīvidere, dīvīsī, dīvīsum (32) I divide
dīvīnus, -a, -um (13) divine

dīvitiae, -ārum, *f. pl.* (17) riches
dō, dare, <u>dedī</u>, datum (5) I give
doceō, docēre, docuī, doctum (6) I teach
doctor, doctōris, *m.* teacher
doctus, -a, -um (29) learned
dolor, dolōris, *m.* (33) pain, grief
domicilium, -ī, *n.* lodging
domina, -ae, *f.* (13) mistress
dominus, -ī, *m.* (21) master
domum (6) (to) home
domus, domūs, *f.* home
dōnum, -ī, *n.* (30) gift
dormiō, dormīre, dormīvī, dormītum (4) I sleep
dubius, -a, -um (30) doubtful
  sine dubiō (30) without doubt
dūcō, dūcere, dūxī, ductum (3) I lead; I draw (water)
dulcis, dulce (29) sweet
dum (11) while
duo, duae, duo (5) two
dux, ducis, *c.* leader

ē/ex + abl. (8) out of, from
eam, eum (3) her, him
eās, eōs (4) them
ēbrius, -a, -um drunk
ecce! look!
edō, ēsse, ēdī, ēsum (28) I eat
efficiō, efficere, effēcī, effectum (17) I effect, do
effugiō, effugere, effūgī, effugitum I flee away, escape
ego (6) I (acc. **mē**)
ēloquentia, -ae, *f.* eloquence
emō, emere, ēmī, ēmptum (5) I buy
enim (17) for
eō, īre, iī, itum (6) I go
eō (adv.) (14) thither, (to) there
epistola, -ae, *f.* (21) letter
eques, equitis, *m.* (31) horseman
equitēs, equitum, *m. pl.* (31) cavalry
equus, -ī, *m.* (9) horse
ergō (27) and so
errō, errāre (11) I wander; I err, am wrong
et (1) and
et...et (15) both...and
etiam (12) also, even
euge! good!
ēvādō, ēvādere, ēvāsī, ēvāsum (16) I escape
ēvertō, ēvertere, ēvertī, ēversum (32) I overturn
ēvigilō, ēvigilāre I wake up
ēvolō, ēvolāre I fly out
excitō, excitāre (13) I rouse, wake up
exemplum, -ī, *n.* (16) example
exeō, exīre, exiī, exitum (6) I go out
exerceō, exercēre, exercuī, exercitum (14) I exercise, train
exercitus, -ūs, *m.* army
exitium, -ī, *n.* (27) destruction

expellō, expellere, expulī, expulsum (31) I drive out
explōrō, explōrāre I explore
expōnō, expōnere, exposuī, expositum I put out; I explain
exspectō, exspectāre (8) I wait for
extrā + acc. (19) outside

fābula, -ae, *f.* (2) story, play
fābulōsus, -a, -um fabulous, from a story
facile (20) easily
facilis, facile (20) easy
facilitās, facilitātis, *f.* (25) ease, facility
faciō, facere, fēcī, factum (5) I do; I make
falsus, -a, -um false
fāma, -ae, *f.* (11) fame, reputation, report
familia, -ae, *f.* (14) family, household
faveō, favēre, fāvī, fautum + dat. (22) I favor, support
fēmina, -ae, *f.* (1) woman
feriō, ferīre (26) I strike
ferō, ferre, tulī, lātum (11) I carry, bear
ferōx, ferōcis (24) fierce
ferrum, -ī, *n.* (32) iron; sword
ferula, -ae, *f.* cane
fessus, -a, -um (1) tired
festīnō, festīnāre (1) I hurry
fīlia, -ae, *f.* (2) daughter
fīliolus, -ī, *m.* (33) little son
fīlius, -ī, *m.* (3) son
fīnis, fīnis, *m.* (31) end
    fīnēs, fīnium *m. pl.* (31) boundaries, territory
fīō, fierī, factus (24) I am made, I become
flamma, -ae, *f.* flame
fleō, flēre, flēvī, flētum (18) I weep
flōs, flōris, *m.* (14) flower
flūmen, flūminis, *n.* (16) river
foedus, foederis, *n.* (16) treaty
fōns, fontis, *m.* spring, fountain
fōrma, -ae, *f.* (13) shape, beauty
fortis, forte (7) brave
fortiter (7) bravely
forum, -ī, *n.* forum, city center
frāctus, -a, -um (22) broken
frangō, frangere, frēgī, frāctum (22) I break
frāter, frātris, *m.* (7) brother
frūmentum, -ī, *n.* (16) grain
frūstrā in vain
fugiō, fugere, fūgī, fugitum (7) I flee
fūnus, fūneris, *n.* funeral
furor, furōris, *m.* madness

gaudeō, gaudēre, gāvīsus sum (9) I rejoice;
    + abl. I rejoice in
gaudium, -ī, *n.* joy
genus, generis, *n.* (24) sort, kind, race
gerō, gerere, gessī, gestum (14) I carry, wear
    mē gerō (30) I behave myself
    rem gerō (30) I conduct a matter

gladius,. -ī, *m.* (26) sword
glōria, -ae, *f.* (14) glory
gradus, -ūs, *m.* (20) step
grātiae, -ārum, *f. pl.* (20) thanks
    grātiās agō + dat. (20) I give thanks
grātulātiō, grātulātiōnis, *f.* congratulations
grātus, -a, -um (29) pleasing; grateful
gravis, grave (17) heavy, grave, serious

habeō, habēre, habuī, habitum (9) I have
habitō, habitāre (10) I inhabit, live
hasta, -ae, *f.* (8) spear
haud (15) not
herī (30) yesterday
hērōs, hērōis, *m.* hero
hīc (8) here
hic, haec, hoc (15) this
hiems, hiemis, *f.* (12) winter
hilaris, hilare (31) cheerful
hodiē (14) today
homō, hominis, *c.* (10) human being, man
honestus, -a, -um (33) honorable
hōra, -ae, *f.* (17) hour
horribilis, horribile horrible
hortus, -ī, *m.* (5) garden
hostis, hostis, *m.* (11) enemy
hūc (8) hither, this way
hūc...illūc (19) this way and that
hūmānus, -a, -um (29) human; humane, kind

iaceō, iacēre, iacuī (5) I lie (down)
iaciō, iacere, iēcī, iactum (7) I throw
iam (4) now, already
iānua, -ae, *f.* (6) door
ibi (12) there
īdem, eadem, idem (31) the same
igitur (17) therefore, and so
ignāvus, -a, -um lazy
ignis, ignis, *m.* (18) fire
ignōscō, ignōscere, ignōvī, ignōtum + dat. I forgive
ignōtus, -a, -um (11) unknown
ille, illa, illud (4) that; he, she, it
illūminō, illūmināre I light up, illuminate
immemor, immemoris forgetful of
immineō, imminēre + dat. (33) I hang over, threaten
immortālis, immortāle (31) immortal
imperātor, imperātōris, *m.* (14) general
imperium, -ī, *n.* (12) order
    imperium Rōmānum (26) the Roman empire
imperō, imperāre + dat. (11) I order
impudēns, impudentis impudent, shameless
in + acc. (2) into, to
in + abl. (5) in, on
incendium, -ī, *n.* fire
incendō, incendere, incendī, incēnsum I set on fire
incertus, -a, -um uncertain

incidō, incidere, incidī, incāsum I fall into
incipiō, incipere, incēpī, inceptum I begin
incolumis, incolume (8) safe
inde (28) thence, from there
induō, induere, induī, indūtum (20) I put on (clothes)
ineō, inīre, iniī, initum (18) I enter, begin
īnfāns, īnfantis, *c*. (33) infant, baby
īnfēlīx, īnfēlīcis (12) unhappy, unlucky
ingēns, ingentis (9) huge
ingeniōsus, -a, -um (21) clever, talented
ingenium, -ī, *n*. (21) character, talents
inimīcus, -ī, *m*. (24) enemy
inquit (3) he/she says
    inquiunt they say
īnscrīptiō, īnscrīptiōnis, *f*. inscription
īnsignis, īnsigne (25) outstanding, distinguished
īnspiciō, īnspicere, īnspexī, īnspectum I look at
īnsula, -ae, *f*. (9) island
īnsum, inesse, īnfuī (23) I am in, I am among
intellegō, intellegere, intellēxī, intellēctum (20) I understand
intentē intently
inter + acc. (9) between, among
interdum from time to time
intersum, interesse, interfuī + dat. (21) I am among, I take part in
intereā (12) meanwhile
intrō, intrāre (1) I go into, enter
inveniō, invenīre, invēnī, inventum (11) I find
invideō, invidēre, invīdī, invīsum + dat. (13) I envy
invītō, invītāre I invite
invītus, -a, -um (19) unwilling
ipse, ipsa, ipsum (15) himself, herself, itself
īra, -ae, *f*. (7) anger
īrātus, -a, -um (2) angry
is, ea, id (14) he, she, it; that
itaque (6) and so, therefore
iter, itineris, *n*. (18) journey
iterum (6) again
iubeō, iubērē, iussī, iussum (6) I order
    valēre iubeō (18) I bid goodbye
iūcundus, -a, -um (29) pleasant, delightful
Iuppiter, Iovis, *m*. (19) Jupiter
iūs, iūris, *n*. (25) right, justice
iuvenis, iuvenis, *m*. (14) young man
iuvō, iuvāre, iūvī, iūtum (2) I help

labor, labōris, *m*. (9) work, suffering
labōriōsus, -a, -um laborious, toilsome
labōrō, labōrāre (1) I work
lacrima, -ae, *f*. (18) tear
laetus, -a, -um (1) happy, joyful
lātus, -a, -um (21) wide, broad
laudō, laudāre (2) I praise
lavō, lavāre, lāvī, lautum (14) I wash
lectus, -ī, *m*. bed, couch

lēgātus, -ī, *m*. (32) deputy, officer, envoy
legiō, legiōnis, *f*. (14) legion
legō, legere, lēgī, lēctum (17) I read
lentē (4) slowly
lēx, lēgis, *f*. (25) law
libenter (29) gladly
liber, librī, *m*. (20) book
līber, lībera, līberum (16) free
līberō, līberāre (16) I free
lībertās, lībertātis, *f*. (31) freedom
licet mihi I am allowed, I may
līmen, līminis, *n*. (30) threshold
littera, litterae, *f*. (6) a letter
    litterae, -ārum, *f. pl.* (25) literature
lītus, lītoris, *n*. (10) shore
locus, locī, *m*. (**loca, locōrum**, *n. pl.*) (14) a place
longē (18) far
longus, -a, -um (18) long
lūceō, lūcēre, lūxī (25) I shine
lūdō, lūdere, lūsī, lūsum (6) I play
lūdus, lūdī, *m*. (4) school, game
    lūdī, -ōrum, *m. pl.* (22) the games
lūgeō, lūgēre, lūxī, luctum I mourn
lūmen, lūminis, *n*. (30) light
lūna, -ae, *f*. (28) moon
lupus, -ī, *m*. wolf
lūx, lūcis, *f*. (13) light

magister, magistrī, *m*. (6) master
magnificē magnificently
magnopere (24) greatly
magnus, -a, um (4) great, big
mālō, mālle, māluī (23) I prefer
malus, -a, -um (5) bad
māne (27) early (in the morning)
maneō, manēre, mānsī, mānsum (3) I stay, remain, await
manus, manūs, *f*. (20) hand; band (of people)
marītus, -ī, *m*. (13) husband
māter, mātris, *f*. (8) mother
mātrōna, -ae, *f*. married woman
maximus, -a, -um (22) very great, greatest
mē (acc.) (6) me
medius, -a, -um (19) middle
memoria, -ae, *f*. memory
mēnsis, mēnsis, *m*. (33) month
merīdiēs, merīdiēī, *m*. (21) midday
meus, -a, -um (6) my
mīles, mīlitis, *m*. (14) soldier
mīlitō, mīlitāre (31) I serve (as a soldier), I campaign
mīlle a thousand
    mīlle passūs a mile
    mīlia, mīlium, *n. pl.* thousands
    mīlia passuum miles
miser, misera, miserum (4) miserable
mittō, mittere, mīsī, missum (3) I send
moenia, moenium, *n. pl.* (15) walls, fortifications

moneō, monēre, monuī, monitum (9) I warn, advise
mōns, montis, *m.* (10) mountain
monumentum, -ī, *n.* monument
mora, -ae, *f.* (23) delay
mors, mortis, *f.* (8) death
mortuus, -a, um (8) dead
mōs, mōris, *m.* (30) custom
   mōs maiōrum (30) the custom of our ancestors
mox (1) soon
mulier, mulieris, *f.* woman
multitūdō, multitūdinis, *f.* (25) multitude, crowd
multus, -a, -um (4) much, many
mūnus, mūneris, *n.* gift; (gladiatorial) show
mūrus, -ī, *m.* (8) wall

nam (3) for
nārrō, nārrāre (2) I tell, narrate
nātus, -ī, *m.* son
nauta, -ae, *m.* (10) sailor
nāvigō, nāvigāre (7) I sail
nāvis, nāvis, *f.* (7) ship
nec/neque (5) nor, and not
nec/neque…nec/neque (6) neither…nor
necesse est it is necessary
neglegō, neglegere, neglēxī, neglēctum I neglect
negōtium, -ī, *n.* (29) business
nēmō, nēminis, *c.* (13) no one
niger, nigra, nigrum black
nimis too much
nimium, -ī, *n.* + gen. (23) too much
nisi (29) unless; except
nōbilis, nōbile (22) famous, noble
nōlō, nōlle, nōluī (15) I am unwilling, I refuse
nōmen, nōminis, *n.* (11) name
   nōmine by name, called
nōn (1) not
nōndum not yet
nōnnūllī, -ae, -a (31) some
nōtus, -a, -um (11) known
novus, -a, -um (9) new
nox, noctis, *f.* (9) night
nūbēs, nūbis, *f.* (28) cloud
nūbō, nūbere, nūpsī, nūptum + dat. (30) I marry
nūgae, -ārum *f. pl.* trifles, nonsense
nūllus, -a, -um (13) no
num? (26) surely not?
numerō, numerāre (24) I count
numerus, -ī, *m.* (17) number
numquam (13) never
nunc (12) now
nūndinae, -ārum, *f. pl.* market day
nūntius, -ī, *m.* (12) message; messenger
nūper (30) lately
nūptiae, -ārum, *f. pl.* (30) wedding
nūptiālis, nūptiāle (30) of a wedding, nuptial

obeō, obīre, obiī, obitum I go to meet, meet; I die
obscūrō, obscūrāre I darken
obses, obsidis, *c.* (16) hostage
obsideō, obsidēre, obsēdī, obsessum I besiege
occīdō, occīdere, occīdī, occīsum (7) I kill
occupātus, -a, -um occupied, busy
occupō, occupāre (32) I seize, occupy
occurrō, occurrere, occurrī, occursum + dat. (11) I meet
oculus, -ī, *m.* (12) eye
offerō, offerre, obtulī, oblātum I offer
officium, -ī, *n.* (31) duty
ōlim once
olīva, -ae, *f.* olive; olive tree
ōmen, ōminis, *n.* omen
omnipotēns, omnipotentis all powerful
omnis, omne (7) all
opprimō, opprimere, oppressī, oppressum (31) I oppress
oppugnō, oppugnāre (7) I attack
optimus, -a, -um (17) very good, best
ōrātiō, ōrātiōnis, *f.* (17) speech
ōrātor, ōrātōris, *m.* (21) speaker, orator
orbis, orbis, *m.* (27) circle, globe
   orbis terrārum (27) the world
ōrdō, ōrdinis, *m.* (24) rank, line, order
ōrō, ōrāre (10) I beg, pray
ostendō, ostendere, ostendī, ostentum (11) I show
ōtiōsus, -a, -um (33) at leisure, idle
ōtium, -ī, *n.* (27) leisure, idleness

paene (19) nearly
parātus, -a, -um (1) prepared, ready
parēns, parentis, *c.* (14) parent
pāreō, pārēre, pāruī, pāritum + dat. (22) I obey
parō, parāre (2) I prepare
pars, partis, *f.* (26) part
partēs, partium, *f. pl.* (32) political party
parvus, -a, -um (9) small
pater, patris, *m.* (7) father
patria, -ae, *f.* (11) fatherland
paucī, -ae, -a (9) few
paulīsper (23) for a little (time)
pauper, pauperis (15) poor
pāx, pācis, *f.* (16) peace
pecūnia, -ae, *f.* (17) money
pellō, pellere, pepulī, pulsum I drive
penātēs, penātium, *m. pl.* household gods
per + acc. (5) through, throughout
perdō, perdere, perdidī, perditum (22) I lose, waste, destroy
perdūcō, perdūcere, perdūxī, perductum I lead, conduct
pereō, perīre, periī, peritum (30) I perish, die
perficiō, perficere, perfēcī, perfectum (12) I carry out, complete
perīculum, -ī, *n.* (10) danger
perlegō, perlegere, perlēgī, perlēctum I read through
perpetuus, -a, -um everlasting, perpetual

persōna, -ae, *f.* character

persuādeō, persuādēre, persuāsī, persuāsum + dat. I persuade

perveniō, pervenīre, pervēnī, perventum (26) I reach

pessimus, -a, -um (17) very bad, worst

petō, petere, petīvī, petītum (12) I ask, seek, pursue

philosophia, -ae, *f.* (27) philosophy

pictūra, -ae, *f.* picture

pictor, pictōris, *m.* painter

placeō, placēre, placuī, placitum + dat. (12) I please
  mihi placet (12) it pleases me to; I decide

plēnus, -a, -um (+ abl.) (27) full (of)

plērīque, plēraeque, plēraque several

plūrimus, -a, -um (22) very many, most

plūs, plūris, *n.* more

poēta, -ae, *m.* (20) poet

pompa, -ae, *f.* procession

pōnō, pōnere, posuī, positum (5) I put, place

populus, -ī, *m.* (14) people

porta, -ae, *f.* (8) gate

portō, portāre (2) I carry

portus, portūs, *m.* (27) port

poscō, poscere, poposcī (16) I demand

possum, posse, potuī (8) I am able, I can

post + acc. (12) after

posteā (14) afterwards

postrīdiē (15) the next day

potēns, potentis (30) powerful

potestās, potestātis, *f.* (27) power

praebeō, praebēre, praebuī, praebitum I offer, give, show

praeficiō, -ficere, -fēcī, -fectum (32) I put x (acc.) in command of y (dat.)

praemium, -ī, *n.* (24) reward, prize

praesidium, -ī, *n.* (16) garrison

praesum, praeesse, praefuī + dat. (32) I am in command of

praetereā (21) moreover

praetereō, praeterīre, praeteriī, praeteritum (24) I pass, go past

praetor, praetōris, *m.* praetor

prīmum (adv.) (10) first

prīmus, -a, -um (6) first

prīnceps, prīncipis, *m.* (7) prince

prō + abl. (26) in front of; on behalf of, for

prōcēdō, prōcēdere, prōcessī, prōcessum (4) I go forward, proceed

procul (15) far from, far off

proelium, -ī, *n.* (15) battle

prōferō, prōferre, prōtulī, prōlātum I bring forward, bring out

prōmittō, prōmittere, prōmīsī, prōmissum (17) I promise

prope + acc. (6) near

propter + acc. (29) because of, on account of

prōspiciō, prōspicere, prōspexī, prōspectum I look out

prōvideō, prōvidēre, prōvīdī, prōvīsum (24) I foresee

proximus, -a, -um nearest, next

prūdēns, prūdentis (27) sensible, wise

prūdentia, -ae, *f.* prudence, good sense

puella, puellae, *f.* (1) girl

puer, puerī, *c.* (3) boy; child

puerīlis, puerīle (25) of boys, childish

pugna, -ae, *f.* (7) fight

pugnō, pugnāre (7) I fight

pulcher, pulchra, pulchrum (13) pretty, beautiful

pulsō, pulsāre I hit, knock

pupa, -ae, *f.* doll

puppis, puppis, *f.* stern

pūrus, -a, -um pure

pyra, -ae, *f.* pyre

quaerō, quaerere, quaesīvī, quaesītum (10) I ask; I look for

quam how (in exclamations); than (24);
  quam + superlative, e.g. **quam celerrimē** = as quickly as possible (25)

quamquam (24) although

quandō? (29) when?

quantus, -a, -um? (26) how great?

-que (8) and

quī, quae, quod (13) who, which

quīdam, quaedam, quoddam (14) a certain, a

quiēscō, quiēscere, quiēvī, quiētum (10) I rest

quis, quid? (5) who, what?

quisquam, quicquam (29) anyone, anything (after a negative)

quō? (22) whither? where to?

quod (4) because

quōmodo? (15) how?

quoque (16) also

rapiō, rapere, rapuī, raptum (22) I snatch, seize, steal

recēdō, recēdere, recessī, recessum I go back, retire

recipiō, recipere, recēpī, receptum (32) I take back
  mē recipiō (32) I retreat

recitō, recitāre (20) I read aloud, recite

rēctē (20) straight, rightly

rēctus, -a, -um (20) straight, right

recurrō, recurrere, recurrī, recursum I run back

reddō, reddere, reddidī, redditum (8) I give back, return

redeō, redīre, rediī, reditum (3) I go back, return

referō, referre, rettulī, relātum (23) I bring back; I report

rēgia, -ae, *f.* palace

rēgīna, -ae, *f.* (11) queen

regō, regere, rēxī, rēctum I rule

relinquō, relinquere, relīquī, relictum (8) I leave behind

reliquus, -a, -um (28) remaining

repellō, repellere, reppulī, repulsum (15) I drive back

rēs, reī, *f.* (21) thing, matter
  rē vērā (21) in truth, really, in fact

resistō, resistere, restitī + dat. (7) I resist

respiciō, respicere, respexī, respectum I look back (at)

respondeō, respondēre, respondī, respōnsum (5) I answer
rēspūblica, reīpūblicae, *f.* (21) public affairs; the republic
retineō, retinēre, retinuī, retentum (23) I hold back
revocō, revocāre I call back
rēx, rēgis, *m.* (7) king
rīdeō, rīdere, rīsī, rīsum (20) I laugh
rogō, rogāre (5) I ask, I ask for
rūmor, rūmōris, *m.* rumour, report
rumpō, rumpere, rūpī, ruptum (16) I burst, break
ruō, ruere, ruī, rutum (27) I rush
rūsticus, -a, um rustic, country

sacer, sacra, sacrum (19) sacred, holy
sacrificium, -ī, *n.* sacrifice
saepe (4) often
saliō, salīre, saluī, saltum I jump
saltus, -ūs, *m.* dancing
salūs, salūtis, *f.* safety; greetings
salūtō, salūtāre (2) I greet
salvē, salvēte! (21) greetings!
sanguis, sanguinis, *m.* blood
satis + gen. (26) enough
saxum, -ī, *n.* (10) rock
scelestus, -a, -um (27) wicked, criminal
schola, -ae, *f.* (20) school, schoolroom; lecture
  scholam habeō (29) I give a lecture
sciō, scīre, scīvī, scītum I know
scrībō, scrībere, scrīpsī, scrīptum (6) I write, I draw
sedeō, sedēre, sēdī, sessum (3) I sit
semper (11) always
senātus, -ūs, *m.* (15) senate
senex, senis, *m.* (14) old man
senior, seniōris (31) older, senior
sentiō, sentīre, sēnsī, sēnsum (30) I feel, realize
sepulcrum, -ī, *n.* tomb
sērō late
servō, servāre (8) I save
sevērus, -a, -um (20) severe
sī (13) if
sīc (9) thus, like that
sīcut (29) just as, like
signum, -ī, *n.* (22) sign, signal, seal
silva, -ae, *f.* (18) wood, forest
sine + abl. (18) without
sinister, sinistra, sinistrum (28) left
  sinistrā (manū) (28) on the left (hand)
sinō, sinere, sīvī, situm (21) I allow
socius, -ī, *m.* companion, ally
sōl, sōlis, *m.* (30) sun
sollicitus, -a, -um (33) anxious
sōlus, -a, -um (8) alone
  nōn sōlum…sed etiam (16) not only…but also
solvō, solvere, solvī, solūtum (28) I loosen, cast off
somnium, -ī, *n.* dream
somnus, -ī, *m.* (11) sleep
sonus, -ī, *m.* (13) sound

sordidus, -a, -um dirty
soror, sorōris, *f.* (21) sister
spectāculum, -ī, *n.* (24) sight, show
spectātor, spectātōris, *m.* (24) spectator
spectō, spectāre (5) I look at
spērō, spērāre (22) I hope
spēs, speī, *f.* (21) hope
squālidus, -a, -um filthy
statim (5) at once
statua, -ae, *f.* (16) statue
stō, stāre, stetī, statum (11) I stand
studeō, studēre, studuī + dat. (18) I study
studium, -ī, *n.* (21) study
stultus, -a, -um foolish
sub + abl. (10) under
subitō (2) suddenly
succurrō, succurrere, succurrī, succursum + dat. (11) I (run to) help
sum, esse, fuī (17) I am
sūmō, sūmere, sūmpsī, sūmptum (25) I take (up); I put on
summus, -a, -um (16) highest; greatest
super + acc. (29) above, over
superbus, -a, -um (24) proud
superō, superāre (17) I overcome
supplicō, supplicāre + dat. (30) I beg, supplicate, pray to
surgō, surgere, surrēxī, surrēctum (4) I rise, get up
suus, -a, -um (14) his, her, their (own)

taberna, -ae, *f.* stall, shop, pub
tablīnum, -ī, *n.* (21) study (the room)
tabula, -ae, *f.* writing tablet
taceō, tacēre, tacuī, tacitum (9) I am silent
tacitus, -a, -um (9) silent
tālis, tāle (22) such
tam (18) so
tamen (17) but, however
tandem (4) at last
tantus, -a, -um (12) so great
tegō, tegere, tēxī, tēctum I cover
tempestās, tempestātis, *f.* storm
templum, -ī, *n.* (11) temple
temptō, temptāre (15) I try, attempt
tempus, temporis, *n.* (18) time
teneō, tenēre, tenuī, tentum (13) I hold
tepidus, -a, -um warm
ter three times
terra, terrae, *f.* (3) earth, land
terreō, terrēre, terruī, territum I terrify
territus, -a, -um (8) terrified, frightened
theātrum, -ī, *n.* (26) theatre
timeō, timēre, timuī (8) I fear, I am afraid
timidus, -a, -um timid
timor, timōris, *m.* (26) fear
toga, -ae, *f.* (15) toga
togātus, -a, -um wearing a toga
tollō, tollere, sustulī, sublātum (10, 30) I raise, lift

tot (indecl.) (32) so many
totiēns (32) so often
tōtus, -a, -um (9) whole
trādō, trādere, trādidī, trāditum (5) I hand over
trahō, trahere, trāxī, tractum I drag
trāns + acc. (15) across
trānseō, trānsīre, trānsiī, trānsitum (18) I cross
trēs, tria (5) three
trīstis, trīste (12) sad
tū (6) you (sing.)
tum then
tumultus, -ūs, *m.* (25) uproar, riot
tunica, -ae, *f.* tunic
turba, -ae, *f.* (22) a crowd
tuus, -a, -um (6) your
tyrannus, -ī, *m.* (26) tyrant

ubi (19) where
ubi (conj.) (4) when
ubīque (19) everywhere
ūllus, -a, -um (27) any
ultimus, -a, -um (26) furthest, last
umbra, -ae, *f.* shadow
umquam (13) ever
unda, -ae, *f.* (10) wave
unde? (23) whence? from where?
undique (23) from all sides
ūniversus, -a, -um all
ūnus, -a, -um (5) one
urbs, urbis, *f.* (7) city
urna, -ae, *f.* water pot
ut (29) as, when
uter, utra, utrum? (29) which (of two)?
  utrum...an? (whether)...or?
uxor, uxōris, *f.* (9) wife

vacuus, -a, -um (19) empty
valdē very
valeō, valēre, valuī, valitum (33) I am strong, I am well
  valēre iubeō I bid goodbye to
vehemēns, vehementis (31) violent

vehō, vehere, vēxī, vectum (24) I carry
vendō, vendere, vendidī, venditum (18) I sell
veniō, venīre, vēnī, ventum (4) I come
ventus, -ī, *m.* (11) wind
Venusīnī, *m.* the people of Venusia
vēr, vēris, *n.* (18) spring
verbum, -ī, *n.* (10) word
versus, versūs, *m.* (20) verse
vertō, vertere, vertī, versum (8) I turn
vērus, -a, -um (17) true
  vēra dīcere (17) I speak the truth
vesper, vesperis, *m.* (22) evening
vestīmenta, -ōrum, *n. pl.* (19) clothes
vestis, vestis, *f.* clothes
vetus, veteris (22) old
vexō, vexāre (27) I worry, I annoy
via, -ae, *f.* (2) road, way
viātor, viātōris, *m.* (28) traveller
victor, victōris, *m.* victor
victōria, -ae, *f.* (24) victory
videō, vidēre, vīdī, vīsum (3) I see
vīgintī twenty
vīlla, -ae, *f.* (32) villa, country house
vincō, vincere, vīcī, victum (7) I conquer
vīnum, -ī, *n.* (11) wine
vir, virī, *m.* (9) man
virgō, virginis, *f.* (16) maiden, virgin
virīlis, virīle (25) manly, of a man
virtūs, virtūtis, *f.* (16) virtue, excellence, courage
vīsō, vīsere, vīsī, vīsum (21) I visit
vīta, -ae, *f.* (29) life
vītō, vītāre I avoid
vīvō, vīvere, vīxī, vīctum (13) I live
vīvus, -a, -um (28) living, alive
vix (10) scarcely
vocō, vocāre (2) I call
volō, velle, voluī (15) I wish, I am willing
volō, volāre (22) I fly
vōx, vōcis, *f.* (13) voice
vulnus, vulneris, *n.* (17) wound
vultus, -ūs, *m.* (20) face, expression

Vocabulary

English – Latin

Regular verbs are given with infinitive only.

about **dē** + abl.
admiration **admīrātiō, admīrātiōnis,** *f.*
affair **rēs, reī,** *f.*
again **iterum**
all **omnis, omne**
alone **sōlus, -a, -um**
and **et, -que**
and so **itaque, igitur**
angry **īrātus, -a, -um**
answer, I **respondeō, respondēre, respondī, respōnsum**
anxious **ānxius, -a, -um**
approach, I **accēdō, accēdere, accessī, accessum (ad)**
arrive, I **adveniō, advenīre, advēnī, adventum**
ask, I **rogō, rogāre**
Athens **Athēnae, -ārum,** *f. pl.*
at last **tandem**
at once **statim**

because **quod**
begin, I **incipiō, incipere, incēpī, inceptum**
better **melior, melius**
big **magnus, -a, -um**
bigger **maior, maius**
board (a ship), I **cōnscendō, cōnscendere, cōnscendī, cōnscēnsum**
book **liber, librī,** *m.*
boy **puer, puerī,** *m.*
bring, I = carry **ferō, ferre, tulī, lātum**
= lead **dūcō, dūcere, dūxī, ductum**
burn, I (= I am on fire) **ardeō, ardēre, arsī, arsum**
but **sed**
by **ā/ab** + abl.

call, I **vocō, vocāre**
can, I **possum, posse, potuī**
captain (of ship) **magister, magistrī,** *m.*
care for, I **cūrō, cūrāre**
carry, I **portō, portāre; ferō, ferre, tulī, lātum**
cast off, I **solvō, solvere, solvī, solūtum**
catch sight of, I **cōnspiciō, cōnspicere, cōnspexī, cōnspectum**
certain, a **quīdam, quaedam, quoddam**
child **puer, puerī,** *c.*
citizen **cīvis, cīvis,** *c.*
civil **cīvīlis, cīvīle**
climb, I **ascendō, ascendere, ascendī, ascēnsum**
come, I **veniō, venīre, vēnī, ventum**
cross, I **trānseō, trānsīre, trānsiī, trānsitum**
crowd **turba, -ae,** *f.*

day **diēs, diēī,** *m.*
every day **cotīdiē**
decide, I **cōnstituō, cōnstituere, cōnstituī, cōnstitūtum**
defend, I **dēfendō, dēfendere, dēfendī, dēfēnsum**
delay **mora, -ae,** *f.*
difficult **difficilis, difficile**
dinner **cēna, -ae,** *f.*
dismiss, I **dīmittō, dīmittere, dīmīsī, dīmissum**
dog **canis, canis,** *c.*
don't! **nōlī, nōlīte!** (+ inf.)
door **iānua, -ae,** *f.*
drag, I **trahō, trahere, trāxī, tractum**
drink, I **bibō, bibere, bibī**

each (of two) **uterque, utraque, utrumque**
easily **facile**
easy **facilis, facile**
eat, I **edō, ēsse, ēdī, ēsum**
enjoy, I **gaudeō, gaudēre** + abl.
every day **cotīdiē**
everything **omnia, omnium,** *n. pl.*
exercise, I **exerceō, exercēre**
expression **vultus, -ūs,** *m.*
eye **oculus, -ī,** *m.*

family **familia, -ae,** *f.*
farmer **colōnus, -ī,** *m.*
father **pater, patris,** *m.*
field **ager, agrī,** *m.*
fifty **quīnquāgintā**
fight, I **pugnō, pugnāre**
find, I **inveniō, invenīre, invēnī, inventum**
fire **ignis, ignis,** *m.*
flee, I **fugiō, fugere, fūgī, fugitum**
for, on behalf of **prō** + abl.
forum **forum, -ī,** *n.*
fountain **fōns, fontis,** *m.*
fourth **quārtus, -a, -um**
freedom **lībertās, lībertātis,** *f.*
friend **amīcus, -ī,** *m.*
full (of) **plēnus, -a, -um** (+ abl.)

garden **hortus, -ī,** *m.*
girl **puella, -ae,** *f.*
give, I **dō, dare, dedī, datum**
glory **glōria, -ae,** *f.*
go in, I **intrō, intrāre**
good **bonus, -a, -um**
very good **optimus, -a, -um**
great **magnus, -a, -um**
greatly **magnopere; valdē**

Greece **Graecia, -ae,** *f.*
greet, I **salūtō, salūtāre**

hand **manus, -ūs,** *f.*
happens, it **accidit, accidere, accidit**
harbor **portus, -ūs,** *m.*
have, I **habeō, habēre**
hear **audiō, audīre**
his/her/their own **suus, -a, -um**
home **domus, -ī,** *f.*
   at home **domī**
   to home **domum**
hope **spēs, speī,** *f.*
hour **hōra, -ae,** *f.*
house **casa, -ae,** *f*; (grand house) **aedēs, aedium,** *f. pl.*

if **sī**
increase, I **augeō, augēre, auxī, auctum**
Italy **Italia, -ae,** *f.*

journey **iter, itineris,** *n.*
joy **gaudium, -ī,** *n.*

land **terra, -ae,** *f.*
last, at last **tandem**
late (adv.) **sērō**
laugh, I **rīdeō, rīdēre, rīsī, rīsum**
lead, I **dūcō, dūcere, dūxī, ductum**
leader **dux, ducis,** *c.*
leave, I = go away from **discēdō, discēdere, discessī, discessum**
   = leave behind **relinquō, relinquere, relīquī, relictum**
lecture **schola, -ae,** *f.*
letter **littera, -ae,** *f.*; **epistola, -ae,** *f.*
listen to, I **audiō, audīre**
live, I **vīvō, vīvere, vīxī, vīctum**
   = inhabit **habitō, habitāre**
long **longus, -a, -um**
   for a long time **diū;** longer **diūtius**
look! **ecce**
look after, I **cūrō, cūrāre**
look at, I **spectō, spectāre; īnspiciō, īnspicere, īnspexī, īnspectum**
look back, I **respiciō, respicere, respexī, respectum**
look for, I **quaerō, quaerere, quaesīvī, quaesītum**
loud (voice) **magnus, -a, -um**
love, I **amō, amāre**

make, I **faciō, facere, fēcī, factum**
man **vir, virī,** *m.*
many **multī, multae, multa**
marry, I **nūbō, nūbere, nūpsī, nūptum** + dat.
miserable **miser, misera, miserum**
mistress **domina, -ae,** *f.*
money **argentum, -ī,** *n.*
more **plūs, plūris**

= more greatly **magis**
mother **māter, mātris,** *f.*
move, I **moveō, movēre, mōvī, mōtum**
moved **commōtus, -a, -um**
much, many **multus, -a, -um**
must, I **dēbeō, dēbēre**

near **prope** + acc.
never **numquam**
nothing **nihil, nihilī,** *n.*
now **iam**

often **saepe**
old **vetus, veteris**
one **ūnus, -a, -um**
   one (of two) **alter, altera, alterum**
open **apertus, -a, -um**
other **alius, alia, aliud**
   the other (of two) **alter, altera, alterum**
   the others = the rest **cēterī, -ae, -a**
our **noster, nostra, nostrum**
outside **extrā** + acc.
overcome, I **superō, superāre**

parent **parēns, parentis,** *c.*
passenger **viātor, viātōris,** *m.*
people **populus, -ī,** *m.*
play, I **lūdō, lūdere, lūsī, lūsum**
please, I **dēlectō, dēlectāre; placeō, placēre** + dat.
praise, I **laudō, laudāre**
prepare, I **parō, parāre**
proceed, I **prōcēdō, prōcēdere, prōcessī, prōcessum**
pupil **discipulus, -ī,** *m.*

quickly **celeriter**

race **cursus, -ūs,** *m.*
reach, I **perveniō, pervenīre, pervēnī, perventum (ad)**
read, I **legō, legere, lēgī, lēctum**
reply, I **respondeō, respondēre, respondī, respōnsum**
republic **rēspūblica, reīpūblicae,** *f.*
return, I = go back **redeō, redīre, rediī, reditum**
   = give back **reddō, reddere, reddidī, redditum**
riot **tumultus, -ūs,** *m.*
rouse, I **excitō, excitāre**
run, I **currō, currere, cucurrī, cursum**
   run towards, I **accurrō, accurrere, accurrī, accursum**

sail, I **nāvigō, nāvigāre**
sailor **nauta, -ae,** *m.*
save, I **servō, servāre**
say I **dīcō, dīcere, dīxī, dictum**
   he/she said **inquit**
school **lūdus, -ī,** *m.*
sea **mare, maris,** *n.*'
see, I **videō, vidēre, vīdī, vīsum**

send, I **mittō, mittere, mīsī, missum**
serve (as a soldier), I **mīlitō, mīlitāre**
severe **sevērus, -a, -um**
ship **nāvis, nāvis,** *f.*
shout **clāmō, clāmāre**
sit, I **sedeō sedēre, sēdī, sessum**
sleep, I **dormiō, dormīre**
slowly **lentē**
small **parvus, -a, -um**
   very small **minimus, -a, -um**
so **tam**
someone, something **aliquis, aliquid**
son **fīlius, -ī,** *m.*
soon **mox**
   as soon as possible **quam prīmum**
speed **celeritās, celeritātis,** *f.*
stand, I **stō, stāre, stetī, statum**
stay I **maneō, manēre, mānsī, mānsum**
step **gradus, -ūs,** *m.*
street **via, -ae,** *f.*
study **studium, -ī,** *n.*
suddenly **subitō**
surely not? **num?**

tavern **taberna, -ae,** *f.*
tell, I = say **dīcō, dīcere, dīxī, dictum**
   = narrate **nārrō, nārrāre**
   = order **iubeō, iubēre, iussī, iussum**
ten **decem**
terrified **territus, -a, -um**
than **quam**
their own **suus, -a, -um**
thing **rēs, reī,** *f.*
this **hic, haec, hoc**
three **trēs, tria**
through **per** + acc.
tired **fessus, -a, -um**
today **hodiē**
toga **toga, -ae,** *f.*
top (= highest, greatest) **summus, -a, -um**
travel, I **iter faciō**
tree **arbor, arboris,** *f.*
turn, I **vertō, vertere, vertī, versum**
   turn round, I **mē vertō**

under **sub** + abl.
unwilling **invītus, -a, -um**

very **valdē**
verse **versus, -ūs,** *m.*
voice **vōx, vōcis,** *f.*

wait, I = stay **maneō, manēre, mānsī, mānsum**
   = wait for **exspectō, exspectāre**
wake up, I **excitō, excitāre** (trans.)
      ēvigilō, ēvigilāre (intr.)
walk, I **ambulō, ambulāre; contendō, contendere,**
   contendī, contentum
want, I **cupiō, cupere, cupīvī, cupītum**
war **bellum, -ī,** *n.*
warn, I **moneō, monēre**
watch, I **spectō, spectāre**
wave **unda, -ae,** *f.*
way **via, -ae,** *f.*
wedding **nūptiae, -ārum,** *f. pl.*
well **bene**
what? **quid?**
when **ubi, cum**
which **quī, quae, quod**
   which (of two)? **uter, utra, utrum?**
who? **quis?**
why? **cūr?**
wife **uxor, uxōris,** *f.*
willing, I am **volō, velle, voluī**
wine **vīnum, -ī,** *n.*
wish, I **cupiō, cupere, cupīvī, cupītum**
with **cum** + abl.
without **sine** + abl.
woman **fēmina, -ae,** *f.*
word **verbum, -ī,** *n.*
work, I **labōrō, labōrāre**
worse **pēior, pēius**
write, I **scrībō, scrībere, scrīpsī, scrīptum**

year **annus, -ī,** *m.*
you (s.) **tū;** (pl.) **vōs**
young man **iuvenis, iuvenis,** *m.*

Index of grammar

Word-building